Parents for Safe Food

The Safe Food Handbook

Parents for Safe Food

The Safe Food Handbook

EBURY PRESS
London

To Lady Eve Balfour,
founder of the Soil Association
and pioneer of the organic movement,
who died as this book was going to press.

First published by Ebury Press
an imprint of the Random Century Group
Random Century House
20 Vauxhall Bridge Road
London SW1V 2SA

Copyright © 1990 Parents For Safe Food

British Library Cataloguing in Publication Data
Parents for safe food.
  1. Food. Health aspects
I. Taylor, Derek II. Cannon, Geoffrey III. London Food Commission
613.2

ISBN 0-85223-823-1

Typeset in Sabon from disk in Great Britain by
Saxon Printing Ltd., Derby
Printed and bound by
Mackays of Chatham Plc, Chatham, Kent

Contents

A note on measurements

Weight

1oz = 28g (grams). In recipes this is rounded up to 30g = 1oz.
1 million micrograms (mcg) = 1000 milligrams (mg) = 1gram (g).
1000g = 1 kilogram (kg) = 2.2lb.

Volume

1000 ml (millilitres) = 1 litre = 1.76 pints. In recipes this is given as a round figure.

Temperature

To convert Fahrenheit (F) to Centigrade (C), subtract 32 degrees, multiply by 5 and divide by 9.
To convert Centigrade to Fahrenheit, multiply by 9, divide by 5 and add 32 degrees.

Energy

Kcal = calories.   1000 calories = 1 Cal = 1 Kcal

Glossary of Abbreviations

ACP Advisory Committee on Pesticides
ADAS Agricultural Development and Advisory Service (government)
ADI Acceptable Daily Intake
BNF British Nutrition Foundation
CBP Chorleywood Bread Process
COMA Committee on Medical Aspects of Food Policy
DoE Department of the Environment
DHSS Department of Health and Social Security (now divided)
EC European Community (formerly EEC)
FAC Food Advisory Committee
FAO Food and Agricultural Organization (United Nations)
FoE Friends of the Earth
GRAS Generally Regarded as Safe
HEA Health Education Authority
LFC London Food Commission
MAFF Ministry of Agriculture, Fisheries and Food
MRL Maximum Residue Levels
MRM Mechanically Recovered Meat
NACNE National Advisory Committee on Nutrition Education
NFU National Farmers' Union
NRDC National Research Defence Council
RDA Recommended Daily Allowance
UKROFS United Kingdom Register of Organic Food Products
WHO World Health Organization

Introduction

by Pamela Stephenson

JUNK! Chips saturated with grease, over-salted potato crisps, horribly chemicalized packet snacks, highly coloured sweets containing coal-tar dyes, juice drinks containing almost no fruit at all, hot chocolate sweetened artificially with a chemical that has been banned in other countries ... do I give these things to *my* children to eat?

I'm afraid the answer is yes. I do – sometimes. When we've been on the motorway for hours, the picnic's run out, they're clamouring for a snack and there's nothing healthy at the garage. When Santa in his chain store grotto offers a treat we can't refuse. On the plane when their ears are popping and the flight attendant presents a plate of adulterated sugared rubbish. When we're at the supermarket checkout, queuing for five long minutes, and at eye level all they can see is wall-to-wall processed junk ....

Yes, I occasionally buy this stuff for them. I'm not happy about it, but I do. Like every parent I'm often faced with impossible choices. A boiled sweet or a tired child throwing a tantrum. I watch them eating this rubbish, and I think angrily – once again, I've been a mug. Putting even more money in the pockets of manufacturers and retailers who couldn't care less about my children's health, so long as *they* make a healthy profit.

This fury at the priority given to economic interests has been the driving force behind the formation of Parents for Safe Food. We can't stop children being children, can we? They are going to demand sweets and treats, no matter what – those Saturday morning TV commercials see to that. But is it necessary for those treats – let alone basic/staple foods – to be made with substances which carry risks of allergies or even cancer?

It was quite a shock for us to discover just how far our children can be guinea pigs for profit. Most parents know that the *obviously* unhealthy, unwholesome foods are best avoided. For example, we now tend to be suspicious of bright orange batter on fish fingers, rotted peanuts or stodgy white fibreless bread. But what about the 'healthy' diet we've been told to follow and give our children – plenty of fresh fruit and vegetables and grains that we know are essential for us all? Surely we can trust those to be safe. But can we?

I must say I thought we could until I learned, for example, that the average English Cox apple is sprayed about a dozen times with various questionable chemicals and dipped in a fungicide before it reaches our supermarket shelves. When Parents for Safe Food investigated pesticides on our children's food, we found that no fewer than 426 of these nasty substances are approved for use on food crops in this country, and many of them don't wash off. Many are suspected of causing cancer, mutations, reproductive ill-effects, allergies, asthma – some of them may even be damaging our children's central nervous systems. If you didn't already know that, I guess it makes rather worrying reading. But the story of Alar should cheer you up a little bit.

Alar, a trade name for the chemical daminozide, was sprayed on millions of apples and pears in Britain to regulate their growth. It is a systemic, which means it gets right inside the pulp and can't be washed or peeled off. Alar had been the subject of controversy ever since independent scientists discovered that when heated, as in the making of apple juice, sauce or fillings, it breaks down into UDMH, a chemical cousin of rocket fuel.

Since they were first weaned, I've fed my own three children an awful lot of apple juice, thinking it was a healthy, safe choice – so I was horrified to learn that the independent research group National Resources Defence Council (NRDC) in the USA has actually estimated that around six thousand children of school age will get cancer at some stage in their lives due to exposure, before the age of five, to Alar and eight other common pesticides.

Not surprisingly, following NRDC's report a major debate followed in the USA. Parents and other consumers were outraged and upset. In Britain Parents for Safe Food, a new organization set up in 1989, pledged to put safety first and campaigned hard. At the end of that year, following withdrawal in the USA, the manufacturers took Alar off the market worldwide.

The argument that the consumers and public health should be given the benefit of the doubt had received a great boost. Nevertheless, the British government's Advisory Committee on Pesticides continued to approve Alar, and in December 1989 gave it a renewed clean bill of health.

While arguments still rage about Alar, we say it should not be used. Our children should not in any way be guinea pigs, especially for a chemical that is a mere cosmetic.

The fact that a multi-national company was persuaded to remove one of its key products is enormously encouraging to everyone who believes in the power of the consumer to promote constructive good. But why did industry, growers and retailers get away with this threat to our children for so long? Alar is not even *necessary* in the growing of apples. The way we feed our children now will affect their health for the rest of their lives. We *must* have a say. We need a *choice*.

We desperately need to know more about our food. We can only eat a good diet and be protected if we're fully informed, and have access to a safe food supply. We have to insist on our right to labelling and information. For all our sakes, we should know exactly what's in food.

After all the worries about food quality and safety in the 1980s it is so important that the 1990s must see the interest of consumers properly represented and our voices heard by food producers. After all, they are supposed to supply what we demand, aren't they? And that's why Parents for Safe Food have prepared this book – to help us all pick our way through the minefield. We will continue to need your help as much as ever. Your voice on Alar was vital in getting the company, supermarkets and fruit growers to see sense. Together we can keep up the pressure to ensure sanity.

We've already had wonderful help and advice from many independent scientists and experts throughout the world – and dedicated journalists and writers have worked hard to publicize the facts – but we'd like *you* to join with us in insisting that industry, farmers, retailers and government put safety first. We all have a right to safe, healthy, wholesome food – a right to a choice. And surely that's a very reasonable request, isn't it?

It's clear now from government sources and farming interests that there is a movement away from the worst of intensive, corrosive farming. It's time to suggest that we see ourselves and government, manufacturers and producers as *partners* in this broad green movement.

With a new attitude and a real organic basis in all of our thinking, we can not only use the resources we've already got to feed everyone in the world, but we can also make the last decade of a messed up century something of which our children really might approve. At last!

Founder Members Speak Out

Jean Boht

Each member of Parents for Safe Food is responsible for a specific area of concern. And not surprisingly, mine is the Better Bread Campaign.

Why should you be concerned about bread, you might well ask – surely any pesticide or fungicide residues remaining in the grain would be removed in either the bleaching or baking processes? Sadly this is not always so. In MAFF tests conducted in 1987, 72 per cent of brown bread and 67 per cent of white analysed showed pesticide residues.

What is more frightening still is that even some organic bread has shown chemical residues. This must mean that the supposedly pure grain from which organic bread is made can absorb the chemical from other sources – storage, perhaps, or breadmaking machinery.

In the Better Bread Campaign, our concern should be that:

- no pesticide should be used unless parents and other consumers can be assured that it is completely safe
- we should be told when the review of data called in by MAFF's Advisory Committee on Pesticides will be complete, and use of pesticides should be suspended until the committee can report complete safety
- information on pesticides should be freely available to the public from government sources.

I am also concerned at the high water content in mass-produced bread. If you ever bake your own, you will see what I mean.

Potassium bromate, a flour improver which was supposed to create a better texture, was recently withdrawn by British bakeries because it was found to be a carcinogen. Then we read that the industry might have to increase the price of the family loaf because more expensive ingredients would have to used. No compensation, you notice, for the possible development of cancer!

I have a dream. Instead of the government paying the farmers to keep land out of production because of the creation of huge mountains of surplus foodstuffs by the use of intensive farming methods, my dream is that it will subsidize the farmers to return this non-productive land to use – organically.

Jenny Seagrove

I have a great hope that one day the experts will get it right. But although asbestos, thalidomide and various food additives were all declared safe in their day, it seems that the lessons still have to be learnt. Shoppers are understandably wary about technologies like irradiation. Neither you nor your food will glow in the dark because of it, but there are still many questions left to be answered.

It is not surprising to discover that the nuclear industry and various individuals associated with it are pushing for irradiation. The scientific bodies advising the government on the safety of this technology have displayed worrying arrogance in evaluating safety tests performed over the past 30 years, but independent scientists are finding implications from their experiments that are disturbing. If the human race is not be used as guinea pigs, and we are to avert the potential 'thalidomide of the nineties', then irradiation must be banned worldwide.

Even if it *were* safe there are other problems – such as using irradiation to cover up bad hygiene in food handling, and the effect of this technology on nutrition. Imagine, too, the kind of risks that would be created by irradiation plants springing up all over the place. Highly dangerous radioactive substances, by-products of the nuclear industry, would be travelling hither and thither to supply these plants. Consider the possible effects of just one accident – and accidents have already occurred.

When I joined Parents for Safe Food I was concerned. Now I know more about it all I am more, rather than less, concerned. Parents for Safe Food is equally concerned about irradiation's impact on food and the environment. Good food doesn't need irradiation.

Victoria Wood

I have a problem with food. I over-eat, and for years I was addicted to sugar, chocolate and Coke. With an immense amount of effort I slowly managed to change my eating habits, cutting out processed food and aiming to eat mainly fresh fruit and vegetables. When I had a baby, I wanted her to be brought up on that kind of food, and was convinced I was doing the right thing for her.

Then Pamela phoned me. 'Does your baby eat apples?'

'Yes, she eats them as if she had a government grant and a time limit.'

'Don't give them to her!'

She told me about Alar, and after that Grace was never given English apples. But I was so angry about it – we'd given her what we thought was the best food available, and it turned out it might have been safer to dish up the baby food with the drawing pins in it.

I believe we have the right to good food available locally and at reasonable prices. Most people don't have the time, energy or money to search out and drive to the one organic outlet for miles, to choose the least wrinkled of three knackered carrots, and come out with 30p change from a ten pound note.

Now I am labelling monitor for Parents for Safe Food. I have loved labels ever since I learned to read. My first word was 'niacin'. We believe food labelling at the moment is misleading and confusing, and needs to be standardized. If people are not told the truth about what's in the food they buy, they can't make an informed choice.

Of course we know that 'full of sugar – rots teeth' is never going to be in large letters across the corner of the packet, but if the weights of the ingredients were given, and labelling standardized throughout the industry, it would be possible to compare one product with another.

Words like 'low-fat' and 'natural' mean as much as 'the funniest show in town' or 'makes wash day a pleasure', but consumers take the wording on food products in good faith, and we believe they are often misled by manufacturers and copywriters. You shouldn't need a thesaurus, a chemistry degree and a calculator to choose something for your baby's tea.

Barbara Bach

When Pamela asked me to join Parents for Safe Food, I jumped at the opportunity to help raise public awareness on such an important matter. Most of us take it for granted that the food we buy from our supermarkets, bakers, butchers, delicatessen and restaurants is safe, but is it? After reading the labels and asking pertinent questions you may be surprised. Some of our most staple products still have secret ingredients.

Ever since Maurice Hanssen's book *E is for Additives* was published, most people seem to know that additives may cause a whole range of ill-effects in people, from rashes and allergies to tumours and cancers. Many parents witness behavioural changes in children such as hyperactivity from chemicals like tartrazine. Yet products containing these substances continue to be sold and millions of pounds are spent on advertising, often targeting children.

The pace of modern-day living doesn't always allow us the time or opportunity to cook all our meals from freshly grown produce, free from preservatives, artificial emulsifiers and stabilizers, anti-oxidants, colours and flavourings. However, we can insist on proper legislation banning harmful and unnecessary chemical additives in our food. High-tech production and distribution must be monitored carefully.

Human beings are creatures of habit, and as parents the eating habits of our children are important to us. We can't make an informed choice if we don't have all the facts.

Julie-Anne Rhodes

For years now, my mother has been sending me printed articles from America on the dangers of drugs and pesticides in the foods we eat. Since becoming a mother myself the concern I felt greatly intensified, and by the time Pamela brought me her vast scrapbook of clippings I realized it was time to do something about it.

I joined Parents for Safe Food hoping that together we might at the very least help educate other parents as to the dangers, and suggest what the choices might be. Ultimately I hope to see a time when testing for residues from drugs or pesticides is carried out much more frequently, and a time when products are labelled 'treated with chemicals' so that we know if they have been. We also look forward to the day when residue levels are very much lower than they are now.

Recently my concern has been growing over the levels of residues from hormones and antibiotics in milk and meat. The latter are often used purely to stimulate growth or for preventive medicine, rather than to treat an illness known to have broken out.

I am frustrated at the way current legislation leaves the benefit of the doubt in favour of the producer instead of the consumer. We don't know the long-term effects of these chemicals. They are loosely controlled. There is insufficient testing for residues, and products should at the very least be labelled as to their content. Without this information we are deprived of choice.

Children are physically more vulnerable to toxins and consume far greater amounts of milk and (in some families) meat than many adults. I am terrified at what I could be giving my child just by giving her a 'well-balanced diet'.

Francesca Annis

Me? Campaigning for safe food? Hang on a moment – like every parent, *of course* I'm concerned about giving my family good, nutritious food. But I'm no food fanatic!

'What's that you say ... BSE? Never heard of it. Come on, if it was dangerous we'd have been told about it – wouldn't we?'

Well, it seems that we wouldn't be. In fact, we weren't.

The statistics are frightening enough by themselves. Since 1986 over ten thousand cattle infected with the fatal brain disease have been recorded.

What actually scared and outraged me were the facts that we don't know:

- where did it come from?
- what is it exactly?
- how does it get passed on?
- how many infected cattle have got through the system and into the food chain?
- can it be passed on to humans through beef and animal products?
- have I fed infected meat to my family?

No one can give us satisfactory answers to these questions.

Me campaigning for safe food? You bet!

Rula Lenska

Since my main source of protein is fish, I was naturally eager to find out as much about waterways and the fishing industry as I could. My research so far – and I'm finding out more every day – has uncovered some frightening facts. You don't have to be an expert to realize that, since our seas and rivers are often horribly polluted, what lives in them *must* be affected.

Since the early days of the Alar fight, Parents for Safe Food have blossomed and gained a great deal of professional and public respect, not least because of Pamela's amazing drive and determination. Now we are expanding into every area concerned with the safety of food.

It alarms me to see how the human race has disregarded and abused nature. And as a parent I intend to fight for my children's future right across the board.

Anneka Rice

I'm as excited about new technology as the next person – but I have to say I've always had some nagging doubts about the safety of microwaves.

My concern centres on a series of major questions:

- do microwaves kill bacteria adequately?
- do they heat food all the way through?
- are the instructions that accompany microwaves adequate?
- are the cooking instructions on food packaging comprehensive?

- do microwave users understand about 'standing time'?

Many of these questions, and others asked by experts, remain unsatisfactorily answered – bacteria remains in food, cold spots exist, instructions are not thorough, many food companies give instructions based on a 650 watt oven although yours may be a 500 watt model, and so on ....

So once more it seems that we've all been flogged a new technology that hasn't been thoroughly researched. Yes, the good old consumer is being used as a guinea pig yet again!

What can we do? Whilst so many doubts exist about microwave safety – including a recent report in the highly respected *Lancet* which suggested that neurotoxins (poisons) are actually created in food by microwaving – Parents for Safe Food will be campaigning for clearer instructions on use, better food labelling and further testing.

But what can we all do now? Short of throwing the microwave out of the kitchen and going back to traditional cooking methods, or devising new uses for it (it can make a very attractive plant stand!), if you do want to continue using it there are some very simple hints:

- keep your eyes on the press and TV to keep updated on new findings
- revise your cooking methods, and if in doubt over-cook
- write to the manufacturer of your microwave asking for updated instructions for your model
- buy a food thermometer to enable you to test the food to ensure that no cold spots exist and that the food is adequately heated.

Olivia Harrison

Most pesticides are toxic to humans, and some are so dangerous that in their undiluted form just a few drops can be fatal. The spraying of these chemicals is a particular concern of mine as my son, who suffers from allergies, attends a school in a rural area surrounded by farmland.

In the spring and summer of 1989 his allergies were completely out of control. When I talked to other mothers we discovered an incredibly high incidence of hay fever, asthma, headaches, runny noses, coughs and so on. Yes, of course there was a lot of pollen about – but what about the coughs that went on for six weeks?

Any parent who has helplessly watched a child suffer from an asthma attack or month after month of hay fever knows that, once the symptoms start, any exposure to chemicals, spray, household cleaners or certain food only exacerbates the problem. I began asking about the farmer whose land lies adjacent to the school:

- what was he spraying and when?
- could the spray be drifting on to the school playing field?
- how long was the pesticide active?
- and most of all, was he a concerned farmer, aware that he shared not only the countryside with these children, but also the air they breathed?

I learned that legally he was under no obligation to notify us when he would be spraying.

One billion gallons of chemicals are sprayed on crops every year. About 20 per cent of that spray is released in droplets so small that it drifts on the air. People sitting in their gardens, joggers on a public footpath, picnickers driving along country lanes and children playing have all been victims of spray drift.

There are a whole range of issues tied up with the thorny question of chemical pesticides. As the mother of an allergy sufferer, I feel my priority is to campaign for firmly enforced legislation that requires farmers to post notices of their intention to spray, together with a clear indication of how long it will be before that area is safe to re-enter. That, at least, will be a start.

1 The Answer Lies in the Soil

Crops and chemicals: the growth of intensive farming and what it means for the food we eat

Farmers, once beloved, are now disliked. Here is Prince Charles, addressing the British Organic Farmers' Conference in Cirencester in early 1989:

> There is no doubt that over the last few years, a growing anxiety has developed amongst all sections of the community about the consequences of modern, intensive farming methods. It is increasingly felt by members of the public that large-scale soil erosion, the destruction of wildlife habitat, and the excessive use of chemicals and unnatural substances are unacceptable and cannot continue unabated without ruining the countryside for future generations and probably causing long-term health hazards.

Members of the British Royal Family may speak truths ignored by governments. A couple of months later, in the Dimbleby lecture broadcast on BBC television, Prince Philip echoed his son's words, with a global perspective, saying that intensive agriculture is against the laws of nature. 'The unpalatable fact is that agriculture has been the victim of its own success,' he said. It has 'caused the biggest of all external disturbances to the ecology of this globe'. He cited 'criticism from the consumer of the quality of the food produced, the methods of production, and the risks to the health of the consumer'.

Don't blame the real farmers

Intensive farming is a fact of life today – albeit an unpalatable one to many of us. But we shouldn't immediately assume that it's the farmer who is at fault. Any self-respecting farmer wants to produce good, nourishing food, to protect his land, and to leave a healthy inheritance to succeeding generations. But in Britain, farmers – people who work the land – are an endangered species.

Fifty years ago the land supported more than half a million farmers. But by 1960 the number had dwindled to 350,000, and it is now under 150,000. The reasons? With the growth of modern farming methods, small farms have become less competitive. The massive increase in mechanization has led to larger farming units employing fewer workers. Indeed the economies of scale which mechanization brings have resulted in amalgamations of farms, so that the proportion of larger farms in this country has greatly increased. As a consequence the number of farms – and therefore the number of farmers – has fallen.

Another result of modern farming methods has been a cornucopia – and, often, a surplus – of cereals, milk and meat. But it has 'been achieved at an enormous environmental and human cost', said the Sunday Telegraph in a major feature in December 1987, 'by tearing down hedges, and turning fields into vast prairies, by shedding labour and heaping on more and more fertilisers and pesticides...'.

Those small farmers who are still working the land are often drawn into this net in order to survive. But they can, and do, reject some aspects of the new farming. One agricultural graduate talked to this book's contributors about her father, who is a caring user of fertilizers and pesticides. He farmed about 400 acres, mainly grain and sugar beet. In order for him to make a living from his land some fields had to be under virtually continuous cereal production and were not allowed to rest fallow for a season and recover. Other means were therefore essential to replace the goodness lost from the soil and to deal with the build-up of pests and diseases.

> Dad's main source of advice on what to use was an agrochemical sales rep, so there was pressure to use chemicals. However, the main pressure was the financial incentive to produce large yields of high-quality crops.
>
> There is a type of short-sighted user, though, with a large acreage. They are not farmers but food producers. Farming involves a responsibility to leave the land in a state at least as good as it was when you began, and to accommodate the wildlife where possible.
>
> So we left the hedges and did not encroach on the wood. The Big Farm attitude is not feasible in the long term, as it does not care for the soil structure – for example, hedges limit soil erosion via wind-blow, and the continuous cropping that is only possible through the use of artificial fertilizers increases the incidence of diseases and pests.

Wartime necessity

The British people, and small British farmers, are suffering the effects of a national policy devised half a century ago to solve wartime problems. At that time government, science and industry, faced with dwindling and erratic supplies from the Empire as food convoys were hunted down at sea, combined in a gigantic experiment designed to manipulate the national food supply. There were two aims: to make Britain self-sufficient in food then and in the future, and to feed the nation with cheap food reckoned to be adequate for growth and health.

Peacetime plenty

The 1947 Agriculture Act, brought in by an energetic Labour Minister of Food, Tom Williams, continued in a similar vein. It set the British agricultural industry the objective of producing as much of the country's own food as was in the national interest, at prices as low as possible consistent with reasonable incomes for farmers and farm workers. To help them achieve this aim farmers were offered a guaranteed price for what they produced; these prices were set each year by the government for a range of farm products (such as milk, pork and wheat). This privileged position for British farmers lasted until the United Kingdom joined the European Economic Community in 1973, when the British people took on the additional burden of subsidizing continental farmers' production of surpluses under the Common Agricultural Policy.

To aid the British farmer in his government-driven sweep to greater production in the fifties and sixties, two mighty interest groups burgeoned alongside – both inheritors of noble traditions. One was the chemicals industry, which had done so much to improve the quality of life in areas such as medicine, and the other was heavy machinery, which had so greatly supported the war effort. Now there was forged a bond between these three which was to prove at first impressive and later awesome.

Poison from the skies

So far along this road have we gone that a thousand million gallons of liquid pesticides now rain down each year on Britain's farms, smallholdings, private gardens, roadside verges, allotments and market gardens. In concentration, the mixture of poisons thought necessary to kill unwanted plants and creatures amounts to 26 million kilograms (well over 25,000 tons) every year. Metric or avoirdupois, pure or diluted, sprayed on the patio roses from hand-held canisters or poured out of light aircraft over barley prairies, pesticides have us hooked. These figures come from the Soil Association (Britain's longest-standing advocates of organic growing) and from Friends of the Earth, two worthy names introduced early in the story and quoted freely so that no one can be in any doubt as to this book's leanings.

Organic farming must be the way of the future, because we are now seeing the folly of chemicals and realizing that the pests, in the ground and above it, will evolve and adapt to defy the worst that all the might of agrochemical conglomerates can throw against them. Great beasts have become extinct in the history of the universe, but the insect is much tougher than the dinosaur. Indeed, as we shall show, they and man's other perceived enemies, the weeds of the earth, grow ever hardier, better equipped, battling it out against our cruel but doomed ingenuity.

Accidents: the awful statistics

In his book *Gluttons for Punishment* James Erlichman says: 'To be sure, most but not all of the pesticide residues found on foods in Britain appear in minute, almost undetectable, quantities. But then so do the carcinogens in individual cigarettes. And the Environmental Protection Agency in the US which regulates pesticide safety say there is "no safe level" of known or suspected carcinogens.'

In 1988 the London Food Commission produced a report entitled *Food Adulteration and How to Beat It*. It stated that, out of 3,009 product brands composed of different combinations and formulations of 426 named chemicals cleared for use on the land, 164 had been implicated as causing cancer, reproductive effects ranging from impotence to birth defects, genetic mutations, or irritant reactions. The report listed:

- 68 possible carcinogens
- 61 possible mutagens
- 93 known irritants
- 35 pesticides linked with possible reproductive effects.

'In total, therefore, almost 40 per cent of pesticide chemicals are linked with at least one adverse effect,' the report concluded. These are appalling figures, but the public can and must speak out.

Serious stuff. For the next few years – even given a massive increase in organic production – it's going to be impossible to avoid food containing pesticide residues. Don't panic. The Government agencies and others do monitor foods. Balancing risks with benefits,

Parents for Safe Food's advice is: continue to eat fresh produce and encourage your children to do so. They mostly don't get enough of this kind of food. Wash all fruit and vegetables very well. When appropriate, give them a good scrub in hot water.

The best advice, of course, is to eat organic if you can buy it fairly easily. If you can't, kick up a fuss – and if you're not certain how to make your opinions heard, or where they will hit hardest, read Chapter 7.

Accidents continue to happen

In *Gluttons for Punishment*, James Erlichman says: 'On the available evidence no one has ever died in Britain as a direct result of eating pesticide residues in food, and it has been more than a decade [he was writing in 1986] since an agricultural or factory worker in the UK was proved to have died from direct exposure to pesticides.' But he goes on to confirm that the relevant authorities have refused to set up the sort of medical monitoring that could prove their claims that pesticides, and the hormones and antibiotics used on animals (see Chapter 2), can be exonerated from causing undiagnosed illness, chronic disease and even death.

This raises an important question, which particularly affects the Third World where, according to the Voluntary Health Association of India, there are up to twenty thousand deaths a year as a result of using pesticides. In 1981, say the World Health Organization, there were 750,000 accidents involving pesticides; today there may be as many as a million every year. At Bhopal in India there were two thousand immediate deaths in that horrifying accident in 1984 involving organophosporous pesticide production.

Who's winning the war?

How are we doing, we humans, against the pests? Not as well as the farmers would like, it seems, for – as mentioned earlier in this chapter – nature is more adaptable than man. The 1 December 1989 issue of *Farmer's Weekly* carried a series of short but revealing reports on a conference held by the British Crop Protection Council. When the agrochemical company Schering Agriculture carried out a survey of nearly 2,500 fields it found:

● the top four weeds of winter cereals were showing remarkable resilience to pesticides
● those four – chickweed, speedwell, mayweed and cleavers – were 'if anything on the increase': 94 per cent of the fields of winter barley or winter wheat contained chickweed, while cleavers, the least abundant, was on 58 per cent of the field

- the figures for 1967 were much less – 77 per cent for chickweed and 49 per cent cleavers
- annual meadowgrass was found to be much more widespread than had been thought
- blackgrass was found on 70 per cent of East Anglian fields

Answering the indictment that weedkillers were failing, Schering said herbicides were generally directed at keeping just a single crop clean. It doesn't seem as if things are all that effective. However, agribusiness is not slow to see a silver lining for its clouded image – Schering also asserted that this resilience on the part of the weeds disproved the claims of some people that herbicides were changing the countryside.

The *Farmer's Weekly* reports contained the news that the Agricultural Development and Advisory Service (ADAS) of the Ministry of Agriculture, Fisheries and Food (MAFF) was indicating that one in ten seed samples was showing some degree of resistance to herbicides. Out-and-out resistance was confirmed in 33 fields on 20 farms across seven counties. ADAS had also found that:

- none of the 14 herbicides tested singly gave better than 75 per cent control
- even sequential treatments of up to four chemicals gave no more than 86 per cent control
- with 95 per cent control needed to keep on top of the weeds in continuously grown, minimally tilled cereal crops, other strategies were clearly required.

Farmer's Weekly quoted reports from across the world, all with the same theme: resistance was building up, and the only solution was rotation of crops (to prevent the build-up of pests and diseases specific to a certain crop) and the application of pesticides at slower rates. None of this was from conservationists, organic sandal wearers, bearded nut-eating weirdos, food terrorists or other such two-legged nuisances – but from the pests themselves. 'We're bigger than you are,' came the message, loud and clear. 'Try us!'

The ones that get away

The use of pesticides is hemmed in with complex rules. There are restrictions of all sorts:

- on their use near watercourses
- on what pests they can be applied to
- about time delays on harvesting and distribution, so that nothing gets 'out there' containing 'fresh' pesticides.

But we all know that human beings are notoriously fallible, and there are obvious loopholes in these regulations. Pesticides can be used against rats and mice, but not against foxes and crows. But don't the latter eat the former? Haven't the regulation-drafters heard of the food chain? And it would be straining credulity too far to believe that growers do not make occasional mathematical errors in relating spraying and harvesting times, between storage and distribution periods. And with the pressures of the marketplace and, say, looming bad weather, time limits may get chopped and risks taken to meet the needs of what we hear so often is the Real World.

And there is no doubt whatsoever that some very unpleasant pesticides are finding their way into our rivers and watercourses. The recent report of the MAFF Working Party on Pesticides and Residues stated that residues of DDT and other pesticides had been found in eels. (DDT, incidentally, had been withdrawn from use way back in 1984 – which widens the meaning of 'residues' considerably. Monitoring of this aspect of pollution continues.) In July 1989 both the *Daily Telegraph* and *The Independent* reported that in the previous year, in 'an unprecedented action', Ministry farm inspectors had destroyed 1,600 lettuces and a lorryload of tomatoes that had started their journey to the shops too soon after being sprayed. The action had been taken under new food and environmental protection legislation.

The paper also confirmed that there had been a number of cases where people in their gardens had suffered sore throats, headaches and other symptoms after farmers had applied chemical sprays to neighbouring fields. There had been 160 suspected poisoning incidents.

A wind of change blowing through the cornfields

By the year's end, 1989 was turning out to be a watershed in terms of opinion and activity. Radio and television documentary items were a regular and persistent feature of the debate for and against pesticides. Newspapers and magazines, by no means all of them notably sympathetic to 'green' organizations, were running special articles and news reports on surveys that revealed anti-chemical attitudes.

Farmer's Weekly of 9 December reported that 'more than half of a very broad survey of farmers and landowners questioned believed that their colleagues were using too many pesticides'. The journal said that land agents Savill's had organized the survey in response to a similar one carried out by the *Daily Telegraph*, which had found that 87 per cent of respondents thought farmers were using too many chemicals.

2 All Creatures Faked and Mauled

Unethical methods of livestock production, and the hazards of infection and pollution

---

Some people say that salmonella is the revenge of a tortured chicken population on the human population. For the food-borne diseases that hit the headlines in 1989 are caused above all by the factory farming of animals. If as a result of the food poisoning scandals of 1989 we give some thought to the fate of animals bred for our food, then we may in future eat meat safely and with an easier conscience.

Meat production in Britain is an industry in deep crisis – a crisis we, as a nation, have made. First, we eat so much meat. Second, we shut our eyes to the facts of factory farming. And third, we demand cheap meat.

Most people in Britain eat meat. On average, every man, woman and child eats over 2lb of meat a week. Our total meat consumption every year is over 5 million tons. That's a lot of animals. And that's where the trouble starts. For in our small island the mass production of meat involves the herding, slaughter and processing of animals in squalid conditions that breed disease.

In 1989 we learned from the newspapers that chickens are fed the ground-up remains of other chickens. Most people were appalled. But this is 'normal practice' in the factory farming of poultry. We also learned to our horror that the ground-up remains of sheep have been fed to cows, which are naturally vegetarian animals. Protein is protein, the scientists said – what's the difference? In the case of cows it means a big difference, for British herds are now devastated by 'mad cow disease', transmitted from the diseased sheep fed to them.

In 1989 our newspapers carried front-page food poisoning horror stories. Inside, the same papers carried full-page advertisements from food retailers, flogging off chicken, meat and meat products at rock-bottom rates. Did we notice the irony? For cheapened, penny-off meat is likely to be unhealthy and eventually unsafe. If as a nation we demand cheap meat, we will get poisoned meat from tortured animals.

What we want and need is wholesome meat free from contamination. This means healthy animals, treated with respect. In turn this requires us all to pay some attention both to the quality of meat and to the quality of life of the animals that are made into meat. Be prepared to eat less meat and to pay good money for good quality: good for your health, and better for the environment.

Should we begin the discussion of animals by launching into horror stories of Britain's abattoirs? Or about infected meat entering the food chain and slipping into the mouths of babies? Times have certainly moved on in British 'husbandry' since that lowing herd wound slowly o'er the lea in Gray's *Elegy*.

Even then, the herd wasn't intended to prettify the landscape – though that it did, and still does in many corners of Britain's verdant, untilled and pleasant pastures. That so-familiar sight of bovine 'contentment', almost still life in black and brown and white on green, is the good side of a messy business. Or is it? This tranquil scene is threatened by a cloud called BST – of which more presently.

And of course with the increase of industrial mass production units where intensively fed and housed beasts replace the grazing herds, we are forced to look upon this business for what it is. Grim. For many of the creatures born to die to please our palates, it is grim from first breath to last gasp.

And that last gasp will probably be made in some of the vilest abattoirs in Europe – in the early months of 1989 it was learnt that conditions in British slaughterhouses were such that 90 per cent failed to qualify for EC export licences. Among the objections were:

- meat smeared with faeces because intestines are commonly ruptured during slaughter
- improperly sterilized knives used for cutting meat
- bad drains
- condemned meat spilling out of bins
- hosing down of meat in crude attempts to clean it.

So James Erlichman informed *Guardian* readers. As if that wasn't bad enough, later that year BBC *Newsnight* ran a horrifying and all too well-documented lead item on diseased animals that had passed into the mainstream food supply. Counterfeit stamps of approval on carcasses are turning rotten meat into vast profit for dodgy middlemen. The meat from their carcasses would have ended up where? Baby's Beatrix Potter dish?

In case the wrong impression has been conveyed by all these arguments, this book is not trying to suggest that you turn vegetarian tomorrow. The choice of whether or not you and your family eat meat is entirely up to you, as a shopper, cook and caring parent. But you can't make that kind of choice without knowing all the facts, good and bad.

Poor cows

Meat and its production are – one hardly needs say it – a very large and complex subject, even without the intensive farming that has made it such a minefield. As our health is indivisible from what may be going into and around the flesh of living and dead animals, birds and fish, we should perhaps examine in some detail the activities of the chemical companies in relation to livestock. It is, after all, one thing to spray an ear of grain and hope that the chemical kills insects. It is quite another to put something into an animal and hope that everything turns out all right.

In her book *The Meat Machine* Jan Walsh points out that from the birth of a calf to the selling of a steak pie, the machine is at work converting every possible part of the carcass into something edible. Along the way, the meat may be given doses not only of hormones and antibiotics, but also of tranquillizers and tenderizers. These may come in the form of additives to their feed, injections or implants in the animal's body. If we eat meat, we also consume whatever residue of chemicals that meat contains.

Antibiotics and hormones

On the face of it prescribed by vets to cure or prevent infections, antibiotics also stimulate growth, and no one in livestock farming in the UK pretends otherwise. At the time of writing, hormone growth promoters are no longer legal in Britain – they are specifically not allowed in medical terms – though they are available on the illegal market. But for most of the 1980s these substances were supplied legally to get animals ready for market as fast as possible.

The obvious concern here is that antibiotics would arrive via the food chain in our own bodies, which in time might develop, in us, a resistance to these life-saving drugs. To forestall this eventuality, clear regulations were drawn up in the Swann Report of 1969. Antibiotics for therapeutic use on livestock were (and still are) available only on a vet's prescription, and could only be used against a known outbreak of disease (in other words there could be no 'just in case' prescribing). And hormones for growth, though freely available without recourse to a vet, were restricted to those discarded for human use and, whether supplied ready mixed into feed or given separately, could only be used in small doses.

In 1986 the EC decided to outlaw the use of hormones for growth, and that ban came into effect early in 1989. The then British Minister of Agriculture, Michael Jopling, initially opposed the ban. Richard Body called the Ministry's 'attitude on hormones ... abysmal' and called for its food functions to be taken over by the Department of Health. No chance. Not yet.

The Italian veal affair

Parents for Safe Food feel that 'farming by needle' is too open to abuse, and that far greater powers of inspection and more staff to implement them are vital. The 1980s had begun with a terrible scandal in Italy, where veal calves were injected in their breast muscles with a synthetic hormone. The meat from the calves found its way into baby food. Male babies developed breasts, female babies commenced puberty in their prams. The drug was stilbene, illegal in Italy then (though clearly available under the counter) but legal in Britain. Fortunately the children affected returned to normal when their diet was corrected, and stilbene is now – quite rightly – banned everywhere.

But Italy is not the Third World and its farmers have not got a monopoly on opportunism – and there is no doubt whatsoever that some British farmers are tempted to muck around with hormones for growth.

More milk that we don't need – courtesy of the lab

In the perfectly legal but secretive world of 'testing', the drug bovine somatotropin (BST) has been used on British cows for two or more years. It is just one part of the biotechnological revolution in farming (of which more in Chapter 3), which may accomplish great good in the world, but if handled carelessly or greedily might equally achieve the opposite effect. Sensible opponents to the use of BST claim that if this drug's use is authorized in the EC it will lead to a whole new series of hormones for pigs, poultry and fish.

BST increases milk yields in cows. In Britain it has recently been tested on certain selected herds, involving about a thousand cows in all. MAFF authorized the trials, decided not to name the herds, and assured the public there would be no danger. It is to be hoped that the government is right, for milk was collected from the treated cows and distributed along with conventionally produced milk. Monsanto Chemicals, the developers of the drug, are anxious indeed to know how 'well' the experiment has worked.

Mad cow disease – 'Made in Britain'

And talking of the health of our cattle, one indisputably nasty insight into the implications of a poisoned food chain is provided by bovine spongiform encephalopathy – BSE, otherwise known as mad cow disease. This awful business began in the early 1980s and is Made in Britain – it is so far all ours. At the time of writing, about 120 new cases were being reported every week. By February 1990 ten thousand visibly infected cattle had been slaughtered and disposed of, some of them at a well-documented and famously photographed burning, and the West Germans (at least) had announced that they would not be buying any British beef because of fears over BSE. Other European countries have quietly banned the importation of live cattle from Britain.

This quite reasonable and tactful blockade began because farmers broke the laws of nature and fed animals to herbivores. Cattle got the disease because they were given processed foodstuffs containing sheep protein infected with scrapie, that most onomatopoeic of diseases that affects sheep's brains. The brains were gathered up in slaughterhouses along with other waste-not-want-not parts of the sheep, and processed into fine powder for cattle feed. The disease jumped species, and thus BSE was born. Then, having leaped from sheep to cattle, it spread to chimpanzees, mice, rats, hamsters and guinea pigs, and even to two antelopes in an English zoo. Dr Helen Grant, a neuropathologist at London's Charing Cross Hospital, points out that 'all these are mammals and we humans are just mammals too'.

Into the food chain

Mr Kenneth Clark, Minister of Health, said that cattle with BSE had got into the food chain between 1985 and 1988. In fact the disease takes as much as eight years to incubate, and there is little disputing that since that time a great many cattle, incubating BSE, have been slaughtered for food. In 1988 allegations were made by the London Food Commission that controls had failed to prevent BSE entering the food chain. By 1990 this was a persistent, widespread allegation.

There is no test during the incubation period which could give hints of the infection and, says Dr Grant, offal – which includes brains and spinal cords, the parts of the animal affected by BSE – has found its way into meat pies, paté and mince. Parents for Safe Food's advice is not to give children meat pies and not to buy prepared mince. And the government has banned the use of offal in baby food.

Fatted calves

Veal production can be a distressing business. In Britain most calves are taken from their mothers a few hours after birth, so that there is no time for bonding to take place. This means that the mother's milk is left in an unstressed condition for human consumption. The poor motherless calf may be kept for subsequent dairy or beef use, according to breed and sex. But far too many will find themselves put into a box alongside thousands of others in similar boxes, unable to turn or suckle or relate to anything, dosed up with antibiotics against infection (widespread in calves), kept in darkness and very soon killed for the restaurant trade. Who would eat veal?

The pig – a horizontal human

James Erlichman, ever apt with a phrase, told his *Guardian* readers in December 1989: 'The pig's fatal flaw is that it will withstand almost any abuse to which man subjects it. It is the near perfect inmate of intensive agriculture.' It has, he says, been called 'a horizontal human .... They are very nice and intelligent, their physiology closely resembles our own. They, like us, are capable of arranging some quite nice lavatory systems within accepted limits respected by their neighbours.'

But in modern farming the pigs are often kept in very closely packed pig units. Since these are a breeding ground for disease their steady diet of (growth-boosting) antibiotics, prescribed for infection which is often real enough, help the farmer get meat on the hook in the shortest possible time. They are chained, kept close together, infecting each other, unable to escape their own and others' filth.

The British love their pig meat – even though the price of bacon increased by 40 per cent in 1989 it remained popular, with ever more specialized bacon (different cures, different flavours) on the up and up. But in bringing it to us, the farmer and those who collude with him are, it is claimed, cutting corners, playing with the 'minimum withdrawal time' before slaughter for all residues of antibiotics to leave the pig's body. Residues have turned up and are continuing to turn up – if in declining numbers, according to the government's chief veterinary officer, Keith Meldrum. In 1985 more than a quarter of pig kidneys sampled contained traces of a substance called sulphadimidine, whereas now, Mr Meldrum informed James Erlichman, residues contaminate just one sample in twenty.

In the *Food Magazine* for January/March 1990 Dr Alan Long of the Vegetarian Society writes:

> Pigs in intensive systems are under constant stress and threat of infection during the five and a half months in which feed and growth boosters fatten them to slaughter weight. Sulphadimidine is added to feed to counter the prevalent infections of the respiratory tract and gut. It is a prescription-only medicine obtained through a vet. Farmers may mix it themselves and the drug ... may be advertised direct to farmers.

Tests conducted in the USA (where it is called sulfamethazine) suggest a link to thyroid cancer in rats and mice – though no evidence has been found that it causes cancer in humans. It is likely, says Dr Long, that from mid-1990 the drug will be banned in America, adding that the US government is already refusing to allow the country's pharmaceutical industry to introduce it in new mixtures for farming use. Yet sulphadimidine is still cleared for use in the UK.

Baa, baa, black sheep

It is almost with relief that we come to sheep, for by and large they are reared in much more natural conditions than most other livestock (farmers would gain little by not doing so, for sheep can thrive on poor, hilly land that would be no good for anything else). There are consequently far fewer worries about hormone or antibiotic residues in the lamb and mutton we buy at the butcher's. However, in tests carried out during the eighties 50 per cent of the sheep sampled contained pesticide residues.

The other concern of the queue at the butcher's is, of course, about the lingering effects of the Chernobyl disaster. MAFF data indicates that sheep and lamb carcasses now being sampled contain levels of radiation too low to cause anxiety.

The real price of cheap chicken

Let us now cross the farmyard of our mind and enter that big shed there. Inside you will find twenty thousand of God's feathered creatures in small cages. They are all eating, laying eggs, eating, laying eggs, on and on and on and on, day in, day out, until they are put out of their misery. There are no egg-holidays in these birds' lives.

In Britain the battery system accounts for 90 per cent of all egg production, and readers will remember that, when she was junior Health Minister, Edwina Currie told a reporter from ITN that most egg production was infected. It cost her her ministerial career. In the final issue of the *Grocer* for 1989, an editorial reviewing the recent conflicts between complainers and providers declared the damage to the egg industry caused by the 1988 'scare' to be 'irreparable'. Mrs Currie's voice had been perhaps the most audible among many during the salmonella outbreaks that year.

It is a sad old business. About 37 million battery hens in this country produce eggs. The birds are often contaminated – they are huddled so close together in their stacked up cages that infection is almost inevitable, and as a consequence the use of antibiotics is rife. And one certain means of infecting hens is to feed them with the processed remains of other chickens. Unbelievably, this imposed cannibalism went on for years. It is said, by the industry, that it has now ceased. Monitoring groups trust that this is so.

Forced moulting and de-beaking

The use of forced moulting is widespread. It involves holding back food and water for about 24 hours while the birds are kept in darkness. Normal light and feeding are then resumed gradually over a few weeks. The shock brings about a sudden moult, which produces another thirteen months of laying.

To prevent serious pecking damage in these cramped conditions about one-fifth are de-beaked, by amputation. It also happens to turkeys in nine cases out of ten (and, regrettably, may also be observed in some free-range birds which have been de-beaked before the way in which they were to be kept was decided).

The broiler house scandal

Roast and barbecued chicken, and chicken pieces, will today almost all be birds reared in broiler houses. Broiler houses are high-temperature, windowless sheds where the birds spend a horrifyingly short, intensively fed and heavily drugged life of six or seven weeks. They are kept for only as long as it takes for them to reach a weight of about 4lb. If it could be done in less, then these baby hens would be gone almost before you could say Chickens' Lib. In theory they could live for several years, but when these birds are taken for slaughter they would, in decent conditions, just be growing out of sleeping under their mother's wings.

Though living creatures, they are called a 'crop'. The process of catching – a terrible affair involving men running to and fro in the dark with several birds to a hand, hurling them into bags, is called a 'harvest'. Yet no fruit or vegetables would be treated with such rough dispatch. Much bruising and many broken bones are the result.

Animal welfare campaigners have helped initiate and fund research into alternatives, and in January 1990 Ruth Harrison (whose campaigning book *Animal Machines* made such headlines 25 years ago) talked of one outcome: a machine called a broiler harvester. She told the *Observer Magazine*: 'Broiler chickens are usually collected roughly by hand ... whereas the harvester picks them up very gently and puts them into modules equally gently; in practice, "untouched by human hands" can be really pleasant.' The harvester is coming into more general use.

Buy free-range if you can

This book recommends that you always attempt to buy free-range eggs and birds. According to the guidelines of Compassion In World Farming and Chickens' Lib, with a free-range system hens should run freely on grass, at a stocking rate of about 150 hens to the acre (though up to 450 is more often the case). Ideally there would be three square feet of aviary house space per bird, and the same out in the open air. The chickens will roam around, of course, but that is the allocation – one square yard per bird. Henhouses are provided for egg laying and shelter and for security at night. Foxes only pose a threat to free-range birds if the flock is inadequately looked after. Properly cared-for birds should be locked away in secure henhouses at night, and if human beings are in evidence during the early morning and evening, when foxes come out to feed, birds will only rarely be taken.

The numbers of free-range birds demanded by housewives, and now increasingly available, are expected to grow substantially in the 1990s – and that can only be good news.

Other systems – don't be deceived

There are other systems which are not battery – but are not free-range either. They can be confusing. The first of these alternatives (again according to Compassion In World Farming and Chickens' Lib – neither of whom, incidentally, approves this system, which they call 'intensive free-range') should give the birds continuous daytime access to open-air runs, with a maximum density of four thousand hens per hectare (about one square foot per bird). Something called deep litter is used – at least a third of the floor space is covered with suitable natural absorbent material such as straw.

And then there is one system that in marketing terms sounds attractive, but in reality isn't. It is called the barn egg or perchery system, and uses an aviary of perches and feeders at different levels. The birds have no access to fresh air, and great density is permitted. This book does not recommend barn eggs.

Muddied waters

Fish of high value are now farmed intensively to produce more food, more quickly and more cheaply for the ever-hungry consumer. Parents for Safe Food suggest that before you buy you should know that there is a very complicated network of activity going on around the lovely, tasty fresh (and that means 'farm-fresh') salmon steaks which many of us can now afford. According to a *Food Magazine* survey at the end of 1989, on a fish-per-penny basis it is only slightly more expensive than the average fish finger. And of course if you want all the fabulous nutrients of salmon (see the A to Z Buyers' Guide in Chapter 8) you would be hard put to beat this succulent pink delight. Now let's look at the down side. Let's note, first, that the 'pink' comes from a dye mixed in with the feed. Their flesh would otherwise be an unappealing grey.

In a report published by the Scottish Wildlife and Countryside Link in March 1988, fish farming was described as 'a giant out of control'. Its statistics suggests its potential. In Britain about ten thousand jobs, direct or indirect, are locked into this industry, which embraces some four hundred onshore trout farms and even more than that number of coastal salmon farms. Output has increased thirty times over since the early 1980s, and salmon farming is said to be already the size of the Scottish beef industry. By 1991 it will be the size of Scottish beef and lamb combined.

Farmed UK trout and salmon are now worth £100 million a year. Contrast this with about £400 million worth of fish trawled in time-honoured ways by the British fishing fleets in 1988. It is clear, therefore, that with wild fishing quotas now on the way down by a hoped-for 20 per cent in 1990 – due to dwindling stocks, over-fishing, and the use of nets that are too small-mesh and catch young fish that should be left to breed – the numbers of farmed fish could soon overtake those of their cousins caught in the wild. A giant out of control? The North Atlantic Salmon Conservation Organization (NASCO), which represents nine countries, says that these farmed fish may prove the greatest danger for ten thousand years to wild salmon, because of inter-breeding.

The incredible growth of the fish farming industry greatly concerns ecological groups, who feel that the industry already imposes quite a strain on the environment from fish farming, and fear that much worse lies ahead if the government doesn't act. Farmed fish are kept in cages, which, just like the broiler houses and piggeries of Farm Factory Britain, breed diseases. It doesn't take an Einstein to see that any food or medication given to fish is going to get into the waters round about – and claims have been made that pesticides are in regular use. Friends of the Earth are particularly concerned about this aspect, and in December 1988 the Marine Conservation Society said that the government was neglecting European Commission environmental safeguards.

There are other ecological costs, too, for fish farming poses a particular threat to wildlife. The herons, cormorants and seals attracted by the fish are shot regularly. Farmers traditionally protect their livestock from predators, and there is no reason to be prissy about these farming methods. It is only natural to protect one's investment, and fish farming is clearly very big business.

Chris Patten, the new Secretary of State for the Environment, has set up a Select Committee to look into fish farming. The industry has developed so fast that you can be sure many (how can we put it?) *difficult* things are happening that won't be permitted when all the facts are known. It will be interesting to see what conclusions the Select Committee comes to when it reports to the Minister, and what legislation is drawn up as a result.

So where does that leave you, the shopper and caring parent – perhaps now aware of some of the truth, but (like most of us) still awaiting the whole truth. Fish are a valuable source of protein for your children, so buy and eat it if it looks good and fresh, but keep alert to the fish farming stories in the press and on TV. Read about it as it comes to you, in serial form, with one cliff-hanger after another. Just as all the salmon once did, this story will run and run.

Poisons in the North Sea

When Nicholas Ridley was Minister of the Environment he said it was not right to infer that pollution in the seas was killing fish. It could be disease, he suggested – and anyway, we over-fished. Of the North Sea, source of that great random harvest of plenty in days gone by, he said it was quite well looked after, 'better than many other seas'.

Friends of the Earth responded: 'To use the seas for a rubbish dump for our effluent is a policy of the most staggering short-sightedness. Those fish we eat have to fight their way through an accumulation of pesticides, detergents, fertilizers, industrial effluents, harbour dredgings, oil spillage, human sewage, chemical wastes and ships' garbage.' Sadly, they are right. For starters, each year Britain dumps something like a quarter of a million tons of liquid industrial waste directly into the North Sea. Greenpeace, Friends of the Earth, the World Wide Fund for Nature and the Marine Conservation Society have joined up to fight this and much more.

There is still government indifference, although we all hope for better policies from Chris Patten. Nicholas Ridley had blamed much of the trouble in the North Sea on our neighbours in Europe: according to him, the Rhine, the Elbe and the Meuse (all draining – a loaded word in this context – into the North Sea) cause 80 per cent of the trouble. There are plans to stop the incineration of toxic wastes at sea by 1994, and this is greatly to be welcomed. How disgusting that we ever did it! And the West Germans have promised by the mid-1990s to halve the volume of heavy metals and chemicals (mostly agricultural) that pours into the Rhine.

The Ministry of Agriculture, Fisheries and Food's view of the North Sea was expressed in a letter to the editors of this book by Mr David Curry, parliamentary secretary to the Ministry:

> The general public is constantly being given the impression these days that the North Sea is badly polluted, that the level of pollution is increasing, that this increasing level of pollution causes an increase in the incidence of fish diseases and that this poses a health risk for consumers. This line of argument is wrong in all respects.

He stressed that the government was taking all possible steps to prevent contamination of the marine environment as a result of pollution.

Protective measures

With all this unpleasantness around it is just as well that at Lowestoft MAFF has a Directorate of Fisheries Research with two hundred scientists as well as administrators and technical and industrial advisers. You may not know if your fish has been lurking in murky waters, but there are good safeguards and the fresh or frozen fish made available for you to feed your family has not been regarded haphazardly. Real care is taken to ensure its – and therefore your – safety.

You have the right, however, to insist that we do not poison our natural resources. The government holds our coastal waters in trust, and is party to major international treaties in relation to the open seas. But never forget that the government is your servant, and if you want to eat fish, you have the right to know that it has come from clean waters.

Spiritual poverty

On the subject of intensive livestock rearing, Parents for Safe Food agree with the Archbishop of Canterbury, Dr Robert Runcie, who has written:

> Of course these systems of extreme confinement are to be abhorred ... history has repeatedly shown that when man exploits his fellow creatures for immediate gain, it rebounds on him eventually and leads to spiritual poverty.
>
> In the end, lack of regard for the life and wellbeing of an animal must bring with it a lowering of man's self-respect: 'Inasmuch as ye do it to these the least of my little ones ye do it unto me.'

3 All Things Wise and Wonderful

The value of going organic, and the
wonders of the biotechnological revolution

Just at the point that everybody got the message about healthy food, the story seemed to change. Meat products, we know, are unhealthy; but also, evidently, fresh meat is unsafe. Cakes, biscuits and confectionery are fatty and sugary; but also, it seems, fresh vegetables and fruit are drenched with poisonous chemicals, before and after harvest. Processed food contains additives; fresh food, we now learn, contains contaminants. No wonder, then, that so many people say 'What can I eat then?' or even 'To hell with it – I'll just eat what I fancy'.

Do not despair; help is at hand. Yes, it is true that food additives and contaminants are a problem. Just how much of a problem, nobody knows. But whole, fresh food is always the best choice. First, food in its natural form is free from unhealthy added fat, sugar and additives, and rich in all sorts of nutrients. Second, the cereals, vegetables and fruit used as ingredients in processed food have also been sprayed with pesticides, herbicides, fungicides and other contaminants. So there is no dilemma. If you are worried about the chemical poisoning of whole, fresh food, that is no reason to eat processed food.

Nor need you be eaten up with worry; because the best choice of all is whole fresh food grown organically to recognized standards. In the 1990s, organic foods should become available to everybody in Britain, at prices that everybody can afford.

When you buy organically grown vegetables and fruit, and organically reared meat, you are doing the very best you can to protect your health and that of your family. You are also investing in sustainable agriculture, which is respectful of nature and good for the environment. Going green, in the food you eat, means choosing organic food. It also means doing your bit to recreate a green and pleasant land. For yourself, and especially for the children in your life, when only the best will do: always prefer organic food.

The meaning of organic food

If you can, you should go organic. That is this book's firm recommendation. Parents for Safe Food suggest that whenever possible you should think organic and buy organic. You can do it just as easily in a city centre as in the country, if you know how. Many supermarkets are now selling food grown without chemical fertilizers or pesticides, and fresh developments are taking place all the time.

Take a carrot, knobbly, noble and pure, full of carotene (vitamin A), and enriched by land fertilized with real farmyard manure. It won't be a bargain. It will not have been beautified. It might not look perfect. But it will probably taste wonderfully of carrot, particularly if you steam it.

How will it have been grown? If it has been produced to Soil Association standards (and the Association's symbol is only granted to those who meet its standards) it will have come from a grower who does not allow the use of:

- synthetic fertilizers
- pesticides
- growth regulators
- antibiotics
- hormone growth stimulants
- intensive livestock systems.

The grower will have relied on:

- rotation of crops to keep the soil reasonably pest-free
- biological pest control to deal with the rest
- natural nitrogen fixation (conversion of nitrogen from the air into a form in which the plants can assimilate it – the natural

way to do it is by bacteria which live on the roots of plants; the intensive way involves chemical fertilizers)

- farm manure and crop residues to fertilize the soil
- decent, humane and therefore ethical livestock systems.

In other words, anything unwelcome in the soil or on the carrot will have come not from the hand of the grower but from something drifting in from neighbours who are still using the chemicals about which this book is so concerned.

Agricultural visionaries

The Soil Association, though by no means the only old hands in organic farming, did get an early start and now has charitable status. It was set up in Bristol in 1946 by a group of clear-eyed visionaries, right against the grain of 'progress' at the very time that jet-age agrochemicals were on the runway.

Its 'founding mother', the late Lady Eve Balfour (granted an OBE in the 1990 New Year's Honours List) wrote an editorial in the very first issue of the association's magazine, *Living Earth*, and it was reprinted in the first issue of 1990. It shows remarkable prescience, and indeed could have been written now.

People have begun to see life on this planet as a whole and Nature's plan as a complicated system of interdependence rather than one based on competition. As an outcome of this interpretation of natural law, they share the belief that the only salvation for mankind lies in substituting cooperation for exploitation in all human activities from soil treatment to industrial and international relations.

As we approach the millennium, much of the world has stopped bickering among itself and has acquired an awareness of the imminence of planetary changes of horrendous dimensions. If we take care, however, we can settle on a better way of life. Parents for Safe Food are also parents for a safe world, and we are all in this together. But it starts right here, in small ways, with the choice on the supermarket shelves.

Whether or not we choose to eat our fellow creatures, they should have rights. In the organic world there are:

- no crated calves
- no slithering infected pigs
- no BST
- no BSE
- no battery chickens
- no de-beaking
- no antibiotics feeding.

In that world – and for those who abide by the rules of the Soil Association it is a real world, not a dream one – there are also:

- no insurance spraying
- no poisons
- no residues
- no additives in the food produced.

The Association's advisers are there to help those who want to go organic. A two-year transition period is insisted on after the last chemically 'improved' crop before organic status can be conferred.

The opposite side of the farm fence

But it is not as practical people that organic farmers and campaigners are characterized. The sandal-wearing beardies of the demonology (fostered by intensive farmers and their lobby) come in for a lot of stick. Consider the opinion of Big Farmer Oliver Walston, an articulate man who is not a fool. 'Organic farming is a rich man's toy, and organic food is a rich man's luxury,' he said when addressing the British Growers Look Ahead conference in 1989. He was responding to remarks made by the Prince of Wales, whose Gloucestershire farm is organic. Prince Charles had pointed out in a speech (part of which was quoted on p.17) that there was growing anxiety at the effects of modern intensive farming on the environment, on wildlife and on human health. The Prince was firm in proposing the new truth: organic farming was gaining credibility as a solution.

Irritation rippled through the world of agrochemicals. Walston, perhaps Britain's most energetic scourge of the organic lobby, aimed at the Prince's unavoidably vulnerable Achilles heel when he replied: 'Unlike the Prince of Wales, the farmers of Britain live in the real world and have real problems ... were I to be a fortunate owner occupier with no tedious distractions to worry about like rent and overdrafts, I too might be an organic farmer.' Walston's view of his own situation, with three thousand acres to farm in Cambridgeshire (two thousand of them rented) is that were he to go organic he would go bankrupt.

At present he appears to be a man of fixed agrochemical dependency, and it was therefore interesting to hear him at the end of 1989 reporting for the BBC on a visit to the Mississippi Delta where, talking to a big cotton farmer, he raised the subject of organics. The farmer was not at all unsympathetic, but said that unless there could be some parity with his neighbours he could not yet afford to go organic. However, he saw with certainty a future without chemicals. It would have to evolve, was the drift of his thinking. Walston, to his credit, remained silent and moved on to other topics. What an excellent spokesman he would be if ever he had a change of heart and pinned his colours to the organic mast!

Meanwhile, in response to his earlier claim to be living in a real world not occupied by such as the Prince of Wales, the organization Wholefood, who are by no means bankrupt in spite of their dedication to the organic movement, commented with a press statement:

> Mr Walston's real world would appear to be one which is solely concerned with economics of a type which would suggest that farmers cannot, without pouring nitrates and poisonous chemicals into the soil from which they produce foods, make a living, and that they cannot repay their borrowings and pay their mortgage without destroying the land that is vital for feeding future generations.

Up to the consumer

And then Wholefood explained why chemical-free food was at the moment more expensive.

> Production and distribution costs are higher and output per acre is lower. The amount of expenditure on research and development on the production of chemically free food is practically nothing, whereas successive governments as well as all of the giant chemical companies spend hundreds of millions each year worldwide on research and development in chemically based techniques.
>
> This will change as more people become less prepared to eat food unquestioningly, simply because of brain-washing by media advertising and fancy packaging. Consumers are demanding more information about the food which they eat, and as the level of awareness of quality food increases so too will the demand for more research and development in organic food.

This is entirely true, and hands the responsibility to us. We consumers can force change simply by going organic – in stages, if you like.

Political cynicism – but not from every quarter

But let's not allow ourselves to be cynically exploited by those in high places or powerful positions. In May 1989 Nicholas Ridley urged farmers to meet the demands of 'green' consumers: 'Public concern for human health and the environment is also manifesting itself increasingly in demands for organically grown produce. I personally view it as a way for you to rip off the customer by charging more for identical produce. But you need a break sometimes.'

However, in the same month the government launched the United Kingdom Register of Organic Food Standards (UKROFS), ending what the Independent's environmental editor Richard North called 'a decade or so of squabbling and uncertainty within the organic movement and some outside it who have sought to cash in on its growing following'. The new standards, like those of the Soil Association, require a two-year changeover period from chemical farming before produce can be termed 'organic'. Firm restrictions are laid down on things like the kind of manure that can be used – no muck from battery hens, for example. Those who are only tinkering at the margins of 'green' concerns will be excluded. The chairman of the UKROFS board, Professor Colin Spedding of Reading University, said: 'Our task is not to promote organic food, but to set standards. The word "organic" is needed to represent a consensus of what ordinary people would mean by it.'

It was a start. There were those in the 'green' movement who said it would have been more magnanimous if the government had handed over the setting of standards to the Soil Association, who had been campaigning so honourably and for so long. But that would have been too much to expect, given the MAFF attitude to the more purist elements in 'green' politics. For now, UKROFS represents an encouraging way to enter the 1990s with some government support, and it should be welcomed – though with some caution. It is not a charity. It is to be hoped that, as well as soil, it has soul.

Government support, please, for organic farmers!

Dr David Clark, Labour's spokesman on agriculture and rural affairs, had been moving around the country making friendly noises towards the organic movement. In December 1988 he said: 'Let us begin by refuting the oft-quoted comment that organic farming is only for "cranks". I believe that there are some very important environmental reasons for farmers opting for organic production. It is a system which has environmental sustainability as a prime objective.' Dr Clark quoted figures which showed that the cost of taking land out of production (as a counter to surpluses) was very much more than the cost of converting to organic. And he suggested government aid for organic farming. Will a future Labour government stand by that?

He went on to state: 'People are now also prepared to pay a premium for organic food.' A National Farmers' Union survey conducted in 1988 suggested that 50 per cent of the public were prepared to pay up to 10 per cent more for organic food. A survey of one thousand shoppers carried out by Presto in 1986 perhaps gives the reason why: 'Seventy-six per cent of them thought that all food should be grown without chemicals.'

A farmer's daughter and agricultural graduate made some very sensible and even-handed comments on this:

> I think many farmers have some sympathy with the organic movement and would like to know more about the financial state and security of organic farmers and what they live on during the conversion period.
>
> I don't think the mainstream of farming perceives there to be a battleground between them and organic farmers. Most are looking to diversify now that the mess of over-production caused by the EC's Common Agricultural Policy is being sorted out.
>
> If financial security could be a result of organic farming, many farmers would be happy to do it. However, until it gets government financial backing on a level similar to that pumped into conventional agriculture it will not be a viable option for any but the most committed. I do think the Soil Association is being over-optimistic with their 20 per cent.
>
> If farmers can afford to manage the land sympathetically, they will – with the exception of agrochemical maniacs. But it is a job, and they do have to make a living. It's not just Suffolk squires in the business!

Growers in the vanguard

The burgeoning firm of Jordan's in Bedfordshire is already employing hundreds of farmers to supply organic and 'conservation-grade' cereals for flour and for their premium-grade bars, breakfast foods and so on. 'Conservation-grade' indicates a halfway house between organic and standard modern methods – some steps have been taken to reduce the environmental damage caused by intensive farming. The company was set up in the 1970s when Bill Jordan returned from the USA with news of the success of organic growing and selling across the Atlantic. Numerous companies and organizations operate on the right lines, and what they all have in common is their desire to be part of the solution rather than part of the problem.

There is no doubt that the days are numbered for the 'heavy-metal' agrochemicalists. This term does not refer to those who are in the chemical manufacturing business – their aims are clear and legitimate, and they will shift their research and development thrust elsewhere. No, it refers to those over-producing growers who for some reason have got hooked on the damn things and can't give them up. Like other addicts, they will have to be helped in their withdrawal. It's up to you, readers and parents, to show them the way by going organic.

Safer ways of dealing with pests

In *This Poisoned Earth* Nigel Dudley points out that there are choices other than total organic conversion. One of these is integrated pest management, which embraces:

- using fewer pesticides, and using these in the best way possible to avoid waste
- making best use of the existing predators by not killing them with pesticides
- timing planting to avoid the times when pests are most active
- using mechanical methods of dealing with weeds
- using mechanical barriers such as netting against pests and weeds
- removing all dead plant material which can harbour pests and diseases
- rotation of crops (growing the same crop on the same land season after season encourages a build-up of pests and depletes the soil)
- seeking out improved crop strains
- using biological controls (introducing new predators).

Biotechnology or genetic engineering

Whatever happens to the soil and to the plants and livestock and wildlife that live off it, in it and on it, it is certain that a major role will be played by the new world of opportunity known as biotechnology. It will change the way plants are produced and animals are structured – and at present most of us know very little about it.

Let's define exactly what we are talking about here. Since time immemorial farmers have always 'selected', in the sense of breeding from the best animals and keeping the seed from the strongest plants. The modern bacon pig, with a long back, bears little physical resemblance to the swine that rooted in the medieval woodlands – he has been bred to produce the maximum number of rashers. No, the innovations of the future will be made by people in white coats in labs. Nigel Dudley described it succinctly in *This Poisoned Earth*:

> When DNA was discovered, and the key to the genetic code was cracked, this opened up the possibility of radically changing the characteristics of

living materials. For the first time in history, desired genetic material could be taken from one species and added to another, effectively giving the ability to create 'new species' with physical characteristics fitted to order. This is the set of techniques which have become known as biotechnology or 'genetic engineering'.

In September 1989 ICI opened a new £8 million research facility at its Jealott's Hill station near Bracknell where, as *The Independent* reported, 130 scientists and technologists 'will reshape such crops as tomatoes, sugar beet, oilseed rape and maize'. The paper's science editor, Tom Wilkie, stated: 'ICI's biotechnologists have already redesigned the genetic blueprint of the tomato. Starting with the variety Ailsa Craig, they have altered the natural processes of ripening and softening to produce a version which tends not to go soft as it ripens.'

We consumers stand to benefit from better-flavoured tomatoes in the shops, while the growers and traders will suffer fewer losses during harvesting and transport. That is the theory. The technique will be transferred from Ailsa Craig to more commercially attractive varieties. But before the results of genetic engineering developments can be released on the public there have to be controls, because this is clearly 'tampering with nature', and the government's 'green bill', introduced in the Queen's Speech in November 1989, is intended to cover this situation.

A very big scheme now under way at ICI, thought to be the ultimate jackpot, involves the alteration of the genetic make-up of maize. The market for this plant's seeds is the most important and profitable in the world. The aim is to produce a plant that makes its own insecticide and is resistant to weedkillers. It is almost certain that the experiment will succeed, and if so it will lead to the discovery of new knowledge about the make-up of other cereals. We should await developments with interest – and caution.

Ethical problems

There are two or three areas of basic anxiety. The first is ethical: Third World crops are being brought into our modern labs and genetically altered without any concern that the country of origin should be rewarded (say by way of a royalty), while the plant thus engineered is sold worldwide for vast sums.

Secondly, the encroachment on genetic variety implied in these experiments is questionable. Are we trying to play God? Changing genes is a deadly serious business, and we cannot know where it will end. Lawyers and scientists must collaborate openly with governments to ensure that what gets out of the lab doesn't go crazy in the natural world. Science fiction must not become science fact.

And thirdly these experiments might, as Nigel Dudley has said, provide more commercial advantage for a chemical company initially to develop crops which are resistant to pesticides rather than to pests. Wider use could then be made of their chemical products for a few more years, generating more profits for the company, by which time the crops could be replaced by the new, non-pesticide-reliant varieties.

Whatever happens, the future is secure for the growing army of scientists involved in this field. And few of us would deny the right of growers to seek a way to sell more goods and make more money without pesticides or artificial fertilizers. If a laboratory can come up with corn that fixes its own nitrogen (instead of this having to be done via fertilizers applied to the soil), and tells its unwanted pests to get lost (without benefit of spraying), then that's a good thing – as long as it doesn't get out of hand. Public debate is essential. Don't forget that spraying was perceived to be a good thing when it first came into farming. Environmentalists share a fundamental and powerful anxiety that diversity will be lost in the race to develop the Perfect Plant.

Great rewards lie ahead

Presenting the case for biotechnology in the *Food Magazine* for January/March 1990, Dr Jonathon Jones of the independent Sainsbury Laboratory (funded by the supermarket chain) at the John Innes Institute stated:

> We have to accept responsibility for managing the global ecosystem. We have to deploy technologies with less environmental impact rather than attempt to revert to some bygone time before we ever messed it up.
>
> It is frequently pointed out that an accidental release of a living organism is different from the release of a chemical because it can reproduce. But if it is an engineered plant which is perfectly safe and easy to eliminate from inappropriate locations with herbicides, so what?
>
> A major commercial objective of biotechnology is to produce plants which are no longer sensitive to plant pests, drastically reducing the need for insecticide spraying. This seems to be an obvious good thing.

Arguing the case against, in the same magazine, Eric Brunner, research associate at the London Food Commission, said:

> Living things do not exist solely for the benefit of humans. We have been around for only ten thousand years while life began four thousand million years ago. How can we usurp creation, the sanctity of life, and believe it is ours to tinker with? Surely, argue some, we must respect life, whether animal, plant or micro-organism, and have faith that nature is no less bountiful than is necessary.

4 The Food Alchemists

All about food processing: from additives to irradiation, and much more besides

As a nation, we British value food less than the people of Continental Europe. We have been trained, especially in the last forty and fifty years, to think that food is good because it is cheap. As with farming, the British postwar cheap food policy had the effect of concentrating food manufacture in the hands of giant businesses. The small food manufacturing businesses that still flourish all over Europe have mostly been wiped out or taken over in Britain. Instead, gigantic, semi-monopolistic firms have gorged the markets.

A cheap food policy means food made from cheap ingredients by giant firms able to make economies of scale. The British food manufacturing industry is now dependent on hard fats, white flour, processed sugar, salt and chemical additives – all the elements of food now known to be unhealthy. The reason is that these substances are good commodities. Hard fats are stable and, like white flour, slow to go rancid. Sugar is the cheapest legal cash crop after tobacco, is compact, uniform, and packs and travels well. Sugar and salt are both preservatives, as are some chemical additives. Other, cosmetic additives are used to make any product look, taste and smell of anything.

The British government believes that the national economy depends on the development of a highly technological, capital-intensive food manufacturing industry making 'scientific' food from uniform ingredients with sophisticated 'processing aids'. British food technology now leads the world.

What we consumers want now, though, is high quality food, not only free from dirt and bugs, but also made from nourishing ingredients. We do not want to eat chemistry sets. The mood in the 1990s, and rightly so, is against malign food technology such as hydrogenation and irradiation, and

in favour of benign technology such as drying and freezing.
One tip: when you shop for processed food, look at the label.
If any of the ingredients are a mystery, put the packet back
on the shelf, and tell the manager you won't buy it.

The food we eat in the Western world is subjected to a vast number of
processes – some of them scary, some of them disgusting, and some
of them (with relief) perfectly healthy and sensible. A packet of
frozen peas, for instance, picked at their prime and frozen immediately, probably contains even more nutritional goodness than
'fresh' peas in the pod, which will have taken some time to travel
from the grower via the wholesale market to your greengrocer or
supermarket. Parents for Safe Food advise you to buy your food as
near to the beginning of the food chain as possible – 'Keep it simple'
should be your motto. But to do that, you need to know what all the
various processes are, and what they mean in terms of what you are
putting into your children's mouths.

The national health needs watching

In Chapter 1 James Erlichman was quoted as saying that nobody was
known to have died of pesticide residues – and people are not
dropping like flies because they drink our nitrate-rich water. Fair
enough. The nation's health, however, is not good. There are, for
instance, 180,000 deaths each year from coronary heart disease. And
it's partly down to what we eat.

Stand at any supermarket check-out and you can count the trolleys
rolling past, filled with what the grocery trade calls 'value-added'
foods: packet cakes full of fat and sugar; tins of fruit in sugar syrup;
low-fibre sliced bread; sausages, burgers and meat pies .... Our
priorities, as a nation, are wrong. We resent paying out on basic
food, but seem to love our junk.

Big business

Our predilection for this kind of food has resulted in the creation of a
small number of very large, very rich companies. Food manufacturing in Britain is concentrated in the hands of fewer firms than in any
other country in the industrialized world. The markets for biscuits,

chocolate confectionery and soft drinks (all staples in Britain), and for packaged bread and cakes and sugar, are each dominated by a mere handful of firms:

- United Biscuits, Nabisco and Rowntree/Nestlé (biscuits)
- Mars, Rowntree/Nestlé and Cadbury/Schweppes (chocolate confectionery)
- Beecham, Cadbury/Schweppes and Reckitt & Colman (soft drinks)
- Associated British Foods and Rank Hovis McDougall (bread)
- Rank Hovis McDougall and Allied-Lyons (cakes)
- Tate & Lyle and British Sugar (sugar).

Unilever, the world's biggest food manufacturing company, which specializes in fats for human consumption, has a strong or dominant position in the markets for

- margarine
- ice cream
- sausages and other processed meats
- soups
- ready-made meals
- chemical additives.

The company announced a profit of £1454 million for 1989.

What is MRM?

Chapter 2 contained some unpleasant truths about the state of British abattoirs. One of the products of these unlovely places is a substance called MRM, which may well end up in those very sausages, burgers and pies to which our children can so easily get addicted – if we allow them to do so.

MRM stands for mechanically recovered meat. It's what's left after a carcass has been stripped to the bone. You might think there would be nothing left – and in the old days whatever was left was deemed fit only for glue, or at best soup. But the bare carcass does in fact contain small slivers of muscle and connective tissue. Jan Walsh, who in her book *The Meat Machine* is very clear about the details of MRM and its importance to the processors of meat, says that up to 2 kilograms (that's well over 4lb) of 'scrapings' can be obtained from a pig's carcass, and four times that much from cattle.

Not the nicest of processes – or the healthiest. This stuff goes into all manner of processed food and – though it shouldn't – frequently contains bits of bone. Additionally, the force used against the meat in the separation process causes the cell walls to rupture, 'destabilizing' it. In 1980 the MAFF Food Standards Committee questioned the general condition of MRM, calling it chemically 'less stable than carcass meat' and adding that it 'presents a greater microbiological risk'. In other words, it is possibly less safe to eat.

A third disincentive – if you still need one – to buy meat products containing MRM is emphasized by Jan Walsh:

> The area in and around the bones is known to contain a higher-than-average count of the bugs which are naturally present in all meats. Poultry is especially likely to carry the dangerous salmonella bacteria (it is one of the reasons why we are always being exhorted to cook poultry thoroughly and not to eat it if it is still pink near the joint). So MRM is likely to start off with a higher bacteria level than any other forms of meat.

Unfortunately, since it is not compulsory to state that products containing MRM do so, you may find it quite hard to differentiate the 'good' sausage from the slurry-filled one. Play safe with your children's health. Buy and eat real meat. You will probably have to pay more, but you will be running a much lower risk of consuming all those connective tissues and tiny bits of gristle that you certainly would have discarded from old-fashioned pies, tinned stews and sausages in days gone by.

The wrong sort of reform

But it isn't only mechanically recovered meat that worries the experts watching our food. It is the wholesale incorporation of all sorts of meat scraps into what becomes 're-formed meat'. By chemically and mechanically brilliant processes, lots of odd little items, such as:

- emulsions of rind and fat
- cereal
- milk protein
- water

can be flaked, pounded, pumped up, blown out, twisted, stretched, tumbled, massaged and, in due course, totally re-formed into a lovely-looking 'ham steak'. It will taste ... mmm, scrumptious! But what is it? We know it once had something to do with the sorrowing pig, but this is born-again meat. Now that we know what it is, surely we want none of it?

The right kind of processing

Yet not all the processes used in the food industry are 'bad guys'. For a change, let's look at some that have a definite place in the thinking parent's fridge and store cupboard.

Drying

The first form of food processing used by early man was probably drying. It is very reliable for certain foods – fruit, cereals and so on – and is still used widely by aboriginal tribes for very much more, particularly meats. Drying does not pose a danger to health as long as the bacteria remain in suspended animation, which they will in the absence of moisture. But once the dried food is restored to its damp state, activity among the bacteria starts up again and the food must be eaten as quickly as if it had been bought fresh.

Canning

A newcomer to processing compared to drying, the first form of canning was patented in 1795 by a Frenchman called Nicholas Appere; while the first actual tin can was manufactured by an American, Thomas Kennett, in 1823. Canning is now considered a rather old-fashioned method in our modern world of frozen and chilled foods, but for several commodities it is as good a means of getting a decent meal quickly as it ever was – tinned tomatoes in their own juice are a very good thing, and there is nothing at all wrong with a tin of baked beans (without sugar).

During the canning process foods are cooked at a very high temperature and for a long time. Only a very few bacteria, at most, remain – but of course as soon as a can is opened the food is subject to the usual deterioration. The main drawback with canned foods is the loss of water-soluble vitamins B and C.

Freezing – but look out for the double-glazed prawns!

It was in the 1920s in the United States that Clarence Birdseye discovered the most effective way of quick-freezing fresh foods, from which a great industry has since blossomed – in Britain in 1986 it was worth £2.421 billion. The basic principle is in fact much older than canning. On 11 December 1663 Samuel Pepys wrote in his diary: 'Fowl killed in December (Alderman Barker said) he did buy and putting into the box near his sled, did forget to take them out to eat till April next and they then were found there and were, through the frost, as sweet and fresh and eat as well as at first killed.'

Today's freezing is a much less hit-and-miss affair and is widely accepted as safe, though as with all processing there may be some very slight loss of nutritional values. The freezing industry claims that it is the method least likely to reduce nutritional content, and emphatically asserts that there is no chance of loss of vitamin C in the actual freezing process. All the important dietary fibre remains, and there is a big advantage in freezing fruits over canning them in that sugar is not required.

There *are* snags in the uses of freezing – regrettably this excellent method of preserving food can be exploited, and the consumer along with it. The water that is double-glazed (no joke – that is the term used in the industry) around, say, frozen prawns is a direct assault on your purse. (At the time of writing, legislation is in the pipeline – called for by the honest majority in the trade who dislike this practice and what it has done to their reputations – which will require the actual net weight of prawns to be stated on the package.) And the retention of water (to create plumpness and weight) by the use of polyphosphates in frozen chicken is to be deplored. But we cannot blame freezing for the ends to which it is put. The steelmen of Sheffield were not to blame for the execution of Anne Boleyn.

No smoking, please!

Curing, as carried out on kippers, haddock, salmon and whiting, is a traditional method of preservation that involves treating the food with salt and sodium nitrate (and nitrite). A form of pickling, it has a long, treasured past. Cookery writer Jane Grigson, discussing the great advantages of modern refrigeration, adds: 'I just hope we have the sense to hang on to old methods as well, that even if curing is now a luxury finish people will not let it go.' Alas, conventional wisdom now has it that we take in quite enough nitrate and nitrite already, thank you, which doesn't commend commercial curing, and there are also suspicions that smoking food, like smoking your lungs, could be carcinogenic.

Cook-chill

Now, after that little historical detour, what is there to be said about a much more modern method of preserving food: cook-chill? The subject is also dealt with on p.98, but in general Parents for Safe Food do not much care for it as an innovation. Nor indeed do the frozen food interests whom the *Grocer* in October 1989 said could be 'left out in the cold as Europeans warm to the convenience and perceived healthfulness of chilled foods, particularly ready-made meals and dishes'. The *Grocer* reported the chilled foods market as forecast to be worth 46.3 billion dollars in Europe by 1993, up from 36.7 dollars in 1988.

Like the freezer, cook-chill is a friend of the microwave, but unlike the freezer it has its critics on health grounds. Professor Richard Lacey of Leeds University, describing the idea as 'appealing in that meals are readily available for reheating at home or, in the case of chicken, eating immediately', goes on to say:

> The problems begin with the transport and distribution of food in a chilled state, often through several staging posts. The temperature at which chilled foods should be kept is ideally 3°C, and the length of refrigeration may be anything from a day or two to three weeks. This complicated distribution and storage system is vulnerable to breakdowns anywhere along the line.

The food is initially cooked to temperatures of about 70°C to bring about the destruction of all but the spores of bacteria. Then the food is quickly chilled, and kept cold enough to stop food poisoning bacteria from growing.

Professor Lacey quotes from data collected in his microbiology department at Leeds, which show that 'out of a hundred cook-chill foods from supermarkets, nearly a quarter were contaminated with listeria. Others have found contamination ranging from 2 to over 50 per cent.' He recommends that vulnerable people – the very young, the elderly and pregnant women – should avoid cook-chill meals.

Short of a health scandal of major proportions, these foods are here to stay in this busy-busy, rush-rush world. But that doesn't mean you have to join. And if you do, ask your supermarket manager to ensure that this kind of food is kept at the 3°C recommended by the Social Services Select Committee in January 1990.

Another innovation, known as sous-vide (or, less elegantly, as boil-in-the-bag), has been pioneered by those well-known chefs the Roux brothers. Since it is largely used by the restaurant trade it is described in Chapter 6.

Food additives: poison or fraud?

In the mid-1980s, British shoppers got a nasty shock. Looking at the labels of popular manufactured foods on sale in the supermarkets, it seemed that their recipes had changed in a strange and sinister way. Instead of familiar ingredients, shoppers were faced with lists of chemical formulations and what came to be known as 'E numbers'.

Chemistry sets

Here, for example, is the ingredients list of 'oxtail soup':

- modified starch
- dried glucose syrup
- salt
- flavour enhancers (monosodium glutamate, sodium 5-ribonucleotide)
- dextrose
- vegetable fat
- tomato powder
- hydrolysed vegetable protein
- yeast extract
- dried oxtail
- onion powder
- spices
- flavouring
- colours E150, E124, E102
- caseinate
- acidity regulator E460
- emulsifiers E471, E472(b)
- antioxidant E320.

As everybody with an interest in food now knows, 'E' stands for 'Europe'; and 'E' numbers indicate chemical food additives approved for use within the European Community. (Additives with numbers but without the E prefix are used in Britain without general European approval – but that's another story.)

What happened in the mid-1980s was that, after years of holding out against European labelling regulations, the British government was finally forced to tell manufacturers to own up and list, in the approved European style, the chemicals they use in their processed foods. The recipes had not changed. But they were revealed for what they are and chemistry sets is a fair description.

Technological splodge

British food technology leads the world. But this is nothing to boast about. Derek Cooper, presenter of the BBC Radio 4 *Food Programme*, and President of the Guild of Food Writers, gives the recipe for scientific food as a 'basic mix of sugars, starches and fats; throw in your colourings and flavourings, and there's a raspberry trifle, or a strawberry pudding. And you can have the illusion of eating the real thing, just by adding water or milk to a packet of powder.'

Most ingredients in modern scientific food are mucked about and manipulated in some way or another; indeed, it's hard to tell where the ingredients end and the additives begin. Additives are not just sprinkled on otherwise wholesome food, like the herbs used to give a meal savour. Without additives highly processed food could not be manufactured, or else certainly could not be marketed.

Soft drinks are one obvious example: without cosmetic dyes and flavours, soft drinks would be revealed for what they really are – sugared water. Writing for the trade magazine *Food Manufacture*, analyst Richard Seal says: 'Flavourings penetrate every aspect of the food and drink industry .... If flavours were banned from foodstuffs, half the food industry would disappear.'

Here are the ingredients of an instant pudding made by a giant food manufacturer on sale today in most supermarkets:

- sugar
- modified starch
- vegetable oil (hydrogenated)
- emulsifiers (propylene glycol monostearate, lecithin)
- gelling agents (disodium monophosphate, sodium pyrophosphate)
- caseinate
- lactose
- whey powder
- flavourings
- colours (carmine, annatto)

What (leaving sugar aside) is all this?

Modified starches are bulking aids, used to fill out and bind or otherwise alter the texture of processed foods. As any cook knows, raw starch won't thicken or swell until it is boiled. But starch can be modified with acids, alkalis and oxidizing agents (some of which are toxicologically dubious); then, as soon as liquid is added, it turns into instant splodge. Modified starches are classed as additives but do not yet have E numbers, so there is no way of knowing which type is in the product.

Hydrogenation hardens oil into saturated fat – the type that blocks up your arteries and causes heart attacks. In the pudding mixture it adds shine.

Emulsifiers bind water (in the milk added to the powder) to the fat, and bind air (from the thorough whisking recommended on the label) to all the ingredients. Gelling agents are for instant solidification. All the emulsifiers and gelling agents in the instant pudding ingredients listed above have their own E numbers, which manufacturers quite legally nowadays tend to drop in favour of the chemical name.

Products of the dairy industry that now glut the market, such as caseinate (milk protein), lactose (milk sugar) and whey powder (left over when cheese is produced) add extra bulk and texture.

And then there are the cosmetic additives: colours and flavours. This instant pudding is 'strawberry flavour', which means, as the ingredients list indicates, that it contains no actual strawberries. (If it did, the label description would be 'strawberry flavoured', a subtle distinction discussed in greater detail in Chapter 5.)

Oddly enough, though, the picture on the packet shows a strawberry resting on top of the sticky solid splurge. This is legal too. It's a 'serving suggestion' – *you* add the strawberry.

This instant pudding is no worse and no better than similar products made by other manufacturers, or than typical packet soups and cakes, and countless cheapened, highly processed products on sale in every supermarket today. As nutritionist Caroline Walker has said:

> Twentieth-century foods are the inventions of some of the best brains in the UK. An imaginative food scientist, with a flair for sculpture and design and an understanding of the latest inventions in machinery, can create an endless array of textures, shapes, flavours and colours, and present them to us as cakes, biscuits, noodles, snacks, sweets, drinks, puddings, sauces, soups. All of them are made with varying proportions of processed starches, sugars and fats, and the odd fragment of real food; and they are stuck together with – you've guessed it – additives.
>
> Basic ingredients can be mixed with emulsifiers, stabilisers, firming agents, gelling agents, aerating agents, anti-caking agents, texture improvers, thickeners, thinners, binders, buffers. Water and air will stand up to order. Crisps will crinkle, drinks fizz, sauces shine; nothing is impossible.

Why sausages spit in your eye

Meat products are degraded by means of additives. Polyphosphates (E450) are added to meat, making it a sponge for water – which is why technological bacon and sausages spit in your eye when fried, and why the scientific Sunday roast shrivels in the oven. The fatty unmentionables and rusk inside the skin of economy sausages are stained with the coal-tar dye red 2G (number 128 – no E as yet) to give a pink colour and thus the impression of meat.

Average consumption of coal-tar dyes in Britain today is about the same as vitamin C consumption. Is this a worry? Speaking as a parent, Agriculture Minister John Gummer would say yes: one of his children is affected by an additive in the dyes in processed food. Speaking as a politician, Mr Gummer says no: the official line is that additives do not cause illness, but that some may trigger 'idiosyncratic' reactions in a few 'intolerant' people – which is Whitehall's way of suggesting that if additives make your child ill, that's your child's fault and your responsibility.

Paint it red and blue

The scientists who give official advice to the British government have always been worried about some of the coal-tar dyes, which, as by-products of the petrochemical industry, may cause:

- birth defects
- mutations
- cancer
- acute illness.

In recent years the finger of suspicion has pointed at two dyes in particular:

- tartrazine (E102)
- sunset yellow (E110).

Both these are used in many foods manufactured and advertised to appeal to children, such as fish fingers and soft drinks (for a list of artificial colourings encountered in fast foods, see pp.60–61). But all coal-tar dyes are toxicologically dodgy, and manufacturers have been persuaded not to use them in baby foods.

The scientists who advise government are currently worried about caramel, or rather caramels, which make up 98 per cent by weight of all colour used in manufactured food. Technological caramels, almost all made by heating carbohydrates with ammonium or ammonium sulphite, have come a long, long way from the sugars children heat in saucepans at home, and are used in a vast number of processed foods.

About two-thirds of world caramel production goes into soft drinks, notably colas. A lot is used in beer, meat products and soups. Manufacturers like to give us the impression that 'chocolate' or 'choc' products are rich in chocolate, so caramel is added to the mixture, together with some red dye swirled in from the food colourist's paintpot. And a yellowish caramel, according to *Food Manufacture*, can give 'baked or microwaved poultry an oven-roasted appearance including light and dark highlights'. What next? Lipstick and mascara?

Unfortunately, though, scientists who test chemicals on animals have found that caramel can cause:

- swollen guts
- swollen kidneys
- diarrhoea.

And human volunteers have also suffered ill-effects from high caramel intakes. Are colours and dyes safe when eaten in normal quantities? Compared with cigarette smoking, the contraceptive pill, asbestos dust, nuclear emissions, and even pesticide residues in food, the answer is probably yes. But over time these and other chemical additives may impose a toxic load, especially on the fragile immune systems of young children. And the average consumption of caramels in this country is about 1lb per person every year.

Additives to avoid

There is now general agreement on which chemical additives are suspect. These are:

- all coal-tar or azo dyes (E102, E104, 107, E110, E122, E123, E124, E127, 128, E131, E132, 133, E142, E151, 154, 155, E180)
- caramel (E150)

Ranges of preservatives including:

- the benzoates (E210–E219)
- the sulphates/sulphites (E220–E227)
- the nitrates/nitrites (E249–252)
- the gallates (E310–E312)
- the antioxidants BHA and BHT (E320, E321)

Also:

- the glutamate flavour enhancers (621–623)
- the bleaches (924–927)
- saccharine, aspartame and other chemical sweeteners (these have neither Es nor numbers).

Most of these additives are banned or otherwise not used in baby food. Parents are well advised to keep their children away from such additives – advice more easily given than taken, because most of the heavily advertised 'fun' foods, and the confectionery carefully located on low shelves near the check-outs in supermarkets, are brightly coloured and intensely flavoured.

Here is a London Food Commission list of additives (with E numbers or plain numbers for those that have them) which are known to carry risks, or about which there is suspicion.

---

colours

E102, E104, 107, E110, E122, E123, E124, E127, 128, E131, E132, 133, E142, E151, 154, 155, E180	coal-tar dyes	may cause asthma, rashes, hyperactivity; some have been linked to cancer in test animals

E120	cochineal (insect extract)	suspected of causing food intolerance
E150	chemically treated burnt sugar	some forms may damage genes; may reduce white blood cells and destroy vitamin B6
E160b	annatto (tree-seed extract	may cause asthma, rashes; poorly tested for safety

preservatives

E210, E211, E212, E213, E214, E215, E216, E217, E218, E219	benzoates	may cause asthma, rashes, hyperactivity
E220, E221, E222, E223, E224, E226, E227	sulphites	may provoke asthma; destroy vitamin B1
E249, E250, E251, E252	nitrates/nitrites	can produce nitrosamines which are linked to cancers; can reduce blood oxygen levels

antioxidants

E310, E311, E312	gallates	may cause intolerance and liver damage, and can irritate the intestine
E320, E321	BHA and BHT	may cause rashes and hyperactivity; linked to cancer in test animals

emulsifiers, thickeners etc.

E385	calcium disodium EDTA	possible link to liver damage in test animals
E407	carageenan (seaweed extract)	linked to ulcers in colon and foetal damage in test extract) animals

E413	tragacanth gum	may cause intolerance, and linked to liver damage in test animals
416	karaya gum	may cause intolerance; is a laxative, so might reduce nutrient intake
430, 431, 432, 433, 434, 435, 436	stearates and polysorbates	possible link to skin and intestinal inflammation, diarrhoea and possibly cancer
E450a, E450b, E450c	di-, tri- and polyphosphates	possible link to kidney damage in test animals; can have laxative effect

flavour enhancers

| 620, 621, 622, 623 | glutamates | may cause dizziness and palpitations; reproductive damage in test animals |
| 627, 631, 635 | other enhancers | may aggravate gout |

improvers and bleaches

| 924, 925, 926 | flour treating agents | may irritate stomach; bleaches destroy natural vitamin E |

sweeteners

| – | saccharine | linked to bladder cancer in test animals |
| – | aspartame | possible link to neural problems |

But the main objection to chemical additives is not that some are toxic contaminants, and as such a direct cause of illness, but it's that most of them adulterate food and are eventually an indirect cause of major disagreeable, disabling and even deadly diseases that usually show in middle age. As one example: hardened, saturated fat, eaten in the quantity typical in Britain and other Western countries, is a contributor to heart attacks. If cosmetic additives used to disguise cheap fat as good food were banned or restricted, consumption of hard fats would fall, because many highly processed foods saturated with fats could not be made palatable.

Legalized fraud

When you think of chemical additives, don't think 'poison' as much as 'fraud'; for, in Caroline Walker's memorable phrase, much of the highly processed food available in the supermarkets now is a form of 'legalized consumer fraud'. Dyes, colours, flavours and other cosmetic additives are used to disguise inferior ingredients as good food. Many new products depend on a sophisticated use of chemical additives, which are also used to degrade and debase traditional branded products. Polyphosphates, salts, starches, celluloses, gums, gels and other bulking aids, which may be quite harmless in themselves, are employed to swell food with water, air or other valueless volume. 'Slimming' foods depend on such additives. Sugars, apart from their traditional role as sweeteners, are also bulking aids and give what is known in the trade as 'mouth-feel'. Generally, chemical additives are the means whereby food manufacturers create fake food: unhealthy fats and sugars, with other cheap ingredients, masquerading as good food. In the nineteenth century traders who adulterated and contaminated food were prosecuted. Now they are protected by the law. The best advice for any concerned parent with additives in mind is this: always prefer whole, fresh food.

Irradiation – the ultimate additive?

We have all heard a lot about irradiation recently, and the debate continues to rage. Is it necessary? Are there any real benefits? The fact is that good food does not need irradiation. The main reason for irradiating food is to cover up deficiencies in quality, hygiene and freshness.

What is irradiation?

The idea is simple enough. Give massive doses of ionizing radiation to food, and the resulting changes will:

- extend its shelf life – like a chemical preservative
- prevent insects from breeding – like a pesticide
- kill some bacteria on the food – like a disinfectant.

That seems like a good thing, especially since these changes are achieved without additives, pesticides and fumigants – many of which are either being withdrawn or are suspect on safety grounds. And as a bonus, it provides a use for some long-lived radioactive materials produced by the nuclear industry.

Properly controlled, irradiation should not make the food measurably radioactive. Within 24 hours, according to the report of the government's advisory committee, the amount of radioactivity will be undetectable against the natural level in the food. As such, irradiation appears to be the ultimate food processor's dream.

A technology in its infancy

Many national and international bodies have declared that there are no associated problems regarding safety or wholesomeness provided that the dose is limited – to around that of 100 million chest X-rays. However, most countries have yet to permit irradiation at all, and some have rejected it outright. Only 35 nations have granted (limited) permits, and apart from South Africa and the Netherlands, most of these countries use it for fewer than three foodstuffs – mainly spices, potatoes and onions. After eighty-odd years it is still a technology in its infancy. Britain, which banned the process in 1967 following a government report on outstanding safety questions, is only now proposing to lift this ban.

But is it safe?

Critics of irradiation are not impressed by assurances of safety – and nor should you be. It matters little who says it is safe. Public health watchdogs would be irresponsible if they did not question the official assurances on irradiation. What they have discovered is a litany of:

- fraud
- bad science
- manipulation of the rules for safety testing.

They have discerned a systematic bias in the way research has been conducted, reported and reviewed by expert committees. And they claim that statements of opinion have been made which are illogical, misleading or inaccurate. It is said, too, that the pro-irradiation lobby has relied on a lot of research which has not been published in independent journals, and has frequently failed to provide references which would allow many of the opinions to be checked against the facts. This apparent secrecy and lack of accountability is outrageous, and should not be tolerated.

Even so, there is a large body of evidence suggesting adverse effects from feeding irradiated food to animals. In *Food Irradiation – the Myth and the Reality*, Tony Webb and Tim Lang draw attention to:

- low birth weights
- reduced growth rates
- kidney damage
- increased incidence of tumours
- lowered immune response
- miscarriages
- genetic mutations
- chromosome damage
- heart lesions and haemorrhaging.

There is also evidence that massive vitamin supplements have been given to suppress these effects in other experiments.

It is not just consumer watchdogs who are critical. Concerns over safety are echoed in a report by the British Medical Association, which said that the British government's advice 'may not sufficiently take account of, still less exclude, possible long-term medical consequences'. An Australian parliamentary committee, with access to expert international advice, has recently called for the World Health Organization to reopen the safety investigation and produce a proper scientific report. Until this is done, consumers would be most unwise to accept the current unscientific opinion masquerading as scientific fact.

Is it good to eat?

There is no dispute that irradiation causes damage to the vitamin content in food. There are:

- losses from the irradiation process itself and accelerated losses during storage
- increased losses because of the longer storage times that irradiation permits
- additional losses from other processing and cooking.

So irradiated food will look fresh but will actually be old, stale and nutritionally depleted – counterfeit fresh! Even if the questions about its safety can be resolved, it will still need to be regarded like any other food that is taken from the freezer, the packet and the can – food that can be eaten for convenience but that should be balanced with fresh food for health. Therefore, as consumers, we must insist that all irradiated food is clearly labelled.

Abuse and exploitation

Incredibly, there is no method for detecting whether food has been irradiated, nor of ensuring that it has not been over-dosed. Numerous cases have come to light where companies have used irradiation to hide unacceptable levels of contamination in unsaleable food – sometimes in food rejected as unfit by national health agencies. These cases include illegal importation, insurance fraud and customs fraud. The use of the irradiation facilities in Europe, especially the Netherlands, has led to the term 'dutching' being coined by the international food trade. A newspaper investigation turned up the fascinating insider slang: 'Send the prawns on holiday to Holland.'

No solution to food poisoning, no farewell to additives

Ironically, this use of irradiation does not remove the risk of bacterial food poisoning. In fact it may actually increase it, because only certain bacteria are killed. More lethal ones such as those which cause botulism remain, but now unaccompanied by any of the competition yeasts and mould, or the bacteria that give a warning smell when food is going off. And viruses (such as hepatitis) and toxins (the chemical poisons created by some bacteria which cause certain forms of food poisoning) will also remain in the food.

Additionally, irradiation creates a false sense of security which may actually increase the risk of food poisoning. If public health laboratories find high levels of bacteria in food this indicates bad hygiene and the possibility of hidden hazards. Irradiation kills some of these bacteria and so makes obsolete existing controls which guarantee that food is safe, wholesome and fit to eat. A new testing system has yet to be put in place.

More stringent controls on temperature will be needed with irradiated food. In addition the food industry will still need preservatives, flavours and colours to hide the effects of irradiation such as flavour, colour and texture changes, vitamin loss and increased rancidity (which makes meat smell like a wet dog); and chemicals will be needed to bind water into meat and reduce bleeding.

Who wants it?

The food industry doesn't want irradiation, because it will only draw attention to problems of hygiene. A recent survey of the leading supermarket chains, undertaken by the London Food Commission and Friends of the Earth, found only one, J. Sainsbury, in favour of selling irradiated food. The majority have no plans to stock it, though a few appear to be fence-sitting – not good for their 'green' image!

Consumers overwhelmingly do not want it. This was clearly revealed in the results of a Consumers' Association survey in 1989.

Where, then, is the pressure for irradiation coming from? The simple answer is the nuclear industry. The search for a peaceful use for atomic technology has been a dream for many. But it has come to be viewed by others as a failed dream – one which occasionally borders on a nightmare. Should we, the public, be forced to accept the risks of this experiment with our food supply in order to provide a justification for nuclear energy?

What's to be done?

You can help the campaign against irradiation in three ways:

- by writing to your Member of Parliament
- by writing to your Member of the European Parliament – an attempt is being made to enforce the legalization of irradiation in all EC countries by 1992
- by writing to your local supermarket – asking where the company stands on irradiated food, congratulating those which have taken a clear decision not to sell it, and persuading the others to think again.

As with all other less than perfect aspects of the food industry, if enough consumers speak up we can create a sizeable lobby and see that something is done.

5 The Shopping Maze

Retailing, advertising, packaging and labelling

There's plenty of nourishing food on the shelves of every well-stocked supermarket. And in the 1980s the giant British food retailing chains, faced with customers demanding healthy, safe food, started to clean up their act. 'There is such a groundswell of public opinion now against food additives,' said Tony Combes of Safeway in 1985, explaining the company's decision to kick 51 toxicologically dodgy chemicals out of its own-label foods. Healthy food is good for business: 'There is', he said, 'marketing advantage in getting ahead of our competitors.'

In the same year Tesco launched its *Guide to Healthy Eating*, pledging that by the summer of 1986 all 1500 of its own-label foods would carry details of the amounts of fats, added sugar and salt they contained. Between 1985 and 1989 Tesco distributed over 25 million of the booklets in its stores; and its annual profits rose substantially.

So after the mid-1980s we had a chance to identify healthy food. But not so safe food: for 1989 was the year of the great bug scandal – a shock for all food retailers. Professor Richard Lacey, the microbiologist who pointed up the dangers of salmonella and listeria poisoning, believes that most pre-prepared cook-chill food, now such a feature on supermarket shelves, is a health hazard.

Retailers are not usually to blame when the food on their shelves is infected. The big stores spend a lot of money and care on quality and safety control. The root causes of the food poisoning epidemics we now live with are factory farming and the unsafe cook-chill method of food preparation. If what we want is cheap, convenient food, unhealthy and eventually unsafe food is what we will get.

Selling us the goods

The butcher, the baker, the candlestick maker – that was what the high streets of Britain used to be about. Now it means all those multiples. But in towns all over the country the occasional speciality stores can still be found: the grocer, perhaps, whose grandfather had the presence of mind to buy his premises cheaply. Today, if he is lucky, his shop will be enjoying a new lease of life as more people are starting to want food produced and presented in the traditional way. His grandfather may have been turning in his grave as the supermarkets' plastic signs sprang up round about, but now he will be smiling to himself as the wheel of fashion turns in favour of his distinguished old shop.

That shop still smells of freshly ground coffee, and bacon, and cheese cut for each new customer, and it has a fine old counter, with stock ranged on shelves up to the ceiling. The atmosphere is relaxed, even when the shop is busy. No one complains. This is not a shop to rush in and out of – and you can be tempted as your eyes roam over the exotic jars and bottles and tins. The family grocer knew all about impulse buying when supermarkets had yet to be dreamt of.

Likewise the fishmonger, with all those lovely translucent fish glistening on his marble slab. Customers wait in line, mesmerized by the speed and skill with which he fillets and skins and wraps. For a little while time stands still, as it did when we were fascinated children with our mums, watching an expert at work. If you don't know how to cook it, you only have to ask – it's all part of the tradition of service. No wonder many supermarkets have gone over to the idea of shops-within-shops, where we queue and point and have our food weighed out just like in the old days.

The high street giants

Whatever their style, supermarkets are here to stay, and the public has grown used to the convenience of filling up large trolleys with things they didn't realize they needed until they saw them on the shelves. Lots of research has gone into the planning of the routes around the store. All the basic ingredients for a family shop are dotted far and wide.

You trudge what feels like miles to buy your tea and dogfood, cheese and breakfast cereals, orange juice and lavatory paper – it often seems easier just to go up and down each aisle, picking out what you may need from each shelf. That is what you are meant to do – to hell with the shopping list, what have they got here that you fancy?

Temptation to buy the most expensive goods is staring you in the face from the most accessible and strategically placed shelves. Top shelves and lower shelves are kept for the less expensive items. 'Loss leaders' – items that are allowed to be sold at a loss – are bought in vast quantities from manufacturers and displayed prominently. They appeal to the thrifty bit of us, for everyone likes a bargain, and they put us in a good mood to spend on other items.

The fruit and vegetables and meat may have their looks enhanced by 'value-added lighting'. When you are standing by these sections, look at the palms of your hands – if they are an unusual purplish-pink colour, you will know that this is 'showbusiness'. Produce displayed in a cosy, nostalgic way invites us to buy. Sometimes, too, there are huge glossy photographs of lovely food on display. Different colours are used to create particular images:

- green for freshness
- white for hygiene
- red to make us act on impulse
- yellow to make us pack up our troubles and follow the 'yellow brick road' around the store.

Maybe it will lead you hungrily to that lovely aroma wafting from the in-store bakery. What does it matter if the bread and cakes are only being heated? Why not buy a couple of extra loaves and some rolls? They smell so good! And good smells are good business.

And now perhaps something sweet and creamy for a treat. This is no time to read the lists of ingredients on the labels too carefully – why be a spoilsport? At the check-out, the final temptations: sweeties, magazines, miniature bottles of liquor and some spare razor blades for himself. Recognizable? Of course.

Beat the clever manipulators

But if you don't want to be manipulated by skilled retail operators, who after all have a job to do and profits to make:

- take a shopping list and stick to it
- eat (and especially feed the kids!) before you shop
- read all 'sell-by' dates and lists of ingredients
- try to pay cash – cheques and credit cards make unnecessary spending too easy
- if you want organically produced food and can't find it, ask for it.

Should you wish to buy confectionery, and processed food, made with unsaturated fat and less sugar and salt, or real meat from cattle whose rearing, handling and slaughtering has been to the highest standards, or free-range poultry and eggs – say so. If you don't, who can blame the retailer for thinking you are satisfied with what's on offer?

After all, it's in their interests that you buy, rather than leave the store dissatisfied. In 1981, in response to market research, Safeway was the first supermarket chain to sell organic fruit and vegetables. Tesco, Waitrose, Sainsbury's and Marks and Spencer followed suit. Now Safeway is pioneering the sale of beef reared to the high standards of the Soil Association. It will be more expensive, but if you want to eat beef reared ethically and with humanity from field to abattoir, free from mad cow disease, the over-use of antibiotics and pre-slaughter stress, you may feel the extra cost is worthwhile.

Shopping round the corner

The elderly and the car-less can't get to these palaces of conspicuous consumption. Just as well, perhaps, because the temptations, and therefore frustrations, for those on a limited income may be too great. But the local alternatives have their drawbacks, and often aren't much good for pensioners trying to eat a decent basic diet, or for young mums with growing children.

The little corner shop has to open long hours to make a profit. Its prices cannot compete with those of large stores; it hasn't got the space for a variety of products; and it can't afford to have much produce around that doesn't have a long shelf life.

In some areas 'convenience stores' have taken over from the corner shop. They, too, are open for long hours and their profit comes from specializing in ice cream and chilled and frozen foods, milk, juices, soft drinks, beer, wine, a deli-service, bread, cakes, cigarettes, newspapers and magazines. Maybe there will be a microwave oven for heating pies and pasties, but there is unlikely to be much of a range of fresh fruit and vegetables or ordinary groceries.

If we want to see more town centres and more high streets able once again to support real food shops, and not just chain stores and estate agents, we will have to demand them and support them. The ones we still have need our custom, and welcome it. The community needs them – use them or lose them!

The persuasion industry

Even before we get inside the shops – multiple or corner – we are pre-programmed to want certain things, to prefer one brand over another, to feel that a particular item is more yummy than its rival. We may like to think we are immune to the gentle or even the more blatant messages of persuasion bombarding us daily from our TV screens, newspapers and magazines, but the chances are that you could name the top advertised products – and without much doubt your children could.

The astonishing fact is that nearly one-sixth of all advertising is for food. In 1988 the industry spent a colossal £570 million, mainly on TV advertising. Given that we all have to eat (whereas we don't all have to buy a new car), why do the manufacturers want to spend so much? The answer is simple. The very fact that we have to eat makes us a target not for food itself, but for brands – the Heinz beans or the Kellogg's cornflakes or the Flora margarine that their manufacturers want us to buy, rather than their rivals' products.

Adding value?

It's all to do with what is called added value. Take the humble potato – it's very cheap, and profit margins are low. But if you're a food manufacturer you can turn it into a bag of crisps – and then you're on to a winner. Slice the potato and cook it in hot oil, add some colours and flavours, put the result in a colourful packet and you've got a product that you can really sell. They're crispier, tastier, in an exciting bag, with more crunch. And what's more, the mark-up you can charge will give you enough money to pay for an expensive advertising campaign that you hope will make you the brand leader. Pretty hard to do that with a straightforward King Edward!

The big spenders

Here's how some of that £570 million was spent by the food manufacturers in 1988, in descending order of spend (source: MEAL/Euromonitor):

chocolate	£81.7 million
cereals	£61.2 million
coffee	£55.1 million
sauces, pickles, salad creams	£29.2 million
margarine	£25.5 million
tea	£25.1 million
frozen meals	£23.6 million
potato crisps and snacks	£20.9 million
sugar confectionery	£19.6 million
biscuits	£19 million
fresh and frozen poultry and meat	£16.5 million
meat and vegetable extracts	£15.9 million
milk and milk products	£14.7 million
cheese	£14.3 million
butter	£9.7 million

Chocolate manufacturers top the league of big spenders on advertising, with sauces, pickles and salad creams, crisps and snacks, sugar confectionery and biscuits all in the top ten – making a pretty unhealthy selection of foods. By comparison, the Health Education Authority found it hard to get together the £2 million it spent on advertising its recent Look After Your Heart campaign.

The 'health' message

But advertisers have woken up to the 'health' message that started to come across in the late eighties, and are keen to put a healthy gloss on their product. Ads for yoghurts, 'health' breakfast cereals and low-fat spreads abound. There is nothing altruistic about this new approach – the manufacturers are still interested in their profits.

Is it all legal, decent and honest? At a time when consumers need factual information, some manufacturers and their advertising agencies have been accused of pushing at the bounds of acceptability by their use of 'health claims' in food advertisements. Under the MAFF 1984 Food Labelling Regulations products cannot make health claims without a product licence.

Who is the target of all this advertising?

Just who are these huge advertising budgets aimed at? According to the marketers, it's those with the money to spend – the ABC1 social groups, as they are known in marketing jargon, and particularly the young. The poorest (social group E, which includes pensioners) aren't considered a profitable market, but they do cause a problem because their numbers are growing and they watch so much television.

What a marketer is interested in is not just any old large TV audience, but a large target audience with the money to spend. So the kinds of programmes that television companies show are of vital interest to advertisers. The breweries were apparently delighted when American football was introduced on British TV – it gave them instant access to young men, a group traditionally hard to target. The young are undoubtedly the most impressionable, lacking as they do an adult's capacity for critical appraisal. In 1984 the Australian Consumers' Association recorded all the TV food commercials shown in Sydney over one week. One-third were for food and beverages, and of these 78 per cent directly contravened the official nutrition guidelines. The worst offenders encouraged the consumption of fat, sugar, alcohol and salt, and the ads aimed at children were the worst of all.

One-third were for products such as sweets, soft drinks, cordials, ice cream and sweet biscuits. The child who is dragged away from the television set to sit down to a meal at six o'clock will most likely have been bombarded by ads for iced treats, chocolates, sweets, crisps, chewing gum and fast food, using cartoons or films of kids having fun, accompanied by exciting music and sound effects. Is it surprising that wholesome 'real' food sitting on the child's plate does not hold the same appeal? Small wonder that so many dinner tables are battlefields.

The lure of alcohol

According to a 1988 survey of 13- and 14-year-olds conducted by The Association of Market Survey Organizations, their favourite TV commercials were those for Carling Black Label, Foster's and Miller Lite. By the age of 15, teenage boys drink an average of five pints a week, with one in five drinking over 12 pints. It would be difficult to say which was cause and which was effect.

In 1987 a government-sponsored report recommended a ban on alcohol advertising on TV and in the cinemas, and a tightening of the voluntary code covering advertisements in newspapers and magazines. But critics say the Advertising Standards Authority has failed to implement even the present weak voluntary codes.

Below-the-line promotion

Much of the most effective promotion of food is done 'below the line' by means less obvious than direct advertisements. Most of the information that puts fats, sugars and highly processed foods in a good light is shaped by public relations companies employed by manufacturers or their trade associations. Some companies also produce a continual stream of free classroom propaganda masquerading as educational material, and the current lack of funds for teaching aids in Britain means that more schools are relying on these books, packs and videos.

Another means of influence is for the industry to host receptions and trips overseas for journalists and doctors, to show how specific products can be used in maintaining health. Food manufacturers may also fund academic research in an attempt to give scientific credibility to their claims.

As commercial sponsorship increasingly becomes a fact of life, fast food companies are seeing new areas open up for promotion. There is, of course, nothing wrong with companies wanting to be seen as caring about children or the environment, but we should not forget that their ultimate purpose is to improve their image and make us feel good about buying their products. Before you fall for one of these promotions, ask yourself if you really want to eat the product in question. If you want to support a charity or to feel you are helping others, there are plenty of other ways of achieving this.

Baby milk promotion – endorsement by 'experts'

The market for prepared baby milks and foods has boomed – we now spend an estimated £70 million on baby milk and nearly £80 million on baby meals in jars and packets. Changes in domestic life, with more women now working outside the home, are one reason. But another is parents' lack of confidence and their concern to give their baby the 'right' diet – a growing concern now that few young mums live near grandparents, who a generation ago would have been on hand to offer help and advice.

In 1983 the commercial baby milk manufacturers agreed with the government a marketing code which allowed them:

- to promote their products through the NHS
- to give presents to health workers
- to advertise to mothers through material given out by health workers
- to give free samples to mothers
- to let sales representatives counsel or visit mothers in hospital wards.

All these practices have been condemned by the World Health Organization as discouraging breast feeding.

Packaging

The advertising message is also carried through in the way the product is presented. These days you won't find many foods that aren't packaged in some way – often several times over. Packaging helps to protect and preserve food and drink by ensuring greater hygiene. It helps prevent food spoilage and provides convenience in handling. That's good news – especially for those of us who remember the bad old days when a loaf of bread, for instance, was but half-covered with a skimpy shift of tissue paper for its journey home.

But the role of packaging is not purely functional. Packaging does not simply contain the product – it is part of it. Just think of the Coca-Cola bottle or the Marmite jar. The image that the packaging exudes is essential in marketing the product. Indeed, many product relaunches may just mean altering the packaging.

Manufacturers like to sell us an image of the food – that it is wholesome, or excitingly delicious or will make us happy – and it is much easier to sell us that image via the packaging. How many times have you served a dish and thought it somehow didn't quite live up to its packaging image – the colours weren't quite as bright, or the portion looked smaller?

The cost of all that packaging

Packaging accounts for 30 per cent of all household waste, and Britain could build seven columns to the moon with its annual waste of non-returnable bottles and cans. Despite the practicality of plastic PET (polyethylene terephthalate) bottles, in which most fizzy drinks are sold these days, they are not without their problems. PET bottles are slightly permeable and stretch when filled with something fizzy. Beer just doesn't keep as long in PET bottles as in glass. Plastic bottles are rarely recycled – or, indeed, recyclable. In Britain we have already thrown about five thousand million PET containers on to the rubbish tip.

On the other hand glass is cheap – it doesn't contaminate the contents and it can be recycled. Milk bottles are good examples – each one does about twenty trips to the doorstep in a lifetime. Non-returnable glass bottles can be taken to a bottle bank.

Consumer pressure is beginning to lead to the introduction of more environmentally friendly packaging, although Britain has been slow to adopt reusability and recyclability. But there is no totally environment-friendly packaging material.

CFCs in packaging

The foam-blown packaging used for egg boxes and meat and vegetable trays, and to keep your take-away hot, can contain CFCs, known to have a damaging effect on the ozone layer. The big fast food chains and most of the supermarkets say they have changed to CFC-free packaging, but some still have packaging containing CFCs on their shelves. Imported products may be slower to change, as could your little local take-away. Ask at your regular shops and take-aways to find out what they use, and encourage them to change if they are still using packaging with CFCs.

Contamination from packaging

Before you buy it is worth checking the packaging of all products – beware of any that are damaged. Never be tempted to buy cheap, dented cans as there is a risk of the food being contaminated. Despite the great advantage of canned foods' long shelf life, they don't last forever. Acidic fruits and juices will last about 18 months or less, depending upon the type of can. If cans are lined with a lacquer-type coating, they should have a longer shelf life. Once opened, unless a can has a resealable lid, any uneaten contents should be transferred to a dish and kept in the fridge.

All food packages and containers absorb minute quantities of the food they contain and vice versa. The amount may depend on the material used, and on the type of food. In most cases there is little to be concerned about, but you should be aware of potential hazards with:

- plastics
- bleached paper
- aluminium.

Plastics are increasingly used in food packaging. Whilst there is little evidence that any of the chemicals used will do you any harm, certain types of plastics may cause problems. Reports have shown that the plasticizers in clingfilm (the chemicals that make the plastic soft and clingy) can 'migrate' into fatty foods like pork, cheese, cakes, buns, pasties, sandwiches and chocolate. Tests on the plasticizer DEHA, used in PVC-based clingfilm, produced undesirable effects in the livers of test animals. The information available is sparse and inconclusive, because not enough research has yet been carried out, but the government recommends that the intake of DEHA in our diet should be reduced. Studies show that some people may be getting more plasticizer than vitamin C in their diets. So if you use this product in the kitchen:

- buy clingfilm labelled 'plasticizer-free' or 'non-PVC'
- don't wrap with clingfilm in a microwave oven.

Evidence from Canada and Sweden has shown very small traces of dioxin in milk, cream and other foods stored in bleached paper cartons and in coffee made with bleached paper filters. Small quantities of dioxin, a highly toxic by-product of commercial bleaching processes, have been found to migrate from packaging, particularly into fatty foods. Consumer pressure has led to manufacturers producing unbleached coffee filters for those who want an alternative, and carton makers say they are reducing the amount of bleached paper used in their other products.

Recent concern over aluminium has highlighted its suspected, but not yet proven, links with Alzheimer's disease. If acidic fruit and vegetables such as rhubarb, spinach or tomatoes are cooked in an aluminium saucepan, some of the metal will be absorbed by the food. It doesn't happen with glass, enamel or stainless steel pans. Similarly aluminium foil will eventually be corroded if it is in contact with acid food – don't wrap fruit cakes directly in foil, but put a layer of greaseproof paper round them first. Aluminium in fruit juice cartons and in cans of soft drinks is lined with plastic, which should prevent contamination of the contents.

Tamper-proof packaging

Following a number of food tampering scares in 1989, particularly involving baby foods (see p.124), many manufacturers have introduced types of packaging which enable the shopper to see straightaway if the product has been interfered with. These include plastic seals, and jars which are entirely shrink-wrapped. If the packaging on baby foods has been damaged in any way don't buy them, and tell the manager of the shop.

New trends

The increased use of microwave ovens has led to the development of new packaging concepts for products aimed at the microwave market. One new development is what are called 'shelf-stable products'. These recipe meals are heat-treated to make them sterile, and then sealed in an oxygen-free atmosphere in plastic trays which can be used in a microwave oven. They appear to carry little risk of bacterial contamination, do not require refrigeration and have a shelf life of up to 10 months.

Another new development is packaging that extends the shelf life of salads, vegetables and fruit for up to 10 days. The process involves packaging the produce in gas-flushed packs, using the normal gases of the atmosphere but in a different ratio, and then keeping the food chilled.

Labels – what's in a name?

The thorny subject of additives, and how to identify and interpret them on food labels, was dealt with on pp.60–62. Here is a guide through the rest of the minefield of trade jargon, ambiguity and imprecision which modern labelling all too often presents.

Heaviest first

The first thing you need to know about labels is that ingredients are listed according to their weight, the heaviest first. Unfortunately some manufacturers cloud the issue here and thus encourage consumers to buy products that they might otherwise reject. One trick is to split up an unpopular or unfashionable ingredient that comes high on the list – then each of its different components can go further down. One particular baby food claimed to be low sugar (though no actual quantity of sugar was stated). It listed sucrose in fourth place and glucose syrup in seventh place – combined, the sugar might have moved up to third or second place. The average mum is simply not going to recognize these ingredients for what they are. (See pp. 81–2 for more on the different kinds of sugar that you may encounter.)

Confusing definitions

One of the functions of labelling – though one that many manufacturers might prefer to forget, if they were able to – is to tell you exactly what's in that colourful, attractively designed jar or packet. There are certain descriptions on food packages which have very specific meanings, but watch out – these may not be what you expect.

Comminuted orange

Here, as an example, are the problems you can encounter when choosing something fruity for the kids to drink. There's a distinct difference, for a start, between what you get in a 'drink' and what you get in a 'juice'. First the 'drinks':

- *orange flavour drink* means no real orange at all
- *orange-flavoured drink* means that some real orange has been used
- *orange drink* means that a proportion of the drink should be real orange, either juice or minced up oranges, but this can be as little as 5 per cent, with the rest all coloured sugar water
- *orange juice drink* means virtually the same as orange drink, but without minced up oranges
- *whole orange drink* means exactly that – whole oranges minced into a pulp, with the skin and pith and all (called on the ingredients list 'comminuted orange').

And now the juices:

- *orange juice* should be pure orange juice, though a small amount of sugar can be added to make it up to a standard sweetness. But if any more sugar is used, the label must declare that the juice is 'sweetened'
- *pure orange juice* should be just that, although in fact it often means that it has been reconstituted from a concentrate and then pasteurized
- *freshly squeezed orange juice* means it has not been reconstituted from a concentrate, and this description is normally used on juices kept chilled and with only a few days' shelf life – however, occasionally manufacturers put this description on labels of pasteurized orange juice with a shelf life as long as 10 months.

Jack Sprat could eat no lean ...

Another example of confusing definitions is found on various meat products. The 'minimum meat' declaration is supposed to indicate how much meat you can expect to find. But what the law allows manufacturers to mean by the word 'meat', and what a customer means, are not the same. Legally 'meat' can include a hefty proportion of fat – for example a beef sausage must be at least 50 per cent meat, but of this over half can be fat, leaving just 22.5 per cent lean meat. 'Lean' meat also has a definition – it includes:

- heart
- kidney
- tongue
- tail meat
- head meat
- chicken gizzards
- chicken necks.

In ready-cooked products, such as canned meats and soups, additional parts can be used:

- brains
- feet
- intestines
- rectum
- udder
- testicles.

A final point on meat is that you don't just get the animal you think you are getting. A big label saying 'beefburger' does not mean all the meat is beef – the regulations allow 20 per cent of other meats, such as pork or poultry. Economy beefburgers can be 40 per cent other meats. And 50 per cent of the meat used in beef sausages can be pork!

When the big print really means something

Food companies employ huge numbers of staff to find ways of convincing us that their products are a must in our shopping baskets. Psychologists, market researchers, copywriters and label designers work hard at making the big print stand out and get your attention.

In fact it is often the small print that can be the most useful guide to the quality of what lies inside. The small print tells you the ingredients and sometimes a bit about nutrition and the methods of processing. The big print tells you only the good news – and not always very truthfully at that.

But one time that you should look at the big print is when there are various signs and symbols claiming to be organic. The symbols of the

Soil Association and of UKROFS both offer a degree of assurance that the organic claims made for that particular food meet high standards. Other groups also print useful symbols, and the flour, cereal and health bar manufacturers Jordan's offer a semi-organic 'conservation-grade' mark.

'Low sugar' and 'high fibre' claims

Claims like 'low sugar' or 'high fibre' are only relative ones – there is less sugar or more fibre than in a regular product, but it is not clear how much less or more. Despite recommendations from its advisory committee, the government has not yet brought in regulations on how these terms should be used. When the London Food Commission looked at cereal bars it found the phrase 'high fibre' on one that contained 2.4 grams of fibre, despite recommendations that at least 6 grams should be present to warrant the designation 'high'. And in the section on baby foods (p.117) we draw attention to the fact that so-called 'low sugar' teething rusks are still exceedingly sweet – they contain more sugar than digestive biscuits! This only serves to show how very sweet the regular varieties must be.

But when the manufacturers say 'low sugar' they are giving us consumers a useful piece of information which we should not overlook. It means sugar is present – so if you don't want added sugar then you might want to avoid products with the 'low sugar' claim.

Unfortunately 'no added sugar' can also be misleading. Of the cereal bars examined by the London Food Commission, several stated 'no added sugar'. There was, however, plenty of sugar in them – one turned out to be nearly 60 per cent sugar, mostly in the form of dried fruit. These bars do contain many useful nutrients, but we must not lose sight of the fact that they are very sweet. 'No added sugar' can also mean that sweeteners such as fruit concentrate or honey have been used.

Sugar by any other name

Unfortunately sugar wears many different hats on packaging labels. As a careful shopper you will want to know what the various kinds of sugar are, so that you can make an informed decision when buying food for your children. All these terms are perfectly valid in themselves – it's only when manufacturers play about with them in an apparent attempt to confuse consumers that things start to go wrong.

- *sucrose* – regular white sugar
- *glucose* – similar to sucrose

- *dextrose* – identical to glucose
- *glucose syrup, dried glucose syrup, corn syrup* – mixtures of sugars
- *fructose* – fruit sugar
- *lactose* – milk sugar
- *honey* – largely glucose and fructose
- *invert sugar* – like synthetic honey
- *maple syrup* – largely sucrose and water
- *golden syrup* – mixture of sugars
- *molasses, dark treacle* – less refined sugar (with some useful iron, calcium and B vitamins, but it is better to get these from other foods)
- *hydrogenated glucose syrup* – mixture includes Sorbitol
- *Sorbitol, Mannitol, Xylitol* – sweet-tasting complex alcohols.

In all but the last two categories, these substances:

- provide a lot of calories but few nutrients (the last two categories are lower on the calories)
- can act in the mouth as a tooth-decaying agent.

And all of them:

- make the food sweet and so might encourage a liking for sweet foods generally.

'Natural' doesn't always mean 'healthy'

The word 'natural' is also used and abused. Betanin, a colouring extracted from beetroot, may be natural, but to claim that it is natural in strawberry yoghurt is surely misleading. Following many complaints from both the public and trading standards officers, the government is drafting guidelines to limit the use of the word.

In the meantime the industry happily uses 'natural' to mean what it wants. 'Natural colourings' can mean lab-produced colourings similar to ones which can be found in nature, including those in:

- burnt vegetables
- insect eggs
- tree bark
- flamingo feathers.

Other so-called 'natural' ingredients in food include thickeners and gels made from:

- seaweed
- cotton
- wood pulp.

Salt, sugar and saturated fat are all called 'natural', but are not necessarily what we want to buy for a healthy meal.

Other phrases can be equally meaningless. 'Traditional' is used in quite odd places – one brand of smoked fish offers a version with no added colouring or the 'traditional' artificially coloured variety. 'Traditional, farmhouse recipe' Cornish pasties can include:

- hydrogenated palm fat
- mono- and diglycerides of fatty acids
- tartrazine colouring
- monosodium glutamate flavour enhancer
- carboxymethyl cellulose thickener.

It's an insult to the Cornish!

Trade tactics – tell 'em what they want to hear

Here is a light-hearted guide to packet claims:

Label says ...	But it might actually mean ...
Low sugar	Sugar added
Low salt	Salt added
No artificial sweetener	Sugar added
Sugar-free	Artificial sweetener added
Naturally sweet	Very sweet ingredients
Natural sugars	Brown sugar
High fibre	Added bran
Nature-identical flavouring	Chemically synthesized flavour
Natural flavouring	Added flavour, including nature-identical
No artificial flavouring	Added 'natural' flavours
No preservatives	Indestructible
All natural	As only processing can make
Succulent	Added water and fat
Traditional	Developed before last week
Farmhouse	Are you kidding?
Rich in vitamins	Vitamins added
Vitamin-enriched	We had to enrich this
Orange flavour	No real orange in this
Whole orange	Pith, skin and all
45 per cent meat	30 per cent lean meat
Other meats	Change the subject ...

Additives

These substances nowadays form far too large a proportion of the ingredients listed on food packaging. They are covered in detail in Chapter 4.

Those lists don't tell you 'how much'

One of the problems with ingredients lists (as mentioned right at the beginning of this section on packaging, when discussing 'low sugar' baby food) is that they don't say how much of each ingredient is in the food. The heaviest may be first, but if the list says 'strawberry juice, water, sugar' there could be 90 per cent strawberry or 40 per cent strawberry. One MP put it succinctly when he remarked that we know more about what is in our socks than in our sausages – socks declare the amount of each fibre used.

Nutritional advice – but of little value

Besides ingredients lists on their packaging, some companies offer nutritional data showing various standard components, for example:

- energy
- protein
- carbohydrate
- total fat.

These are often of very little help – for a start they do not relate to health advice to cut back on saturated fat, sugar and salt and to increase dietary fibre. The government has done no more than make a range of recommendations, and for the time being all nutritional information is given on a voluntary basis by the manufacturer – who can choose to give none at all. The best data tends to be that given by the larger supermarkets on their own-brand produce, but for many people even this fails to tell them the things they want to know:

- is the product better than similar ones?
- is it relatively high or low in sugar, fats, fibre or salt?

The 'sell-by' date

Another bit of small print worth reading is the 'sell-by' date or 'best before' date. These indicate the shelf life of the product and hence how fresh it is. There are safety margins, but generally it is best to avoid any outdated food.

Cooking instructions

These, especially when they concern microwaving, or thawing frozen food, should be read and followed carefully. The output and characteristics of microwaves vary from one model to the next, and any packet instructions may have to be interpreted in relation to the manufacturer's instructions supplied with your particular oven.

Missing information

However hard you look on labels, you won't find much information about some of the processes the food has been through. Nothing will be said about the fertilizers, pesticides, storage methods, fumigants, processing methods, solvents, lubricants or packaging used to bring the product to you. Yet, as this book shows, all these aspects affect the quality of the food inside the package.

Furthermore, even the normal information is not given on many foods, for instance:

- loose fruit and vegetables
- unwrapped bread and baked goods
- loose sweets and small wrapped sweets
- fresh, unwrapped meat and fish
- food at delicatessen counters
- sandwiches and take-away foods
- food in cafés and restaurants.

In all these cases Parents for Safe Food are tired of buying more than they bargained for. Because in the last resort, even if we consumers don't read the labels ourselves, the fact that manufacturers have to give information on the label about what they are selling us means that they may think twice about what they are putting in the pack.

6 All about Safe Eating

Storing and cooking, convenience foods,
food poisoning and eating out

In Europe a meal at home is a centre for family life. But in Britain family meals are now uncommon, and real cooking has become a hobby for the enthusiast, no longer an everyday skill. Eating is being replaced by snacking; snacking in turn by 'grazing' from high street fast food joints. We British have been brought up to think of food merely as fuel, and to take little interest in its quality.

Most of the middle-class, middle-aged men who decide British food policy know nothing about food: they eat in clubs and restaurants, and their wives do the shopping and cooking at home. Most doctors know nothing about food: nutrition is not on the syllabus for medical students. And future generations in Britain will know little or nothing about food: parents are losing the skills of cooking, and home economics is not included in the new curriculum for schools.

No wonder, then, that the British people eat so much food that is unhealthy and unsafe; as a nation, we can't tell the difference between good and bad food. Less so in European countries with an unbroken peasant tradition, where people are still in touch with the earth and its fruits. In French street markets shoppers poke and smell the produce; only in Britain do street traders display notices saying: 'Don't touch me till I'm yours.'

It's quite easy to tell when food is unhealthy, stuffed with fat and sugar. But it's not so easy to tell when food is unsafe, crawling with bacteria. And no one is immune. After a reception at the House of Lords in 1988, peers were described as 'scuttling down the corridors' after being served contaminated food.

If you don't know what's in the food you eat, you are in for trouble. Professor Richard Lacey has become a food sleuth. At London's St Pancras Station in the summer of 1989 he spotted British Rail burgers stacked in a stuffy room, waiting to be loaded on to trains, then to be stuffed into microwaves and passengers. 'If our society wants this food, it's very sad,' he says.

The lesson to be learnt from the great bug scandals of 1989 is: care about food.

Storing food safely

How long a food can be kept will depend upon its shelf life. 'Best before', 'sell-by' and 'eat-by' dates can indicate how soon a food should be eaten – but there is confusion, and we need a simpler system of marking the shelf life of foods (see the section on labelling on p.78).

In the home, food can be stored either at room temperature, or in a refrigerator, or in a freezer. Labels that say 'keep cool' mean storage somewhere between refrigeration and room temperature, about 10 to 15°C (50 to 60°F), which is fine for certain products such as cheeses. This would have been the temperature in old-fashioned pantries or cellars. Unfortunately few of us now have such a facility.

The freezer

Freezing does not kill bacteria, but prevents them growing. The temperature inside your freezer should be kept within the range −18 to −23°C (0 to −10°F) and it is a good idea to use a thermometer to check this. A chest freezer is preferable to an upright model (if you have the space) as cold air does not 'fall out' when the door is opened. Shelves with sides are considered a good idea in upright models.

The star ratings on foods are guidelines on the maximum length of storage possible while still maintaining the quality of flavour, taste and texture. They are not intended to be a guide to microbiological safety.

- one star indicates one week
- two stars indicate one month
- three stars indicate three months.

It is quite safe to keep foods in the freezer for longer than these suggested periods if you are happy with their quality. But this does not apply to food kept in the fridge.

Basic freezer maintenance should cover these points:

- after shopping, get frozen food home and into the freezer as quickly as possible to prevent it defrosting
- defrost the freezer about once every three months, unless it has a built-in defrost cycle
- remember to keep it clean with warm water and bicarbonate of soda (don't use detergent or any other household cleaning product which would make the food smell)
- label foods with dates of freezing and use oldest packages first
- keep a notebook with details of what you froze when – it helps ensure there are no stray oddments floating around for too long
- wrap foods to prevent cross-contamination
- raw foods such as poultry, meat and fish should never come into contact with foods that will not be cooked before eating, such as cakes

When you defrost foods from your freezer, remove any wrapping and place the food on a dish, ideally in the bottom of the fridge. This is to prevent any spilt juices from contaminating other food. A cool room with a temperature of no more than 15°C (60°F) can be used instead. Once thawing is under way the giblets can be removed from poultry.

If you are using a microwave to defrost, follow the instructions carefully. The food may start to warm up in places, allowing bacteria to grow, while at the same time it may remain frozen in the centre. Don't start to cook food until it is completely thawed right through to the middle.

The refrigerator

Most of us rarely check the temperature of our fridge or ensure that it is working properly. A fridge should be kept between 0 and 5°C (32°F and 40°F) to prevent the growth of food poisoning bacteria, even though at this temperature listeria may not stop growing completely. One survey found temperatures between 8 and 14°C (45 and 60°F) in 40 per cent of domestic fridges.

Few fridges have a built-in thermometer, so you'll need a separate one, placed near the centre. The temperature should be checked after the door has been closed for some time, such as first thing in the morning. The top of the fridge will be warmer than the bottom. Heat rises!

Some advice on keeping a healthy and efficient fridge:

- it is better to keep your fridge too cold than too warm
- defrost regularly, as a build-up of ice will prevent the fridge working efficiently

- even if it has an automatic defrost, remember to keep the inside clean with warm water and bicarbonate of soda
- don't overload. Cold air won't be able to circulate to keep all foods cold in an overstocked fridge. Beware of this particularly at Christmas, when we all tend to fill our fridges to the brim
- don't leave the door open for longer than necessary, and check occasionally to ensure the door seals are fitting snugly
- don't put warm foods in the fridge – the temperature will rise and take a long time to cool again
- dust on the housing at the back will make the fridge less efficient – don't place your fridge next to the cooker or a radiator, as this could affect its performance (and put your electricity bills up!)

Storing foods in the fridge:

- after buying your perishable and chilled foods, get them home and into the fridge as quickly as possible
- it is very important that cooked and raw foods are kept separate
- cover foods to prevent cross-contamination and to stop food drying out or making the fridge smell
- follow 'eat-by' instructions (see the table below for advice on how long foods should be stored in a fridge). Apart from food which should be consumed within two days, a good guideline is a maximum of five days, although unopened cheese, bacon and other packaged products may be safe for longer.

Recommended storage times for food in a refrigerator

Type of food	Days in the fridge
raw foods	
beef, pork, lamb	3–4
poultry	2
mince	1–2
offal	1
sausages	3
bacon (without preservative)	3–5
bacon (with preservative)	according to packet instructions
vegetables and salads	1–5 according to appearance
fish	1–2
shellfish	1

Type of food	Days in the fridge
cooked foods	
meat joints	3
casseroles	2
ham	2–3
pate	2–3
poultry	2–3
meat pies	1
sliced meat	2
stock	2–3
contents of opened cans	2
gravies, sauces, custards made from packets	never
dairy products	
milk (pasteurized)	3–4
cream	2
eggs	6–8

There is conflicting advice over whether eggs should be stored in the refrigerator. The argument against is that the yolks of eggs removed from the fridge will be very cold, and cooking times may not be sufficient to ensure that any salmonella bugs are killed.

Storing food at room temperature

It is perfectly safe to store unopened canned food at room temperature, as long as the cans are not dented or damaged in any other way. Dried foods such as flour, rice and lentils will keep well as long as they don't get damp, when bacteria can start multiplying. Airtight containers will keep out damp and pests. Cans or jars of pickles, sauces, ketchup, mayonnaise and other dressings can be stored at room temperature until opened, when it is advisable to keep them in the fridge unless the label states otherwise.

Kitchen hygiene

- keep all working surfaces scrupulously clean
- wash all utensils and chopping boards after they have come into contact with raw meat, poultry or eggs, to prevent cross-contamination with foods that will not be cooked
- wash your hands before preparing food
- wash all food thoroughly, including salads and raw fruit and vegetables

- wash dishcloths and tea towels regularly. Leaving washing up to drain or using a dishwasher is more hygienic than using a tea towel
- don't leave food standing around in the kitchen
- cool cooked foods as quickly as possible
- keep waste bins covered and away from food. Clean them regularly with disinfectant
- keep pets off work surfaces and away from food.

Cooking

Dealing with bacteria

We cook food for two reasons: to make it more edible, by altering the texture, taste and smell; and to make it safe. Cooking to high enough temperatures (70 to 80°C/160 to 180°F) should kill any harmful bacteria and destroy any toxins. Lower temperatures may produce the same results if the food is cooked over longer periods.

The most effective way to destroy food poisoning bacteria is to boil or fry foods. Generally, heating occurs much more quickly in food cooked in hot liquids than in those cooked in hot air.

When you are frying larger items such as pieces of chicken, or foods with coatings such as breadcrumbs, you will need to take special care to ensure the food is cooked right through. Do it more slowly, and turn it frequently.

Cooking chickens and turkeys can pose particular problems, for the insides of the carcass may be contaminated with salmonella or campylobacter bacteria. Don't stuff poultry when roasting it, as this prevents hot air circulating – cook your stuffing separately.

A meat thermometer can be useful to check that the inside temperature of a joint of meat has reached 70 to 80°C (160 to 180°F). An alternative, traditional method is to insert a skewer – if the juices run clear, the joint should be thoroughly cooked. This method works on the principle that when blood is heated to temperatures needed to kill bacteria it solidifies, so cannot run out of the hole made by the skewer, whereas transparent fat that has been liquefied by the heat can do so.

Microwave ovens

Frozen meals and chilled ready-made meals have been one of the food industry's few growth areas promoted by the increase in microwave oven ownership. Nearly half of all households now own a microwave, and after a long day at work it can certainly seem an advantage to be able to pop a ready-meal in the microwave and have it sitting on your plate in just a few minutes.

But that promise has turned somewhat sour. Tests have shown that microwave ovens are less efficient than conventional ones at destroying food poisoning bacteria. They fail to heat foods evenly, leaving so-called cold spots where temperatures may not be high enough to kill potentially harmful bacteria such as salmonella and listeria which have been found in cook-chill foods and other products, particularly poultry. Sixty per cent of poultry on sale in supermarkets has been found to be contaminated with salmonella.

Researchers cooking salmonella-infected chickens, following manufacturers' instructions, found that eight out of nine microwaved samples produced some type of positive culture, and five out of the nine had very heavy growth. Professor Richard Lacey at Leeds University found that microwave reheating of cook-chill ready-made meals contaminated with listeria did not kill the bacteria. Of the 27 dishes tested, listeria was killed in only five.

In 1989 the government tested 70 of the most popular models of microwave oven and found that one-third failed to heat food evenly and thoroughly to 70°C (160°F), their guideline temperature for ensuring that food is safe. And 10 of those had minimum temperatures below 60°C (140°F). At present there are no adequate standards, in respect of ability to heat food evenly and thoroughly, to which microwave ovens should adhere.

So, with all this confusion, the sensible advice is that it is safe to use your microwave for:

- cooking foods that carry little risk of food poisoning, such as vegetables (including baked potatoes)
- heating sauces, drinks and soups made from 'safe' ingredients
- reheating recently cooked food.

But:

- avoid using your microwave to reheat foods such as chilled meals and poultry, which are known to carry a risk of food poisoning bacteria. This is particularly important for pregnant women, the very young or old, or people with suppressed immune systems.
- if ready-meals don't have microwave cooking instructions, assume that they are unsuitable for reheating in a microwave oven
- do whatever you can to ensure foods are properly cooked – 80°C (180°F) is a safer guideline than the usual 70°C (160°F)
- don't ignore standing time
- if possible stir foods

- keep your microwave clean – a build-up of grease can lead to leakage, and there is also a risk of bacteriological cross-contamination of foods
- have your oven regularly serviced, particularly if it is an older model. If you are worried about leakage contact a service engineer or your local environmental health department, who may be able to arrange leakage monitoring – don't rely on home leakage testers
- don't be tempted to use your microwave to heat your baby's bottle. Government advice warns against this because the heating does not ensure the bottles are sterile, and there is a risk of scalding – as the bottle itself does not get hot, this can give a false impression of the temperature of the liquid inside.

In the USA the most common use of microwave ovens is for making coffee – perhaps in the light of all these potential dangers it is about the safest use for your microwave oven.

Convenience food

Many people don't want to spend a great deal of time shopping, preparing and cooking food. But is it possible for the food industry to produce good-quality, unadulterated convenience foods that enable us to eat a healthy, balanced diet? The answer is yes, for not all convenience food is unhealthy and some of it can be extremely useful for quick main meals:

- frozen: peas, other vegetables and fish
- canned: tomatoes, other vegetables (drain off the salty, sugary water), tuna, sardines and other fish, baked and other beans
- pasta: quick-cook varieties are OK – look for wholemeal and the green (spinach), red (tomato) and egg types

But avoid:

- most made-up meat products like pies, burgers, sausages and tinned meat, which are likely to be high in fat and salt and to contain colourings and preservatives.

Food poisoning

We expect the food we buy to be safe and not likely to harm us. But the salmonella in eggs affair and concern over listeria in cook-chill foods and soft cheeses and patés have highlighted the risk of food poisoning.

The number of reported cases of food poisoning in the UK has trebled in the last 10 years, with some experts estimating that the real incidence may exceed 2 million cases a year. Whilst the symptoms are often mild – an upset stomach or headache – sometimes food poisoning can be more serious, causing vomiting, diarrhoea, severe pain and fever. It can even lead to death. In 1984, in one of Britain's worst outbreaks, 450 patients and staff suffered salmonella food poisoning at the Stanley Royd Hospital in Wakefield. Nineteen patients died.

What has caused this increase? No one knows the whole story, but methods of modern food production, together with poor hygiene controls in some parts of the food chain, may have added to the problem. Animal feeds have been found to be contaminated with salmonella and botulism. Inadequate regulations over temperature control of foods, and lack of registration and training for those working in food premises, may also have increased the risks.

The end result is that shoppers have rightly become wary of the food they buy. New regulations in the Food Safety Act 1990 give extra powers to local authority food enforcement officers to ensure improved hygiene standards throughout the food chain, from the farm to the shop. But the way we buy, keep, prepare and cook food is also important.

Who is at risk?

Food poisoning can affect anyone, but some people are more at risk, including:

- the elderly
- the very young
- those who are ill or recovering from illness
- those with impaired immune systems
- pregnant women.

Foods in which food poisoning germs grow best

- cooked meat and poultry: these should be thoroughly cooked and, if not eaten straight away, kept in the fridge after cooking
- eggs and egg dishes: the government has advised us not to eat raw eggs or uncooked foods made from them, such as home-made mayonnaise, mousses, ice cream or raw eggs mixed with drinks. Those at greatest risk from food poisoning should ensure that any food containing eggs is cooked until both yolk and white are solid. Commercial margarine and ice cream do not (unless stated otherwise) contain raw eggs
- milk and cream: people who are most at risk should avoid unpasteurized milk
- chilled ready-made meals
- shellfish, especially raw.

Salmonella

This kind of food poisoning is a serious problem in the UK. The bacteria have been found in the majority of the chickens that we buy and in samples of eggs. There are two thousand strains of salmonella which can produce toxins in our gut, causing

- diarrhoea
- nausea
- vomiting
- headaches
- fever
- aching limbs.

The incubation period is anything from six hours to two days, and victims can take up to a week to recover. The cost in terms of treatment, lost working days and tracing the sources is considerable.

Campylobacter

Cases of campylobacter have also increased, affecting more people than salmonella, though it is rarely fatal. Symptoms tend to be more unpleasant and can include

- severe stomach pains
- the passing of blood with diarrhoea as the bacteria causes inflammation of the stomach wall.

Campylobacter is found in contaminated poultry, in unpasteurized milk and even water. But it can also be picked up from other sources, including pets.

Staphylococcus aureus

This is another common bacterium that may be found in meats (particularly chicken), creams, custards and baked products containing fillings. If these foods are kept warm for several hours, the bacteria can multiply in large numbers. As the toxin is resistant to normal cooking, the reheating of contaminated food will not make dangerous food safe. Staphylococcus can also thrive in salty meats such as ham and bacon, but is commonly found in our own bodies and can be transferred to food from our hands – for example after blowing one's nose. Symptoms include

- vomiting
- diarrhoea
- abdominal pains

but they tend to last only 24 hours.

Clostridium botulinium (botulism)

What is commonly called botulism is extremely rare in this country, but in 1989 there were several cases caused by contaminated hazelnut yoghurt. Generally found in unhygienically canned or bottled food, it is a very serious form of food poisoning which can easily prove fatal. Survivors can take up to six months to recover. It can thrive in anaerobic conditions (lacking oxygen), and some experts fear that the new food process of sous-vide (see p.98) could increase the risk of botulism poisoning.

Listeria monocytogenes

This very resistant bacterium can grow at temperatures as low as 3°C. Numbers of cases have risen in recent years, and there were about three hundred confirmed cases in 1988. But Professor Lacey at Leeds University estimates the real number of cases as about eight to nine hundred, with two hundred or so deaths annually.

Listeria can grow at very low temperatures, and it is thought that refrigeration, whilst reducing the risk of salmonella and botulism, may actually encourage listeriosis. If pregnant women contract listeriosis the effects can include miscarriage, stillbirth or severe illness in the newborn child.

It has been estimated that a high number of chickens contain listeria, but thorough cooking should eliminate the small number of bacteria in raw meat and poultry, although microwave cooking has been found to be less effective (see p.92).

Dangers also arise if listeria grows at low temperatures in foods such as prepared salads, soft cheeses, patés, cooked meats and cook-chill convenience foods. It has been estimated that between one-tenth and one-half of raw salads on sale contain listeria. Particularly vulnerable are those which do not have dressings, as the acidity in the dressings tends to destroy germs. When preparing your own salads it is of course important to wash all ingredients. Bought salads are stored in chilled cabinets – low temperatures are vital, and are not always rigorously observed.

What to do if you think you have food poisoning

Whilst not every upset stomach is a case of food poisoning, the majority of the estimated 2 million genuine food poisoning cases a year remain undiagnosed and unrecognized. This happens either because the symptoms are relatively mild, or because the doctor does not report the incident.

If your symptoms persist for more than 24 hours, contact your doctor. But if the symptoms are particularly severe or the sufferer is elderly, very young, pregnant or already ill, consult the doctor as soon as possible. It is important to keep your fluid levels up by drinking at least half a pint of liquid every two hours. Avoid eating anything until the worst is over. Essential minerals can be replaced by rehydrating solutions that can be bought at the chemist, or else make up your own from:

- just under 2 pints of water
- 8 teaspoons of sugar
- 1 teaspoon of salt.

The sugar is required in the event of severe diarrhoea, leading to under-nutrition. The quantity of salt must not exceed the amount stated.

Whilst you are ill, and for a few days afterwards, be extra careful about hygiene. If possible, don't handle or prepare food for others; wash your hands thoroughly with soap and hot water, particularly before and after using the lavatory, and use strong disinfectant to clean surfaces and utensils with which you have been in contact.

Children under five who attend nurseries or playgroups should be cleared by an environmental health officer before returning, as their standards of personal hygiene may be much lower than those of older children.

The majority of people who suffer from suspected food poisoning fail to report the incident to their local environmental health officer, whose job it is to follow up such cases. EHOs can try to pin down the source of the illness. One government survey in 1985 found that of 463 outbreaks of food poisoning, 259 were traced to the home and only 64 to restaurants, although larger numbers of people are likely to be affected by restaurant sources.

Eating out

Our eating habits have undergone a revolution in the last couple of generations. The traditional 'meat and two veg' is no longer the staple diet for most people. Foreign holidays have given us a taste for different and more exotic foods, and back home the increasing multi-racial mix has meant that the Chinese take-away and the Indian restaurant are part of most communities. The growing popularity of snack foods, fuelled by our busy lives, means that eating on the run, or grazing, is increasingly popular.

But do we really know what we are being served when we eat out? At home we are more likely to know what is in our meal, but when eating out it's much more difficult. Would you guess that there could be:

- nearly 2oz of fat in a half-pounder hamburger
- artificial colourings in the fish batter rather than real egg
- fries deep fried in beef fat sprinkled with sugar, colour and preservative
- no strawberries in the milkshake (but possibly 8 spoonfuls of sugar, seaweed, wood pulp derivatives and once again artificial colourings)?

You may fondly imagine that behind the restaurant kitchen door there are a whole army of chefs preparing your meal from fresh ingredients. But caterers, particularly those at the middle and lower end of the market, now rely increasingly on pre-packed, pre-prepared food and ingredients.

Even in the most expensive restaurants there is no guarantee of freshly prepared foods. The Roux brothers have pioneered what is known as the sous-vide technique of food preparation. Whole or part meals are prepared to a chef's particular recipe, then pasteurized and vacuum sealed in anaerobic (no oxygen) conditions. These foods are refrigerated and can be kept for several weeks before distribution to restaurants around the country, where they are then reheated before serving. On the plate they resemble a freshly prepared meal.

But there are fears that, like cook-chill, sous-vide could present new food poisoning dangers. Poor handling or inadequate temperature control could increase the risk of botulism.

The fast food revolution

As a nation we now spend £17 billion a year on food eaten out of the home, whether in a café, restaurant, works or office canteen or take-away. And it's not just those with expense accounts – in one survey of fast food eaters in an inner city area of London nine out of ten people claimed to eat fast foods at least once a week, and nearly a third said they ate some form of fast food at least once a day.

'An edible part of the entertainment industry' is just one description of the fast food business. The last decade has witnessed the phenomenal rise of fast food retailing. Fish and chip shops have been with us for a long time, but burger bars and pizza parlours are a much more recent innovation. Never before have we eaten so much food so quickly.

The world's largest burger chain, McDonald's, serves 13,000 customers worldwide every minute of the day. When Kentucky Fried Chicken opened its Marble Arch restaurant in London in late 1987, it found it was getting a massive 3500 customers every day. That's an awful lot of burgers and fried chicken, and a whole heap of wrappers and cartons. And a lot of cash, too, with the big three, Wimpy, McDonald's and Kentucky, selling £500 million worth of products in the UK every year.

What good is fast food to us?

Is it possible to eat a balanced diet if you patronize these places regularly? Only with difficulty, say the experts. Some fast foods are loaded with colourings and preservatives, while many, such as fish and chips, burgers, kebabs and pizzas, are very high in fat and often very low in dietary fibre.

And you won't find any labels on fast food. Without basic information on nutrition and ingredients, it's impossible to make an informed choice. Vegetarians beware, too – despite government health advice to use polyunsaturated vegetable oils, some of the chains cook their fries in the less healthy beef fat.

Manufacturers are keen to dispel the image that they are selling junk. Their promotional leaflets claim that fast food plays 'a very valuable part in a healthy diet' and is a 'valuable contribution to healthy eating'. On the surface these pamphlets can look very impressive; the products appear to contain vast quantities of the nutrients necessary for a balanced diet and a healthy life. Certainly a typical meal of large hamburger, large french fries, apple pie and regular cola can provide over 60 per cent of a child's daily energy needs but:

- only 8 per cent of the vitamin A
- 26 per cent of the vitamin C
- 32 per cent of the iron
- 34 per cent of the calcium.

What emerges in reality is a meal with a high proportion of fat (especially saturated fat), too much salt and a fairly low level of nutrients for the calories provided.

Colourings in fast food

As you would expect, a wide selection of colourings is used in fast food. In autumn 1988 the *Food Magazine* published a useful list of what you might expect to be consuming, including:

- fish batter – tartrazine (E102), annatto (E160b)
- mushy peas – tartrazine (E102), lissamine green (E142)
- chips – tartrazine (E102)
- noodles – tartrazine (E102)
- pilau rice – sunset yellow (E110), ponceau (E124)
- vinegar – caramel derivative (E150)
- soy sauce – caramel derivative (E150)

- onion bhajis – tartrazine (E102), sunset yellow (E110)
- tomato sauce – sunset yellow (E110), carmiosine (E122), indigo carmine (E132)
- saveloy sausage – red 2G (E128)
- hot dog sausage – brown HT (155)
- sausage roll – red 2G (E128)
- beef chow mein – tartrazine (E102)
- spare ribs in sauce – sunset yellow (E110)
- pickled onions – caramel derivative (E150)
- milk shakes – tartrazine (E102), sunset yellow (E110), amaranth (E125), caramel derivative (E150)
- orange drinks – sunset yellow (E110)
- cola drinks – caramel derivative (E150)
- microwave pizza – annatto (E160b), turmeric (E100)
- burger cheese – annatto (E160b), beta-carotene (E160a)
- burger meat – red 2G (E128), caramel derivative (E150), tartrazine (E102).

It's your children they're after

Much fast food advertising and many promotional offers are aimed at young children, often through the medium of cartoon or fantasy characters. And with good reason. Market surveys have found that children have a lot of influence over where the family eats – what harassed parent has the strength to argue with a small child determined to go to his or her favourite fast food restaurant? No parent should feel guilty about the occasional burger or birthday treat. But they can justifiably feel angry at the trade's promotion of fast foods as glamorous and desirable products, with no concern for the consequences.

Fast can be healthy too

But adult fast food eaters do have a shrewd idea that they aren't doing themselves any good. A survey conducted by the London Food Commission found that only 20 per cent of people questioned thought the fast food meal they had just bought was good for them. The vast majority thought that it would not do them any good, even though many were eating such food every day. Convenience often seems to be a barrier to good eating habits. But there are some healthier options:

- pizzas: some chains have wholemeal pizzas
- baked potatoes: choose a low-fat filling
- Chinese: choose steamed and stir-fried dishes with lots of rice; avoid fatty meats and rich sauces. Ask for foods without monosodium glutamate – the 'flavour enhancer'

- Indian: avoid rich dishes and choose drier foods like tandoori-cooked meats; go for vegetable curries, chapatis, rice, dal and channa (chick peas)
- Greek: grilled shish kebabs have less fat than doner kebabs; go for pitta, humus and salad.

Too many cowboys in the catering trade

One of the great problems about the catering trade, at all levels from greasy spoon to upmarket nouvelle, is that at present anyone can set up an outlet. Ian Coghill, Birmingham's senior environmental officer in charge of food, said in the summer of 1989:

> Any Tom, Dick and Harry can open a food business. It's one of the biggest start-and-fold businesses around. Under present law you can have grossly insanitary food premises, full of rat and cat droppings, and leaking with human effluvia: and we have no powers of immediate closure. People then try to mend drains and poison rats, while at the same time trying to feed people. It's farcical.

But it's not all bad news for environmental health departments. A number of them, in conjunction with local health authorities, have rightly sought to encourage those places that do observe the rules. Awards are given to restaurants and cafés that provide healthy menu choices and meet good standards of hygiene.

Inadequate resources

The scandal of British catering gave the government the vapours in 1989, and the new Food Safety Act will give law enforcement officers powers to close premises that are poisoning the public. But the new Act is incomplete – training will be introduced for everyone who handles food, but it fails to require premises to be licensed before they can open for business. Which brings us all too smoothly on to our next subject – the children's meal out, where you get more than you bargained for.

School dinners

A national survey conducted by Taylor Nelson and published in 1989 revealed that most British children now eat virtually no fresh vegetables and fruit, and have switched to fatty, sugary fast food. Commenting on *The Diets of British Schoolchildren*, an official report also published in 1989, Health Minister David Mellor said: 'Children in all social classes were well nourished and thriving but ate far too much fat.' And then, in one of the most outrageous examples of 'victim-blaming' since Edwina Currie told poor people in the North of England that it was all their fault if they ate lousy food, Mr Mellor added: 'We all know that diet is linked to cardiovascular disease and some cancers, so I urge youngsters to give as much care to their choice of food as they give to their choice of clothes and career.'

In the light of this you would expect your child to be served good, nutritious food at school – not a bit of it, for the 1980 Education Act abolished nutritional standards for school meals. Some local authorities have abolished them completely, whilst others, squeezed by cash limits, have ended up selling crisps, chips, soft drinks and sugary foods in an attempt to attract kids wooed by TV advertising and promotions.

But one initiative supported by school caterers throughout the UK has gained some success in reversing this decline. The FEAST (Fun Eating at School Today) campaign has sought to educate children's palates to enjoy healthier food and to learn its value. In the dining rooms of sensible schools today you can find:

- wholemeal rolls, pizzas and pastry
- fresh vegetables and fruit
- fruit juices without additives
- skimmed milk
- yoghurt.

One local authority which promoted jacket potatoes with tasty, healthy fillings found that its children now eat 40 per cent fewer chips and 100 per cent more jacket potatoes.

Some schools have introduced 'traffic light' menu labelling schemes indicating:

- red: stop and think before you eat too many of these foods (the ones high in fat, sugar and salt)
- green: go, go, go! These are the Good Guys, so eat plenty of them (foods high in fibre)
- amber: go carefully, and eat these foods in moderation (the rest).

And great emphasis has been laid on making the school dining room an attractive place to be, with music, competitions or theme days which provide an opportunity to sample different cuisines.

If your child isn't offered this kind of food at school, read Chapter 7 for advice on how to initiate changes.

Nurseries and playgroups

Half a million snacks and several thousand meals are provided every day in nurseries and playgroups. But children under five need more than just a good diet – food is fun and educational too. Some nurseries and playgroups now organize activities which encourage an understanding of the social and environmental context of food.

One nursery in the North of England arranged a trip to the wholesale fish market. It was a great success. Several of the children had never seen fish with heads on – only fish fingers and cod balls! Other nurseries get the children to play games, using the play house or play kitchen to make and sell foods, either real or made from play dough. Children can also make their own mid-morning snack or experiment in growing (and eating) fresh foods like bean sprouts, alfalfa and cress.

Recommendations for healthier diets mean moving away from packaged and processed foods and towards more fresh ingredients. But there can be a bonus for staff. As one nursery cook said: 'At last I am doing something interesting, using skills that I had forgotten I had.' Tim Lobstein's book *Children's Food* gives some excellent suggestions for improving food in nurseries and playgroups. If children are encouraged to acquire good eating habits when they are still very young, and learn to distinguish between good and bad food, we shall be setting them up for a healthy life.

7 Stand Up and Be Counted

Lifting the veil on secrecy and vested interests: who to complain to, and how to be heard

Encouraged and informed by this book, you and your family can enjoy safe, healthy food all the year round. Your choices can make all the difference, in the shops and at home, for yourself and for the people closest to you in your life. You can make a difference for the better every day, starting today, as a shopper.

And you will have friends. In 1990 the Conservative MP Jonathan Aitken wrote in the *Food Magazine*: 'The crusade to promote good health through good food is likely to have a high priority on the political and parliamentary agenda in the 1990s. I hope to see Britain's appalling heart disease mortality statistics fall dramatically during the 1990s .... This will be achieved only through national diet, lifestyle and food manufacturing changes on a big scale.'

Six years earlier he had initiated a parliamentary debate on the prevention of heart disease, bringing a touch of theatre to the proceedings. He asked his colleague John Patten, then junior Health Minister, to consider the difference in contents labelling between the two items he was holding up.

> I have here a pair of socks. They are well labelled, as the law requires .... They are 80 per cent cotton, 20 per cent nylon, they were made in Hong Kong, they should be washed in warm water and given a minimum spin. All information which is very helpful.
>
> I also have with me here a packet of sausages, and the labelling might be described as a highly edited version of the contents. There is a long list of such contents as colour, spices, salt and so on, but there is no mention of the quantities involved. Rather puzzlingly, there is also no mention of fat,

though even an O level chemist such as myself could easily discern a large quantity of killer fat in these sausages.

Jonathan Aitken's advisor was the nutritionist Caroline Walker, who had made it her business to contact a sympathetic MP – as anybody can do. As Jonathan Aitken told the story later: 'Half an hour or so before the debate, she strode into the Palace of Westminster, wangling her way past the security guards, with a shopping bag in which there were two colourful props – a packet of pink socks, and a pound of supermarket sausages.'

Talk to shopkeepers and supermarket managers. Write to food manufacturers and retailers. Make friends with, and influence, your MP and MEP. You will make a difference.

Fight the good fight

As a consumer and parent you are up against very powerful forces, forces which can spend millions advertising unhealthy products to your children on prime-time TV and even getting their promotional material into your children's classrooms. So you have to keep up the pressure. After all, your children have a right to good-quality foods, made to high standards. And the person who can defend their interests is you.

You can 'vote with your purse' by choosing only the best products – the information in this book can help you make these choices. Slowly, your buying patterns might get reflected in company sales sheets, and the key decision makers at the top of the company might start to take notice. But this must be about the slowest and most inefficient way of communicating with these senior decision makers. Better by far if you could speak to them directly. And you can.

It is not a waste of time making a fuss. A company that has an eye to the future will, deep down, welcome criticism and complaints – it is from these that they can spot new markets and the potential for new products. Consumers' voices are the source of many a good idea for company bosses, and they are happy when you feed them information on what you want them to feed you.

Take it back

If a product you have bought is not satisfactory, don't be afraid to take it back. If you are uncertain, ask questions about it before you buy. Shops compete for your custom. They don't want to lose you, and they need to hear what you have to say, no matter how uncomfortable it may be for them.

Put it on paper

Writing letters can have an influence, especially if you indicate that copies are being sent to local community groups, the trading standards department of your local authority, your MP and national consumer organizations. It is usually best to write to the customer relations department of the company in question, spelling out your views and making your suggestions. The address should be printed on every own-brand package. If you want to mention a specific product, try to indicate exactly which one you mean: give its name, the size and any codes you can see on the pack. It may also help if you indicate where and when you bought it.

Call in the professionals

If you think a product may be dangerous or is breaking the law – like a piece of glass in the purée, or a misleading label – get some professional help. The people to turn to in such cases are the environmental health and trading standards departments at your local town hall. Besides taking up your concerns and, if it comes to it, prosecuting offending companies, these departments can offer advice and information on the law and how you can use it, and can give you pamphlets and guides on how to make complaints.

These departments have a good record of success on behalf of consumers, but if you don't feel satisfied with the service you get you can take the issue one step higher – local authority departments are answerable to elected councillors. So get in touch with your local councillor if necessary – don't be tempted to do nothing just because it doesn't seem worth the hassle. If you don't know who your own councillor is, ask at the town hall. The staff will tell you who he or she is, and how to make contact.

Complaints about eating out

Not all food, of course, is sold to us in retail shops. With restaurants, take-aways, cafés and pubs you can first complain to the manager, who should be prepared to listen to your complaints rather than lose your future custom. It may help if you do your complaining in front of other customers. If this fails and if it is a question of the fitness of food for eating, or of cleanliness, turn, as before, to the environmental health department at the town hall. Hygiene is especially important in catering because so many people can be affected if, for example, a batch of contaminated food is served.

Problems with school food

Where schools are concerned there are more possible sources of help to which you can turn. Your children's school may have a parent-teacher association (PTA), at whose meetings other parents and staff can express their views and perhaps give you encouragement and support. If you feel you need to make your case more formally, contact the school governors. They include parent representatives, and it might be valuable to have a chat with one of these first. It may also be worth tallking to the head teacher or deputy about your feelings. Although they are not directly responsible for the school meals services, they do have a responsibility for the well-being of all their children.

Ultimate responsibility rests with the senior catering managers. They are the ones who can answer questions about:

- nutritional standards
- menu labelling
- the authority's present policies on matters like additives
- the changes they are proposing for the meals service
- the possibilities of changing suppliers.

The appropriate senior catering manager is the person on whose desk your letters are likely to end up – but, of course, these will carry more weight if you have the support of the PTA, the governors or the catering staff. If you don't like the answers you get from the senior catering managers, go to your local councillor.

Campaigning

If you can, get some people on your side. Better still, get an authority on your side: try asking the health professionals to support a healthy eating campaign as a way of putting pressure on your local authority. At your local hospital, contact the following:

- the district dietitian; in some dietetics departments there are community dietitians whose main function is to work with groups in the community
- the health education officer; often he or she can provide posters, leaflets, videos and other materials
- the district dental officer, who can be particularly good for campaigns on sugar, teeth and diet, and may have leaflets and posters to offer

And at your town hall try:

- the environmental health department, who may help with posters, leaflets etc. on hygiene and food handling to prevent contamination and food poisoning.

Changing policies

It may turn out that what you want is bigger than you thought, and it needs a change of political will to see it happen. This means getting the policy makers and legislators to take notice. It means putting pressure on local councillors and at the town hall, on Members of Parliament and on government departments. It means working alone and with others to get your voice heard, and making sure that it cannot be ignored.

Brick walls

One problem with bureaucrats – especially those in large government departments – is that they are very skilled at writing letters which don't really help. They may try to fob you off with a variety of excuses and half truths, such as:

- 'Thank you ... we shall look into the matter in due course'
- 'The Department considered this issue last year as part of its review of impending legislation. The findings will be published at a time yet to be determined'
- 'We have received no complaints about the matter you raise'
- 'We are unable at present to allocate any resources to an investigation of the issues you raise'
- 'This is a matter for individual choice and not for government legislation'
- 'There is no scientific evidence that a significant problem exists.'

Don't be surprised at these sorts of replies. You won't be the first person to be brushed off like this, and you won't be the last. Over the centuries bureaucracies have developed some sophisticated ways of avoiding issues. If you press for changes they will put up brick walls in the hope that you will go away.

Who is to be trusted?

Who can we trust to give us impartial, independent information on our food? As we have become increasingly aware of what a healthy diet means, those vested interests in industry who feel most threatened have attempted to muddy the water – sometimes in the guise of 'scientific research' about whether their products are good for you.

Manufacturers and their trade associations have a right to put their case and defend the interests of their products. It is when they exert undue influence over government policy, or dominate government advisory committees, that their role is open to criticism.

Have you heard of the following:

- the Sugar Bureau
- the Butter Information Council
- the Biscuit, Cake, Chocolate and Confectionery Alliance
- the Salt Data Centre
- the Food and Drink Federation
- the Snack, Crisp and Nut Manufacturers' Association?

They are just six of the two hundred-odd food and drink industries trade associations listed in the *Food Trades Directory*.

The power of the food industry

The Ministry of Agriculture, Fisheries and Food has long been criticized for its close links with farmers and the National Farmers' Union, but perhaps of greater influence in recent years has been the food processing industry. Many scientists have direct or indirect links with the food, drink, farming or chemical industries. Industry is a chief employer of food scientists and technologists who, as their careers progress, may also move into and between universities, research institutes and government. Academic scientists may accept research grants or consultancies from industry (an increasing necessity as central government funding diminishes), or work for an institution supported by the food industry.

Sweet talk is double talk

In December 1989 the government's Committee on Medical Aspects of Food Policy (COMA) published its report on *Dietary Sugars and Human Disease*, which gives clear advice that everyone should cut down on their sugar intake. The report makes it plain that sugar is linked not only to tooth decay, but to a number of diseases and conditions such as:

- diabetes
- raised blood pressure
- high cholesterol
- heart and artery disease
- gallstones.

But if you had read the press releases from the Sugar Bureau or the Biscuit, Cake, Chocolate and Confectionery Alliance or even the government statement that came out after the publication of the COMA report, you could have been forgiven for thinking that sugar had been given a clean bill of health.

The Health Education Authority and the problems of sponsorship

In recent years the government-funded Health Education Authority has come under considerable pressure to find commercial sponsorship for its health education campaigns. This has become necessary because its own advertising budget does not compare with those of commercial interests.

The government has bowed to industry pressure and refused to introduce mandatory nutritional labelling on foods, but many manufacturers have been less than keen to introduce even voluntary nutritional labelling, particularly for those 'less than healthy' products. During its Food for the Heart campaign in autumn 1990 the HEA plans to endorse products whose nutritional content and labelling are in line with its own recommendations.

But this policy of endorsing particular products has been criticized by health promotion campaigners, who emphasize that our eating advice must concentrate on the benefits of an overall balanced diet.

The role of MPs

And what about our elected representatives? Many Members of Parliament have direct or indirect links with the food, drink, farming and chemical industries. In *The Politics of Food* Geoffrey Cannon lists 250 out of a total of 650 MPs who are or have been connected with the food industry. They included half of all Conservative MPs. This is not to imply that a company will necessarily put improper pressure on MPs, but it would be normal practice to seek to have its interests and those of its shareholders protected. Who is representing the consumer? It is time to right the imbalance, and this is what Parents for Safe Food are all about.

Secrecy – the British disease

Access to information is vital to enable consumers to make an informed choice. Secrecy, although known as the 'British disease', is not something you would generally associate with food. But there is considerable secrecy and lack of information when it comes to the contents, the processes and the health risks of many of our foods. For what you won't find on packaging labels see p.78. This section looks at official government secrecy and 'misinformation'.

In many areas of our lives official secrecy prevents individuals gaining access to perfectly straightforward information. The climate of opinion in Britain is now slowly changing, although we are still a long way from the USA's Freedom of Information legislation. As opinion has begun to shift, MAFF has seen its close relationship with the industry come under increased scrutiny and criticism, and has sought to give the impression of greater openness.

But whilst there have been changes in the Official Secrets Act as it applies to government committees, commercial confidentiality is now the reason given for withholding information. Companies argue that commercial rivalry necessitates secrecy over such matters as ingredients, market share and technology. The government claims that companies will only let the civil service be party to such secrets if it in turn agrees to keep them secret.

So fearful was MAFF of losing the goodwill and cooperation of the microwave oven manufacturers, for example, that in 1989 it promised not to release the results of safety tests to consumers. The MAFF press release omitted to mention that in these tests 24 out of 70 models had failed to heat food thoroughly and evenly to the temperature required to kill bacteria.

Access to the data

Before a new additive or pesticide can be used in the USA, the company must submit all its test data for approval. In the UK companies need only submit that data which they feel supports their case. Access to safety testing data is an issue of great importance for consumer groups. In the USA such groups can obtain copies of safety studies while the approval process is under way, but in Britain that data is only available, if at all, once the relevant government committee has made its recommendations – at which point it may well be too late in the process for independent bodies to have any significant impact on the final decision.

Things you never knew

- the NACNE report was kept secret for two and a half years because its message about dietary improvements was opposed by powerful food industry interests
- the preliminary results of a 1983 DHSS survey of schoolchildren's diets, commissioned after standards for school meals were abolished, showed that many children ate a poor diet. These were only published after details were leaked to the press, and it took six years for the full report to see the light of day
- for over 20 years all evidence relating to pesticide safety was an official secret. After a public outcry the Advisory Committee on Pesticides published its first report in 1986, but it still keeps basic data on pesticide toxicity secret

- with the exception of a 1979 report on colour additives, MAFF does not publish estimates of the amount of additives we eat. It even denies that such figures exist, although they are used by the Committee on Toxicity to interpret safety studies and to give clearance to additives
- MAFF can even mislead its own scientific experts who supervise its work. MAFF's own evidence suggests that at least 30 per cent of food has detectable pesticide residues. Yet the chair of MAFF's Scientific Sub-committee said on a 1986 Radio 4 *Food Programme* that only 1 per cent of foods sampled had detectable residues
- the Committee on Toxicity's report on sweeteners gave full clearance to a new sweetener, Acesulfame K. That report contained references to toxicity studies – every one an unpublished study presented by the company wishing to market the sweetener. MAFF says the studies are the private property of manufacturers. Yet in the USA the CSPI recently obtained safety studies on Acesulfame K which suggest increased cancer risk in some tests on rats and raised cholesterol levels in diabetic animals. As a result of public pressure the government has agreed to place some safety studies in the British Library in future, but this will not apply to reports that have already been produced on Acesulfame K or the 313 other additives already on our permitted lists

Freedom of choice?

It is perhaps ironic that this present government, so committed to 'freedom of choice', is loath to allow consumers the kind of information they need to make real choices. As Ronald Reagan said in 1985: 'Consumers need both information and education if they are to reap the full benefits of the marketplace. They need the information, the facts about goods and services: they need to be educated so they can analyse those facts before making a purchase.'

8 A to Z Buyers' Guide

Your guide to the supermarket shelves: everything you need to know about individual foods

Confused and worried about food? It's no wonder if you are, for food, and its health and safety, have been hitting the headlines throughout the 1980s.

In the early 1980s the stories were about how fatty, sugary, processed British food causes many disagreeable, debilitating or deadly diseases. In the mid-1980s attention shifted to chemicals, and we were told how many chemical additives, food dyes especially, are used to tart up inferior ingredients and how some make children and other vulnerable people ill. By the late 1980s pesticides sprayed on crops, and drugs stuffed into farm animals, were in the news.

In 1989 the messages became more urgent and more alarming, as the great food scandals were followed by wave after wave of bug scandals. And we learned that the vile practice of feeding the ground-up remains of animals to other animals was making cows go mad and die. Bubbling under in 1989 was frightening news about the British water supply. The European Commission proposed to sue Britain because our drinking water is contaminated with lead, aluminium, nitrates and other poisons. As bugs crawled into eggs and chickens, worms crawled out of kitchen taps in London.

And all that, perhaps, is why you are reading this book and hoping that the following pages will tell you what you want to know, to ensure that your food, and that of your family, is safe and healthy.

The basic message is: eat whole, fresh food. This is the right way for everybody, of all ages, in health and in sickness. Best of all, choose food of vegetable origin, grown organically to recognized standards, when you can find it.

Food matters. Your health may well be in your own hands.
You can help yourself and your family to good health by
buying, preparing, eating and enjoying delicious food. And
now, if you read on, you can get the detailed as well as the
basic message. Good health! Long life!

Alcohol

If what's good for business is good for Britain, booze is the best thing
since mother's milk. Three-quarters of a million people are
employed, full-time or part-time, in the manufacture, distribution,
advertising, marketing and selling of alcoholic drinks. And the tax
on alcohol now generates over £6 billion a year for the Exchequer –
over a quarter of the cost of the National Health Service.

Waste of money and lives

If what's bad for public health is bad for Britain, booze is the worst
thing since cigarettes. The total cost of alcohol abuse in terms of
absence from work through sickness, unemployment, hospital costs
and premature death is reckoned at around £2 billion a year. Cynics
might say that the tax revenue more than compensates for this loss.

The carnage and calamity caused by alcohol is horrible: half of all
murders are committed by people who are drunk, and one-third of
all car accidents involve a driver over the legal limit. Drinking is also
involved in two-thirds of suicides, one-fifth of child abuse cases, half
the deaths from fire, three-fifths of serious head injuries and one-
third of domestic accidents.

Around one in every four men and one in every ten women drink
so much that they are liable to lose their friends, family, career,
health – or all four. In the 1930s and 1940s, the lightest drinkers
were young people between 18 and 24. By the 1980s this trend had
reversed and these young people were by far the heaviest drinkers.
Tell your children the unpleasant truth, and make sure they leave this
aspect of 'growing up' to others.

Boozers make lousy lovers

Booze is what makes the world go round, in many people's minds.
Pubs, wine bars and parties are places to be sociable; lunch and
dinner are also times to do business. Drink is celebrated as one of the
pleasures of civilization. And getting legless and boasting about it is a
hobby for many men, despite the fact that boozers make lousy lovers.

What it does to our health

There's no glamour about alcohol's effects on the human body. Heavy drinking wrecks the liver and pancreas, and is an important contributory cause of heart attacks. Alcohol is also a significant cause of stomach ulcers and cancers of the mouth, throat, oesophagus and stomach. Bingeing occasionally kills even young people, from strokes.

Just like saturated fat and sugars, alcohol contains calories but no nourishment. Of the British food supply now:

- 20 per cent is saturated fat
- 20 per cent is sugar
- 6 per cent is alcohol.

So virtually half of what the average person consumes is empty calories. To put it another way, as a nation we depend on half our food for all our nourishment.

But anybody who drinks more than a pint of beer or two glasses of wine a day is liable to go beyond this figure, and three pints of beer or a bottle of wine a day amount to around a quarter of total calories. Cutting out alcohol can make all the difference to anybody with a weight problem.

As far as your health is concerned, it doesn't make a lot of difference what you drink. Roughly the same amount of alcohol is contained in:

- half a pint of beer or lager
- a glass of wine
- a single measure of whisky, gin, vodka or other spirits.

These amounts are all known as 'one standard drink'. The sweeter the drink, the more calories it contains – sweet cider, sweet wine, sherry, port and liqueurs are fattening.

Don't drink during pregnancy

Here's an important warning for women – and men too. If you are planning to have children, stop drinking. An established but little-known fact is that alcohol is a teratogen, literally a 'creator of monsters'. The drug thalidomide is a teratogen. So is nuclear fall-out. Women who drink alcohol after conception increase their risk of giving birth to a deformed or retarded child.

Is there a 'safe limit' for drinking alcohol?

The Health Education Authority says there is and propose:

- for men: 20 standard drinks a week
- for women: 13 standard drinks a week.

Per day, this is equivalent to:

- for men: one and a half pints of beer, three glasses of wine, or three single measures of spirits
- for women: one pint of beer, two glasses of wine, or two single measures of spirits.

Regular social drinking well above this limit will deprive your body of nourishment, decrease your resistance to disease and lower your performance.

Most of us know the immediate symptoms of drinking too much: headaches, dry mouth and skin, and stomach disorders. All too soon these can lead to shakes and palpitations, inability to eat, and vomiting or dry retching. The psychological effects of self-pity, resentment and remorse are no less familiar.

The real truth is that the 'safe limit' is a bit of a fiction. You are unlikely to come to any harm if you drink within the guidelines, and this book is not preaching teetotalism; but in reality, the less alcohol you consume the better. An occasional glass of good wine, or a refreshing pint, or a single measure of spirits or liqueur after a good meal, is one of life's pleasures: but don't imagine they are doing you any good apart from cheering you up and tasting delicious.

Chemical hangovers

Hangovers are caused not only by alcohol but also by chemical additives. Sulphur dioxide, in particular, is added in high concentrations to much beer and wine. Regular drinkers are liable to be over the World Health Organization's maximum safety limit for sulphur dioxide, a cause of chest pain and asthma. Booze manufacturers are not obliged by law to declare chemical additives on the labels of their products, so they don't.

So on the whole, real ale and organic wine, made by time-honoured methods, are preferable. Most people say the taste is better, and the morning after is brighter. And anybody who cares about the environment will want to support traditional methods of manufacture, which encourage craft skills and small businesses.

Alternatives to alcohol

If you decide to cut down or cut out alcohol, treat yourself. Don't swap to pop, which is fattening and full of chemicals. Drink pure fruit juices. Try a variety of herb teas. Become a connoisseur of mineral waters.

If you drink alcohol only occasionally, go for quality. Don't drink fizz or plonk, but savour real ale, a vintage wine or a malt whisky. If you drink in pubs and like beer or lager, mass-produced no-alcohol varieties are now readily available.

Baby food

Formula feed

Although breast feeding may be best for the baby, this book does *not* say that bottle feeding is wrong. Nor should any mother feel guilty if she chooses to bottle feed after hearing the facts and considering her own needs. But no mother should ever allow herself to be pressurized into bottle feeding by hospital staff or manufacturers' claims.

The downward spiral

Food manufacturers have long attempted to replace a human being's first taste of food from mother's breast with something saleable from a packet. Once fed on infant formula, however, a baby will be less hungry at the next breast feed. Less will be taken from the breast. After this has happened a few times the mother's milk supply will begin to decline. The baby will therefore be hungrier at the end of a breast feed, and the temptation is to give a bottle.

The downward spiral is easily begun. It is perhaps not surprising that in Britain a third of all babies who started off being breast fed have stopped by the age of one week. And it is a regrettable fact that the longer a mother and baby stay in hospital, where ready-made commercial feeds are freely available, the more likely they are to give up breast feeding.

Little difference between formulas

For a mother who chooses to bottle feed, one of the main questions must be: is commercial formula feed all right to use? The answer is, first, that it is the best thing to use if you are not breast feeding, and second, that it may be adequate but it is not as good as breast milk.

There is little difference between the formula feeds. All of them have to conform to basic standards, which are fairly good but not ideal. There are slight differences in the ingredients used – most contain animal or vegetable fats, vitamins and minerals, but some are based on cow's milk while others use soya milk.

Breast milk: too complex to imitate?

Manufacturers have been trying to 're-create' breast milk for years, but it is difficult to match the careful blend of minerals and vitamins found in it, let alone the 'live' immunological elements that help protect babies from infection in their first few months. Commercial attempts to replace breast milk have often put the baby in the role of scientific guinea pig. By the mid-1970s, when National Dried Milk was finally withdrawn because the government decided branded products were better, many companies were calling their milks 'humanized' and close to mother's milk.

What happened during the late seventies and early eighties (mainly in the USA, but also in other countries) was that formulas were found to have dangerous, or at least worrying imbalances of ingredients, and problems with contaminations.

In cases where baby milks have been suspected of salmonella contamination, the whole of the relevant batch is normally withdrawn from sale. But this is not completely effective, as Milupa discovered when it had to withdraw Aptamil and Milumil. Both the manufacturers and the Department of Health assumed that the other party would contact wholesalers, *The Independent* reported in July 1988, and as a result potentially contaminated feed was still on sale many days after it should have been taken off the shelves.

But babies weren't out of the wood yet. It wasn't just the formulae but the teats on their bottles, too, that seemed to be out to get them:

- 1985: latex teats were suspected of leaking a cancer-causing agent (nitrosamine)
- 1986: silicon teats used on both bottles and dummies were withdrawn in Britain because they were suspected of fragmenting and causing choking.

Small wonder that in 1989 Professor Morley, head of London University's Institute of Child Health, said he would sue any hospital that fed his baby a formula feed without his wife's permission. 'Just one formula feed can be harmful,' he stated, 'particularly in families with allergic history such as asthma, hay fever and infant eczema.'

The worry of aluminium

An issue which concerned mothers a lot in the late 1980s was the level of aluminium in formula milk. A newborn baby may not be able to prevent aluminium in the gut getting into the bloodstream, and until the kidneys are fully functioning they cannot remove aluminium from the blood into the urine. If fed milk with high aluminium levels, premature babies, in particular, run the risk of poisoning, with the likelihood of high levels of aluminium being left in the brain and bones.

When MAFF scientists analysed 21 samples of baby formula much higher levels of aluminium were found in soya-based products than in cow's milk ones. The difference was, they said, to be expected 'given the higher levels naturally present in vegetable materials such as soya'. Despite finding large differences, also, between the various products they declined to name them. Instead, the Ministry pointed out that such soya formula is available only on prescription – 'formulae with the highest levels of aluminium are likely to be consumed only by infants under medical supervision'. And that was the end of their statement, leaving many parents quite in the dark.

There is no legal standard for aluminium levels in formula feeds, and manufacturers do not declare the amounts on the pack. Values may change from pack to pack, and from feed to feed depending on the amount of aluminium in the water with which the feed is made up. Between 1986 and 1989 the London Food Commission researched data relating to brands and published it in the *Food Magazine;* but it should be emphasized that the products may change and the methods of preparation may also make a difference, so these figures cannot be relied on as absolutely accurate. Treat them as guidelines only, and if in doubt contact the supplier.

Aluminium levels found in baby milks

	micrograms/litre
Pregestomil	1570
Mysoy	1210
Cow and Gate Formula 5	800
Nenatal	590
Ostermilk	360
Cow and Gate Premium	190
Prematalac	170
Cow and Gate Babymilk Plus	130
Osterfeed	100
SMA White Cap	85
SMA Gold Cap	80
breast milk	under 20
EC water regulations	under 200

Current medical opinion suggests that once a baby is a week or two old, and has normal kidney functions, aluminium in the diet should not be a particular problem. But recent evidence has revealed increased risk of pre-senile dementia among people living in areas where the water has high aluminium levels. As a result there is continued concern that formula manufacturers should do more to remove aluminium from their products, and to indicate the aluminium levels on their labelling.

Drinks

Follow-up milk – an unnecessary product

Although there are no biological reasons for cutting back on breast milk as the main drink, even in babies a year old, there are often practical reasons why a baby will be offered other drinks. Dietitians usually suggest weaning on to cow's milk after six months, or else continuing on breast milk or formula. Only if the baby is refusing to eat a range of foods would there be any need to supply additional nutrition through drinks.

In principle, microbiologically safe water is all that is actually needed if the baby is still getting some breast milk or formula and is starting to eat a variety of foods. But food companies wouldn't make much money offering you bottles of plain water – they want mothers to think that water may not be enough and that babies require products which are 'enriched' in some way. Follow-up milk drinks are designed to be given to babies above the age of six months. When Professor Michael Crawford analysed the contents of follow-up milk he found that the balance of fats and other nutrients made it suitable for mammals that needed to put on a lot of weight in a short time. Just the sort of thing, he said, for a baby rhinoceros!

Fruit juice drinks – dentists say no

These often sell themselves on their rich vitamin C content. For a one-year-old, a pint of fresh cow's milk can provide a third of the recommended daily vitamin C requirement. If the child also eats some fresh fruit and vegetables, including potatoes, that should be enough. If he or she also takes the vitamin drops supplied by the clinic that will be more than enough.

The story of Alar showed that fruit juice drinks can increase the risk from pesticide residues because processing the fruit into liquid form makes the chemical even more dangerous. There is no data available on the residues in baby juice drinks (although there is some for regular fruit juices – see **Juices and soft drinks**). But data does exist about another type of hazard: sugar. The television programme *That's Life* highlighted how these sorts of drinks give babies not only a sweet tooth but also many rotten ones. The bad publicity fell mostly on the rose hip and blackcurrant syrups. In both instances mothers are encouraged to buy the product on the strength of its vitamin C content, but they are getting an enormous load of sugar thrown in as well.

Writing in the *Lancet* in March 1988, dentists at the University of Leeds revealed that in a study of baby juice drinks every sample had been found to contain sugar in one form or another:

Sugar in baby juice drinks

	teaspoons of sugar in 125ml (half a baby bottle), diluted as recommended
Robinson's Apple/Cherry	4.1
Robinson's Apple/Plum/Orange	4.1
Cow and Gate Pear/Peach	3.9
Cow and Gate Apple/Blackcurrant	3.5
Robinson's Apple/Orange	3.3
Delrosa Apple/Cherry	2.4
Delrosa Apple/Blackcurrant	2.4
Delrosa Apple/Orange	2.3
Cow and Gate Summer Fruits	2.2
Beecham's Baby Ribena Orange	2.0
Beecham's Baby Ribena	1.9
Robinson's Apple/Blackcurrant	1.5

The Leeds dentists recommended that if these drinks were to be fed they should only be provided at mealtimes, and that drinks between meals should be milk (without added sugar) or water. Fruit juice is not usually recommended by dentists, as the acid it contains can react with the natural sugars present and attack the teeth, even if the juice is diluted.

Baby herbal teas

These are commercial drinks made largely of sweetened water. The amount of actual herb (such as fennel) in these drinks is minute – less than 5 per cent of the sachet contents – and there is no certainty that any active ingredient is still there after it has been through the various manufacturing processes. Made up as instructed, the drink is nearly as sweet as Coca-Cola.

Cow's milk

Only full-cream milks are recommended by the Department of Health for young children aged six months to two years, with semi-skimmed as an alternative for children above the age of two. But there is nothing on any of the other types of milk products to indicate their suitability or non-suitability for young children. (See *Milk*, under **Dairy Products**.)

Gripe water

This product is sold as a cure for a restless, fretful baby. Besides minute quantities of herbal extracts, its main nutritional ingredients are:

- sugar: 15-25 per cent
- pure alcohol: 5 per cent.

The alcoholic strength is higher than that of many commercial lagers and beers, and two teaspoons for a baby can be, weight for weight, equal to an adult drinking half a measure of gin. According to the manufacturers, this sort of dose can be given up to eight times a day. In answer to a recent parliamentary question, the Department of Health acknowledged that over 50 cases of babies being poisoned by the alcohol in gripe water had occurred in the previous two years.

First solid food

Many parents happily mash up the same food that they eat themselves, and even store it in the freezer in ice trays for easy portioning. But the multi-nationals need to convince us that they have better things to offer – and we seem to be convinced. In a government survey reported in 1988, mothers of recently weaned babies were asked what foods they had offered their baby the previous day; 82 per cent had given commercial baby foods. Knowing that parents have become increasingly concerned about quality, baby food manufacturers have jumped at the chance to claim the superiority of their products – their nutritional benefits, their purity, their freedom from additives and so forth.

Herbicides and pesticides

Milupa's advertising says that all the ingredients used in its Infant and Junior recipes are screened for herbicides and pesticides. This may be so, but they don't tell us the results. Nor could they possibly test for all the 426 different chemicals currently permitted to be sprayed on crops.

Heinz, too, is aware of the problems. Indeed, in the mid-1980s the US company announced that it was banning 12 pesticides from its suppliers' farms. When questioned, Heinz UK said it had in fact banned three pesticides – captafol, didnocap and daminozide – several years earlier, but that otherwise the company accepted government assurances that the residues were not a cause for concern. This was said after a government advisory committee had recommended 'that efforts should be made to reduce residue levels in infant foods as much as possible'. As a Heinz spokesperson said: 'Controlled use of pesticides is necessary to produce sufficient quantity and quality of raw materials at acceptable costs.' It's the usual story – if you want organic you have to pay. One company, Granose, is importing West German baby food which claims to be entirely organic. If you can find it, it will cost you about twice as much as regular baby food. A cheaper and simpler alternative, of course, is to eat organic food yourself and just mash some in a sieve or put it through the blender.

Additives

On the additives front, most baby foods contain very few as it is illegal for them to include colourings, artificial sweeteners or flavour enhancers. Some preservatives are also banned, but vacuum-packed jars and dehydrated cereal mixes shouldn't need them anyway. Vitamin and mineral additives are often thrown in – partly as a selling point and partly because the processing can leave rather low levels in the food.

Aluminium again

The presence of aluminium in baby food may also be a problem. As with some formula baby milks, the levels can be surprisingly high. In babies old enough to be weaned, the aluminium content of their food should not be a cause for concern – the baby's gut can stop most of it entering the blood, and the kidneys are able to get rid of what does enter. Nonetheless, there is room to be careful and not expose babies to unnecessarily high levels (particularly if aluminium is already present in the water). There is little available data on the actual levels in baby foods except for a small survey conducted by Warwickshire County Council Trading Standards Department, which in some instances found quite large quantities.

Aluminium in baby foods

	micrograms/litre
savoury chicken and rice	3700
beef stew and vegetables	3100
infant formula	840
soya drink	720
cauliflower cheese dinner	600
baby drinks	330

The amounts actually involved may not be dangerous. We just don't know – only future generations can tell us.

Foreign bodies

Objects such as pieces of glass, metal or bone in baby food are often the result of poor production control. Heinz had to withdraw 300,000 tins of strained beef and oxtail dinner in 1986 following the discovery of fragments of bone. And Cow and Gate were prosecuted for having broken glass in their chicken dinner after an accident at their factory. The only answer is for manufacturers to establish and monitor scrupulous quality control procedures, and for the law to impose substantial fines for any slip-ups.

Deliberate tampering

But there have also been incidents of deliberate tampering with products (see Chapter 5), threats to which baby food firms have to react promptly and effectively. Cow and Gate and Heinz withdrew over 100 million jars after a series of incidents involving contamination with glass, drawing pins, caustic soda and razor blades, and have now replaced their packaging with plastic-wrap jars that show when they have been opened. Nonetheless, the manufacturers came in for criticism for allowing the tampering to continue for six weeks before they withdrew their products. During this time ransom money was being paid to the blackmailer in an attempt to trap him.

Teething rusks

Dried bread, crusts and toast can make perfectly adequate teething rusks (see p.132, under **Bread**). In fact they are probably better than sugar-packed purchased rusks – supposed to be designed for newly emerging teeth! Writing to the Maternity Alliance about the company's policies on adding sugar to baby foods, Cow and Gate declared that the sugar in their Liga rusks was 'necessary in this type of product if it is intended to break down in breast milk, baby milk or water and hence provide a source of nutrients in the baby's diet'. The same company produces glossy leaflets stating, quite correctly: 'It is not recommended that babies are fed foods which are highly seasoned or flavoured, particularly with added salt or sugar .... Sugar is used to sweeten the flavour of foods and although a useful energy source, provides no further food value,' and 'That is why Cow and Gate have developed a rusk with such a low sugar content.'

'Low sugar' is a subject all of its own (see p.81), and as the following table shows, Cow and Gate are not the only manufacturers whose products contain more sugar than a caring parent would want to find. The table compares the sugar content of commercial rusks with those of bread, doughnuts and biscuits.

Sugar in rusks

	percentage of added sugar in each biscuit	cost per ounce
Farley Original	31	9-15p
Farex Fingers	28	8p
Boots regular	26	7p
Farley Low	23.5	9-15p
Milupa Fruit Rusks	19.5	15p
Boots Apricot Low	19	8p
Cow and Gate Liga	16	12p
chocolate digestive	29	7p
ring doughnut	15	5p
plain digestive	14	4p
bread	2	3p
Bikkipegs	0	41p

Bag snacks

Parents for Safe Food aren't in favour of bag snacks, believing them to be empty, over-priced Ultimate Junk. This book has already inveighed against these fattening, nutritionally valueless packets of puffed up, flavoured and coloured cereal in the chapter on food processing (see pp.99–100). In *The Food Scandal*, Caroline Walker and Geoffrey Cannon drew attention to why they are so bad for us: 'It is the generation of the starch from the rest of the nutritious fibrous plant material that is harmful. The shops are full of foods that are made in this way. Potato and corn starch turned into crunchy snacks.'

The Real Thing?

Ah, but they weren't always like that, were they? Smith's crisps were the original bag snack, and the brilliant marketing device that took our childish fancy and made them so special was the inclusion in every bag of a little royal blue paper screw of table salt. Now crisps were crisps in those days – they were the Real Thing. But then again, that may just be nostalgia. They were still a 'value-added' product, a way of making a cheap potato turn in a great deal of profit.

Ingredients and additives

Let's look at a typical list of ingredients from a modern bag snack packet:

- wheatflour
- vegetable oils
- maize
- seasoning (flavourings, flavour enhancers 621, 635; acidity regulator, E262, citric acid)
- soya protein – potato starch
- salt
- emulsifier E412
- colour: annatto.

No need to point out which are the items you might prefer your children not to stuff themselves with!

Apart from these delights, some of the anti-oxidants used in bag snacks (and, indeed, in other processed foods) come into the 'definitely avoid' category. They are

- butylated hydroxyanisole (BHA)
- butylated hydroxytoluene (BHT).

Additives: Your Complete Survival Guide says they 'pose perhaps the most serious chronic hazard from food additives; both are still subject to intensive safety research'.

We know that bag snacks are full of fat and salt – neither substance being much good for us in any great quantity. But how much do they contain? Here are some examples:

- 100g of typical regular crisps contains 35g of fat and 550mg of sodium (chemically, salt is sodium chloride)
- 100g of roasted salted peanuts contains 440mg of sodium.

The full nutritional content of 100g of typical regular crisps looks like this:

- protein 6g
- fat 35g
- carbohydrate 50g
- sodium 550mg
- calcium 40mg
- iron 2mg
- vitamin C 15mg

The good news

Children and teenagers love bag snacks – and we all tend to nibble them at parties, whatever age we are. What can we go for, if anything, that's better for us?

- go for unsalted plain peanuts, bulging with dietary fibre and nourishment; avoid roasted and dry roasted peanuts – the former have added oil, the latter are covered in artificial flavourings and colourings
- go for the additive-free Hedgehog brand, made from organically grown potatoes cooked in unsaturated oil; avoid the regular kinds of potato crisps.

The message that comes across from Hedgehog is that people *can* make a living selling decent stuff. Whether manufacturers are selling healthy or unhealthy food, real or artificial, it all turns on the matter of profit. It is perfectly understandable that if they can make up to 50 times more profit on a potato which is processed and prettified and popped into a packet, they will do so. What is not forgivable is that they should seek to do so without considering real nutritional values when they have the power, the science, the profit-potential and the marketing and promotional skills to do so.

Humans may not safely graze

One serious question needs to be posed here, even if we buy the 'right' bag snacks. Are Britain and other Western countries following the transatlantic lead and quietly falling for the creeping attractions of 'grazing'? In an article in the *Listener*, food writer Derek Cooper asked:

> Could it happen here? Could we become a nation of fatties? My American consultant thought it highly likely. 'If you create a society where continuous eating becomes the norm, then naturally you're going to have problems.' Snacking on rubbish has not yet reached American levels here, but the food industry is working on the project with great persistence. There is, unfortunately, a lot of money to be made out of making people overweight.
> See also **Salt**.

Bedtime drinks

Cocoa, hot chocolate and their ilk are the comfort drinks – what children often have after supper. But they are fattening (as are all the typical bedtime drinks). Make them with skimmed milk, or milk and water, and go easy on the sugar, if and when you add it. Above all, regard these drinks as a food substitute, not an extra.

Derived from the seed of a tropical plant, cocoa was first brought to Europe from Mexico by the Spanish conquistadores in the early 1500s. In Britain it acquired social significance in the 17th and 18th centuries, when fashionable coffee and chocolate houses were the setting for unofficial political debate and intrigue.

With modern growing methods there is an enormous cost to human health both in the distant cocoa plantations in South America and the Far East, and during transportation and processing. The Pesticides Trust states: 'Brazil is a major consumer of pesticides; there are over 8000 sales points for agrochemicals in the country.' In January 1989 the Trust's newsletter listed all manner of horrors: infected eyes, genital areas eaten away in Malaysia, sick workers sacked, fainting dockers in Amsterdam complaining of headaches and nausea while unloading cocoa.

If you buy the less bitter-tasting cocoa-based drinking chocolate you are buying all these worries, plus (typically) sugar in four forms:

- dried whey
- dried glucose syrup
- sucrose
- dried skimmed milk.

It is a soothing drink, but deceptively so, for it is full of fats and sugars. And it usually contains additives as well.

Ovaltine, Horlicks, and various other branded and own-brand equivalents are malted milk drinks with long histories and friendly associations with cosy times round the fire with the wireless set. They contain some good minerals and vitamins, protein, carbohydrate, calcium and so on. For the elderly and the very young, malted milk drinks can be good sources of these nutrients, but they will make you put on weight if you are already getting enough energy-providing nutrients by other means.

See also **Sweets and chocolate**.

Biscuits

What could be more comforting than a cup of tea and a biscuit? Or two? Or three? You reach for the biscuit tin when you are upset, or tired, or feel in need of a little treat. It's such a cosy habit, and it's so easily passed on to the children. So what's wrong with doing it? Well, for a start:

- refined flour
- processed sugar
- saturated fats
- salt
- additives.

Hooked on biscuits?

In the last 20 years the number of people suffering from diabetes has risen alarmingly. In his book *Pure White and Deadly* Professor John Yudkin associates long-term British sugar consumption with several other diseases as well:

- dental decay
- short-sightedness
- dermatitis
- gout
- heart disease
- cancer.

Britain is the third highest consumer of biscuits in the world, after Finland and Holland – on average, we each munch our way through more than 1.1 kg (2¹/₂lb) a month. We also gobble up further large quantities of sugar in shop-bought cakes and candies (see **Cakes** and **Sweets and chocolate**).

What the biscuit tin really contains

Let's look at the contents of a typical packet of nice iced party biscuits from any supermarket shelf:

- flour
- sugar
- hydrogenated palm oil
- palm kernel oil
- glucose syrup
- salt
- baking powder
- sugar syrup
- dried whole milk powder
- gelling agent (gelatine E430)
- artificial flavour
- emulsifier (lecithin E322)
- artificial colours E102, E110, E132, caramel E150.

What a lot of potential for trouble in a plate of pretty iced biscuits! While children's immune systems remain immature, they are more vulnerable to harmful additives, even in small amounts. Now, combine these additives with the refined flour, four sorts of sugar (the fourth, in case you didn't recognize it, is the dried milk powder) and two oils (both high in saturated fat). Oh dear!

Limit the damage

Children raised during and just after World War II were not used to eating biscuits or sweets, since sugar was rationed. Bread was a popular snack food – and if it was all right then, why not now? When your kids want a snack or an edible comforter, why not offer them a good thick slice of fresh wholemeal bread with a scrape of polyunsaturated margarine or peanut butter, and a teaspoonful of no-sugar-added fruit preserve? Encourage your children to eat more fruit if they enjoy it – and if they don't, help them to learn.

If, however, biscuits do have you hooked, look at the labels and see which offer the most healthy/least unhealthy ingredients. Doves Farm, for example, uses flour from organic farms recognized by the Soil Association in its sugar, carob chip, spicy orange and oatmeal biscuits. These biscuits also contain no artificial colourings, flavourings or preservatives. Unfortunately its carob digestive biscuits, though delicious, also contain sugar in several forms, plus palm oil – nearly 50% saturated fat.

Let's look at another 'better for you' brand, Prewett's. This company makes a range of wholemeal biscuits with fruit and/or nuts. They too contain no artificial colourings, flavourings or preservatives, but again there's lots of sugar, even if it does come in the form of raw cane sugar, raisins and honey, and not as empty calories.

Biscuits for cheese

Of course, not all biscuits are designed to taste sweet, but even crackers sold for eating with cheese have sugar in them – as the table below shows. Don't be tempted to buy the 'cheese sandwich' type of biscuit (a sort of cheesy custard cream). They are loaded with fats and sugars and additives (to be fair, they do contain cheese – though frequently described as 'powdered cheese'). If you want the flavour of cheese, a lovely piece of natural cheese and a plain biscuit will do you far more good and taste much better.

What biscuits contain

	per 100g (approx. 4oz)		
	total fat	total sugars	sodium/salt
sweet			
chocolate biscuits, fully coated	28g	43g	160mg
chocolate digestives	24g	29g	450mg
cream sandwich (custard etc.)	26g	30g	220mg

	per 100g (approx. 4oz)		
	total fat	*total sugars*	*sodium/salt*
ginger nuts	15g	36g	330mg
Jaffa cakes	11g	57g	130mg
plain digestives	21g	14g	600mg
semi-sweet (Osborne, Rich Tea, Marie)	17g	22g	410mg
short sweet (shortcake, Lincoln)	23g	24g	360mg
shortbread	26g	17g	230mg
wafer filled (assorted)	30g	46g	70mg
plain			
matzos	2g	4g	17mg
oatcakes	18g	3g	1230mg
rye crispbread	2g	3g	220mg
water biscuits	13g	2g	470mg
wholemeal crackers	11g	2g	700mg

With biscuits, as with so much else, Parents for Safe Food recommend that you read the packaging, choose the least unhealthy product and don't buy them too often.

Home-baked is best

But, of course, home-baked biscuits are quite another story. You know what goes into them. Find one or two good, simple, low-fat recipes and make an occasional batch as a treat. Try passing on a simple baking skill to your children – with a minimum of effort you can teach them something about good food values. See also **Bread and flour** and **Cakes and other baked products**.

Bread and flour

Even in this confusing world, some foods are simply good enough to make you stand up and cheer. The consumption of *all* kinds of bread should be encouraged for its nutritional value in our diet, said the Department of Health's Committee on the Medical Aspects of Food (COMA) in 1981. And if you can find wholemeal bread baked from organically grown 100 per cent wholemeal flour, you are fortunate indeed.

So what does it contain that's so good for us?

- carbohydrates, which provide the body with energy (but may be converted to body fat if you eat too much and don't use up that energy)
- bran, which prevents constipation – it combines with water and greatly assists the passage of digestible materials and waste products through the intestines
- proteins, which provide materials (called amino acids) for growth and repair of damaged body tissues; they can also be converted into carbohydrate and used to provide energy
- fats, which provide energy in a more concentrated form than carbohydrates (they too can form body fat if you don't dissipate the energy)
- minerals such as copper, iron, magnesium, manganese, phosphorus, selenium and zinc, which are needed for growth and tissue repair and help to regulate body processes
- vitamins, which help to regulate body processes; vitamin E and the B vitamins (including thiamin) are particularly important in bread, but when it is toasted its thiamin content is reduced – down 15 per cent in thick slices, and 30 per cent in thin ones.

Use your loaf

Bread is the original and quite the best fast food for people of any age, and it really is inexpensive when compared to so much of the junk food in supermarkets. It is also very good cut into 'soldiers' and baked in the oven for an hour at 150°C (300°F/gas mark 2) for babies to suck on when they are sitting up and eating solids – much better for them than sugar-packed bought rusks (wholemeal bread contains less than 2g in every 100g).

Basic kinds of flour

Flour is the foundation of all breadmaking. There are three main kinds of wheat, all varying in the amount of gluten (see below) that they contain:

- hard (used for modern breadmaking – see below)
- soft (used for cakes, pastries, biscuits and crackers)
- durum (used for pasta).

The good things in wheat

- wheatgerm: the embryo plant – a good source of vitamins, minerals and protein
- bran: the outer layer of the cereal – a major source of fibre, minerals and vitamins

- endosperm: the inner and greater portion of the grain (more than 80 per cent) – good for providing protein and starch
- gluten: the plant protein found in wheat which, when mixed with water, gives dough the sticky semi-liquid property it needs to hold the gas, generated by yeast, that will raise and expand the mixture to make bread.

There are three main varieties of bread: white, brown and wholemeal. Each is made from a different type of flour:

- white is baked from white flour, which includes the endosperm, but most of the wheatgerm and bran have been taken out
- brown is baked from brown flour, which includes much of the wheatgrain, with the exception of part of the bran; such flour used to be known as wheatmeal
- wholemeal is baked from wholemeal flour, which must by law use the whole of the wheatgrain; some wholemeal meal is stone-ground, using traditional methods, but if steel rollers (the modern way) are used there is no loss of nutrients and little difference in taste.

Additives – good and bad

Now let's take a look at some of the other things that go into the flour you buy for home baking, and into the flour that is used for commercial breadmaking. The processing required to make white flour and brown removes some of the important minerals and vitamins. Since certain ingredients must be present in flour by law, supplements are added. They include:

- iron
- minimum quantities of the B vitamins (thiamin and niacin)
- calcium carbonate.

White bread contains almost as much protein as wholemeal and is low in fat, so despite the bad press the British white loaf has received (the writer Sir Compton Mackenzie summed it up nicely: 'You are offered a piece of bread and butter that feels like a damp handkerchief and sometimes, when cucumber is added to it, like a wet one'), it remains a valuable source of nutrition. On the other hand wholemeal cereals, so lauded and approved, have a drawback: the fibre and phytic acid they contain can reduce the absorption of minerals such as calcium and zinc.

Flour 'improvers' must also be listed on the packaging of wrapped bread, and must be displayed where unwrapped bread is on sale. A chemical improver known as potassium bromate was formerly used as an oxidizing and bleaching agent. But lengthy tests have indicated that it could be carcinogenic, and it is now banned.

Other additives include:

- vinegar to stop the bread going mouldy
- caramel colour (see p.59) to make the loaf look darker and more nutritious; some dark bread is little more than white bread in disguise
- ascorbic acid (vitamin C): the only additive allowed in wholemeal bread, it is a raising agent that helps to produce a less dense loaf
- raising agents 500, E450a and E341 are added to wheatflour. 500 (bicarbonate of soda) is safe. E450a (disodium dihydrogen diphosphate) is used as a buffer, emulsifier, stabilizer and sequestrant. It may have a link to kidney damage in test animals, and can have a laxative effect. E341 (acid calcium phosphate), used as a buffer, yeast food sequestrant and texturizer, is safe.

Many loaves today state that no bleaching agents have been included. In any case, EC food law directives will attempt to outlaw the use of bleaching agents and other additives in bread as the single market approaches in 1992.

The modern industrial breadmaking process

Traditionally dough is allowed to ferment (or rise) for about three hours before baking, but in the past 20 years methods in the bakery industry have changed. Today, three-quarters of all British bread is made by what is called the Chorleywood Bread Process (CBP), which uses twice as much yeast as conventionally made bread in order to produce rapid fermentation. The three hours' rising is replaced by two to four minutes of intense mechanical excitation. The result is bread that can be produced more quickly and sold more cheaply. But, as this book has said many times in other contexts, cheap is not always good.

Some bakers believe that the shorter fermentation time affects the flavour. A higher proportion of water is added to maintain consistency than is used in conventional breadmaking. A study carried out by the Food Additives Campaign Team (FACT) and the Consumers' Association revealed that there was a much higher moisture content in breads made by the Chorleywood Bread Process than in those produced traditionally in craft bakeries. The highest moisture content was in a large sliced CBP wholemeal loaf, which contained up to 45 per cent moisture compared to 40 per cent in a similar large white loaf.

Now, if more water can be incorporated at the dough stage, the manufacturer is obviously saving by selling water rather than dough. And as CBP wholemeal loaves are more expensive than white, then are we not paying a higher price for our good health intentions *and* buying more water?

Another reason why all bread made by the Chorleywood method is cheaper than its traditionally made equivalent is that it enables the big bakers to use more British wheat and less North American, which carries import levies. But British wheat is 'weak' or 'soft', whereas US and Canadian wheat is 'hard' or 'strong' and richer in protein. People on low incomes are naturally tempted to buy the cheaper loaves, but they are buying reduced nutritional content. Everyone should try and spare the few extra pence for the better bread made by the time-honoured method – it's worth it.

Speciality breads

Our national bread consumption is around 10 million loaves a day. Wholemeal and brown bread have fallen from their peak in 1986, while white bread is now increasing its share of the market, which is at present about 70 per cent. New varieties such as soft grain with added fibre and premium white bread have become popular. Indian, French, Greek-style wholemeal, Italian rye, German coarse-grain rye and other interesting and unusual products are available from many of the large supermarkets and chains and small craft bakeries. They are growing in popularity with the consumer.

British Bakeries, for instance, have started to produce a wholemeal sliced loaf using a blend of Canadian and English wheat grown without artificial fertilizers and pesticides, and milled in the traditional way between stones. Sunnyvale, part of Everfresh Natural Foods, offers a range of yeast-free loaves suitable for vegetarians, vegans and those with special dietary needs. They are made from stone-ground flour, and organic ingredients are used whenever possible.

Avoid pesticides – buy organic

Unfortunately, the greatest concentration of pesticide residues tends to be found on the husk of the grain – the valuable bran (see p.137, under **Breakfast cereals**). Residues may be present in non-organically produced wholemeal flour, and may even survive the baking process.

Few supermarkets conduct their own tests for pesticide residues. Asda and Tesco do, but Safeway, Gateway, Spar, Sainsbury's and Marks and Spencer leave it to their suppliers. However, Marks and Spencer and Sainsbury's do produce their own organic bread, and some branches of the Co-op stock Doves Farm's organic loaf.

Baking your own

Here are two bread recipes – the first is an easy one that doesn't need yeast; the second is a gluten-free variation of a basic wholemeal bread recipe for those who cannot digest this otherwise valuable substance.

Quick and easy brown soda bread

> 12oz/350g 100 per cent wholemeal flour (organic and stone-
>   ground if possible)
> 12oz/350g plain white flour (organic if possible)
> 1 teaspoon salt
> 1½ teaspoons bicarbonate of soda
> scant 1½oz/35g butter *or* margarine
> approx. ¾ pint/15 fl.oz buttermilk

Pre-heat the oven to 200°C (400°F/gas mark 6). Sift the flours, salt and bicarbonate of soda into a large bowl. If there is any bran left in the sieve, add it to the bowl. Rub the fat into the flour mixture until it resembles soft breadcrumbs. Mix in the buttermilk to form a soft dough. Turn the dough on to a floured board and shape it into a plump, round loaf. Score a bold X on top and down the sides (so the loaf won't crack while baking). Place on a floured baking sheet and bake for 40-45 minutes. The loaf is done when it sounds hollow if you turn it on its side and tap the base. Cool on a rack before cutting. This loaf is best eaten fresh when just cool from the oven.

Gluten-free variation on basic wholemeal bread

For those people who are allergic to wheat, try this adaptation from the American Dietetic Association. For 4oz/125g wheatflour, substitute one of the following:

> 4oz/125g barley flour
> 4oz/125g cornflour
> 4oz/125g fine cornmeal
> 3oz/90g rice flour
> 3oz/90g potato starch flour
> 5oz/150g rye flour
> 5½oz/160g oat flour

Bake at 25°C 75°F lower than the normal temperature for bread, and use less fat. The texture of quick non-yeast breads is improved if the dough is allowed to stand in the tin for 20 minutes before baking. Finished quick breads will hold their shape if left in the tin for 5 minutes before removing. Make them in small quantities, as they don't keep as well as yeast breads.

See also **Cakes and other baked products**.

Breakfast cereals

The majority of children start their day with a bowl of ready-to-eat packet cereal. In the last 40 years British consumption of porridge oats has dropped 70 per cent, while processed breakfast cereal has risen to replace it. The trouble is that the processing destroys some of the nutrients and instead of oats, many manufacturers have used nutritionally inferior grains like corn (maize). This brings us to a story we have met before: refined processed foods which are so lacking in nutrients that they have to have vitamins and minerals added (which the manufacturers turn into a special selling point) to make them worth eating. Wholegrain cereals lose few of their nutrients during processing.

Bran

The health professionals encourage us to eat cereals because they contain dietary fibre. But once again this is an area in which the highly processed cereals are lacking, and several manufacturers add extra fibre to compensate.

Some cereals have pure bran added, and some are largely bran with some salt and sugar to make it palatable. Manufacturers are selling this sort of bran-enriched food as being beneficial to our health and – in the case of oat bran – because there is some evidence that oat fibre helps reduce blood cholesterol and so lessens the risk of heart disease.

But adding pure bran to one's diet can prevent some essential nutrients, especially zinc, from being absorbed. Wheatgerm, however, contains zinc, and so bran eaten as part of the whole grain is rather better. The digestive system is designed to work best with a variety of types of fibre (from fruit, vegetables and pulses as well as cereals) eaten in their wholefood forms. We simply do not know whether pure, refined bran is an adequate substitute for dietary fibre from wholegrain sources.

Quantities of bran in cereals

	fibre per 100g
wholegrains	
rye	12g
wheat	9g
oats	6g
rice	4g

	fibre per 100g
bran-enriched breakfast cereals	
All Bran	30g
Bran Buds	28g
Farmhouse Bran	18g
Sultana Bran	16g
Fruit 'n Fibre	10g

Pesticide residues in cereal grains

A further problem associated with bran is that pesticide residues tend to be found at their greatest concentration on the coat of the grain – the bran. Relying on high levels of added bran as a means of keeping up your levels of dietary fibre can expose you to that extra risk.

Most grain consumed in Britain is grown here, and it is very likely to have been treated with pesticides in the field and after harvesting. In tests conducted for the latest government surveys, low levels of pesticide residues were found in:

- 7 per cent of wholewheat breakfast cereals
- 10 per cent of bran-based breakfast cereals
- 55 per cent of wheatgerm
- 93 per cent of pure bran.

Products claiming to be organically grown were also tested. Residues were found in both of two samples of bran, and in seven out of 12 samples of bread.

Besides wheat, some samples of imported brown rice, rye and oats were tested. Residues were found in:

- 16 per cent of processed oats
- 18 per cent of rye products
- 24 per cent of rice.

Of three samples of 'organically grown' rice and one sample of 'organic' rye bread, none showed traces of pesticide residues.
Some discoveries:

- an 'organic' claim may not necessarily be a guarantee that a product is residue-free
- cereal products, including processed breakfast cereals, appear to show less contamination than the grains they are made from, suggesting that the processing may destroy some of the residues.

In this context, processing appears, for once, to be a good thing!

Candy for breakfast?

Recent years have seen a new interest in 'healthier' forms of cereal, most of them based on mixes such as muesli. In its original concept muesli was a mixture of wholegrain cereal, fresh fruit and some nuts. But in the hands of the modern food industry it has become a concoction of sugar, dried fruit, cereals (some wholegrain, perhaps), more sugar, dried milk powder, extra bran, nuts, salt, still more sugar .... The sugar levels in some cereals advertised as 'healthy' muesli-type mixes can be as high as those in many conventional 'sweetened' cereals (see table below).

And watch out for the fat levels, too. Particularly in the case of the 'crunchy' mixed wholegrain cereals, apparently healthy-looking packs can be concealing a fair dose of fat. Even the type of fat used can be a problem: palm and coconut oil are among the manufacturers' favourites, but since they contain high levels of saturated fat these are not a healthy choice.

Many brands of cereal are promoted on children's prime-time television. They have one thing in common: compared with the rest of the cereals on the supermarket shelves, they are all high in sugar. In fact the top two contain as much sugar, weight for weight, as fruit gums and Bounty bars!

Sugar content of breakfast cereals

	sugars as % of weight
Bounty bar	54
fruit gums	43
products aimed at young children	
Sugar Puffs	57
Frosties	42
Ricicles	40
Honey Smacks	39
Coco Pops	38
Start	32
other brand leaders	
Rice Krispies	11
Cornflakes	7
Weetabix	6
Shredded Wheat	1
Puffed Wheat	0

	sugars as % of weight
products with a 'health' image	
Sultana Bran	33
Fruit 'n Fibre	27
Bran Buds	26
Country Store	24
Farmhouse Bran	23
Tropical Fruit Alpen	22
Special K	18
Harvest Crunch	18
All Bran	15
Ready Brek (flavoured)	9
Ready Brek (unflavoured)	2
porridge oats (quick-cook)	1
porridge oatmeal	0

And don't be misled by the tempting word 'honey'. When it comes to teeth, honey does just as much damage as other sugars. (See **Honey**.)

And a dose of salt, too

Salt (sodium chloride) is a substance which many people want to reduce in their diet, as it increases the risk of high blood pressure and circulation problems (see **Salt**). But food manufacturers realized long ago that the two cheap ways of turning something over-refined into something tasty were to add sugar and salt. And into the breakfast cereal it goes.

Salt content of breakfast cereals

	sodium in a 35g serving
highest	
Bran Flakes	300mg
All Bran	490mg
Rice Krispies	420mg
Special K	380mg
Cornflakes	370mg
lowest	
porridge oatmeal	10mg
Ready Brek	8mg
Sugar Puffs	3mg
porridge oats (quick-cook)	3mg
Shredded Wheat	3mg
Puffed Wheat	1mg
potato crisps, ready salted	190mg

Additives

Look carefully at the labels before you buy your breakfast cereals, to see what has been added to make the product appear extra-attractive. Some cereals are coloured, either with a rainbow assortment of obviously false colours, or with yellow and brown colourings to enhance the toasted or chocolate appearance. Some have flavouring agents added, but the present labelling laws do not require the manufacturers to declare what flavouring they have used. And then there is preservative: few dried cereals need it, but dried fruits added to cereals are frequently preserved with sulphites – which are known to provoke asthma attacks in sensitive people.

Farina breakfast pudding for pernickety eaters

scant ³/₄ pint/15 fl.oz milk
2 tablespoons runny honey
3oz/90g farina or fine bulgar wheat
1 dessertspoon melted butter
2 free-range eggs, separated
1 teaspoon vanilla essence
1 teaspoon grated lemon rind (organic if possible)

Pre-heat the oven to 180°C (350°F/gas mark 4). Boil the milk and add the farina and honey. Stir over a low heat until the mixture is thick. Remove from the heat, add the butter, and leave for a few minutes to cool before adding the egg yolks one at a time. Stir well and add the vanilla and lemon peel. Whisk the egg whites until stiff but not dry, and fold them into the farina mixture. Grease an oven dish and pour the mixture into it. Place the dish in a baking tray full of water, and bake for 30 minutes. Delicious hot or cold.

See also **Cereal bars**.

Butter
See **Dairy products**.

Cakes and other baked products

More than any other food, a cake seems to express love from the baker to the baked for. Small wonder that we find them so enjoyable, and it's a rare person who can say no to a piece of cake warm from the oven. Do a little detective work – track down a few simple, low-fat, low-sugar, whole flour recipes and bake your own cakes from time to time. It would be a pity to deny ourselves, family and friends this pleasure, for fear of all things sweet and fat.

A *feast of fat and sugar from the supermarket shelves*

Unfortunately it's clear from supermarket shelves and bakeries that many people have developed a taste for regular cake eating. But this is not wise. 'Consistent over-eating and not the occasional over-indulgence results in obesity,' says MAFF's 1989 *Manual of Nutrition*. Cakes are treats, not staples.

Manufacturing in bulk presents certain problems which aren't present in small-quantity home baking. 'No amount of whipping', wrote Debbie Taylor in *New Internationalist*, 'will make 100,000 eggs hold the amount of air necessary to raise 50,000 kilograms of sponge mixture to the requisite light and fluffy consistency. But with the help of chemical additives and highly questionable colourings, refined flours, sugars and saturated fats can be made to look and taste like almost anything.' Here is the ingredients list of a typical packet of small iced cakes. The various sugars have been starred.

- sugar*
- wheatflour
- animal and vegetable fat
- glucose syrup*
- whole egg
- skimmed milk powder
- fat-reduced cocoa
- rice flour
- whey syrup*
- salt
- preservative: potassium sorbate
- colours: cochineal, crocin
- emulsifiers: 471, lecithin
- flavouring
- modified starch
- citric acid.

We know there's a whole bundle of sugar there. Now let's have a look at the additives:

- potassium sorbate (E202) is used to prevent the growth of bacteria; it's presumed generally safe, but can be hazardous to some people
- cochineal (an insect extract) is suspected of causing food intolerance
- crocin is included in a list of colourings soon to be prohibited by law, since their safety has not been established
- 471 (mono- and diglycerides) are presumed safe, but are still controversial

- lecithins (E322) are safe
- citric acid (E330) is assumed to be safe.

Many of these additives appear so frequently in people's daily diet that it makes a nonsense of the concept of the 'acceptable daily intake' (known in the food trade as ADI). So there are clearly many reasons why cake should not be a regular feature on the shopping list.

Nutritional content of typical bought cakes and baked products

| | | per 100g of food | | |
	fat	sugars	sodium	fibre
cheesecake, frozen, with fruit topping	10.6g	22.0g	160mg	0.9g
Chelsea/Bath buns	13.8g	21.4g	330mg	2.2g
chocolate cake with butter icing	29.7g	34.3g	420mg	2.9g
crumpets	0.9g	1.7g	720mg	2.6g
currant buns	7.5g	15.1g	230mg	1.8g
custard tarts, individual	14.5g	12.8g	130mg	1.2g
Danish pastries	17.6g	28.5g	190mg	2.7g
doughnuts, iced, ring	17.5g	30.7g	170mg	2.4g
doughnuts, jam	14.5g	18.8g	180mg	2.5g
eclairs, with chocolate icing and cream filling	23.8g	26.4g	150mg	0.5g
Eccles cakes	26.4g	41.1g	240mg	2.0g
fancy iced cakes	14.9g	54.0g	250mg	2.2g
fruit cake, Dundee	12.5g	38.8g	220mg	3.4g
fruit pies, individual	15.5g	30.9g	210mg	2.3g
jam tarts	13.0g	36.0g	130mg	2.5g
lemon meringue pie	14.4g	24.8g	200mg	0.8g
Madeira cake	16.9g	36.5g	380mg	1.3g
muffins, bran	7.7g	19.5g	770mg	8.5g
muffins, plain	6.3g	2.6g	130mg	2.7g
scones, fruit	9.8g	16.9g	710mg	3.6g
scones, plain	14.6g	5.9g	770mg	2.2g
scones, wholemeal, fruit	12.8g	14.2g	650mg	5.2g
scones, wholemeal, plain	14.4g	5.9g	730mg	5.0g
Swiss roll	4.4g	41.0g	130mg	1.0g
Swiss roll, chocolate	11.3g	41.8g	350mg	2.4g
teacakes	7.5g	14.8g	270mg	4.2g

Great cakes can be healthy cakes

Let's be fair – if you shop around you can find a number of excellent bought cakes in large supermarket chains, health food stores, small shops specializing in organic and wholefoods, and some craft bakeries. Freshly baked cakes, meant to be eaten quickly, do not need additives to ensure their shelf life, and if they are made with fruit, spices or nuts they should not need large amounts of sugar.

If you *can* find time occasionally to bake your own, here is a recipe that will enable you to give your family and friends a treat without feeling guilty.

Yoghurt and cottage cheesecake

First, the nut-crumb pie crust:

    4oz/125g ground nuts (e.g. almonds, cashews, mixed etc.)
    4oz/125g biscuit crumbs (e.g. digestive or wholemeal, organic if
        possible)
    4 tablespoons sunflower oil

Blend all the ingredients until smooth, then press into a 9inch/23cm spring-form cake tin. Chill for 30 minutes before filling with the mixture below.

    8oz/250g low-fat plain yoghurt
    3 free-range eggs, separated
    1 teaspoon pure vanilla extract
    1 tablespoon lemon juice
    1 tablespoon grated lemon rind (organic and unwaxed)
    4-5 tablespoons runny honey
    1/4 tablespoon sea salt
    1oz/30g wholemeal flour (organic if possible)
    1lb/500g low-fat cottage cheese

Pre-heat the oven to 190°C (375°F/gas mark 5). Mix all the ingredients except the egg whites in a blender until smooth. Then beat the egg whites until stiff and fold them into the mixture. Bake for 30-35 minutes. Cool completely before removing from the tin. See also **Bread and flour**.

Cereal bars

Sales of cereal bars have shot up since they were introduced to us in 1981, at the start of the 'healthy eating' phase. That year the bar business was worth £500,000. By 1984 sales had rocketed to £10 million. Three years later the total was £38 million and by 1988 annual sales were topping £67 million. We must really like cereal bars!

On the fast track to energy

They are marketed as a healthy snack alternative to ordinary confectionery and biscuits, and we are told they contain no artificial colourings and preservatives. Indeed they don't – credit where credit's due. The ingredients include:

- a mixture of oats, crisped rice, flaked wheat and maize
- bran
- nuts

That's all fine so far. But then there's a whole lot of sugar, masquerading under a variety of names:

- brown sugar
- corn syrup
- dextrose
- dried fruit
- fruit juices
- fructose syrup
- honey
- glucose syrup
- invert sugar
- lactose
- malt extract (maltose)
- molasses
- muscovado sugar
- raw cane sugar
- soft brown sugar
- syrup
- unrefined sugar

together with:

- salt
- colourings
- oils
- flavourings
- emulsifier
- dried milk.

In the London Food Commission's 1989 survey of cereal bars, a carob bar was found to contain 47 per cent sugar – even higher than a traditional chocolate bar. (But perhaps this is not surprising since carob, always presented as a healthy alternative to chocolate, is very rich in sugar.)

Fruit bars have the biggest calorie count of all. A typical 45g fruit and nut bar with honey would supply 8 per cent of the recommended daily energy intake for a grown man, and 11.6 per cent of the amount recommended for a six-year-old child. And those marked 'No added sugar'? Forget it. One fruit bar marked thus was found to contain 60 per cent sugar, mostly in the form of dried fruit. The average was 40 per cent.

Little fibre

There are certainly valuable nutrients in these bars – empty calories they are not. But don't be misled into thinking that they supply much fibre. The government's Food Advisory Committee recommends that bars are labelled 'high fibre' only when they contain more than 6g of fibre. But the maximum discovered during the London Food Commission survey was 5.6g – the least contained less than 1g. So read those ingredients lists carefully before you buy – though unfortunately not all manufacturers supply adequate nutritional information on their wrappers.

Know your ingredients – make your own

So cereal bars are marketed on the basis of a healthy image – yet few of them would seem to live up to that image. You may think there's not much difference between giving your children so-called 'healthy' snacks and a bar of chocolate. But there is a third choice – make your own.

Oatmeal, sesame and raisin crunch

^{1}/$_2$ cup/140ml clear honey
^{3}/$_4$ cup/225ml unsaturated oil
1 free-range egg, beaten
2 tablespoons skimmed *or* semi-skimmed milk
8oz/250g wholemeal flour
8oz/125g medium oatmeal
1 teaspoon ground cinnamon
^{1}/$_4$ teaspoon sea salt
3oz/90g seedless raisins, chopped
3oz/90g sesame seeds

Pre-heat the oven to 190°C (375°F/gas mark 5). Lightly whisk together the honey, oil and egg. Then stir in the remaining ingredients until well blended. The dough should be stiff: if it is too thick add more milk; if too thin, add more flour. Grease a shallow baking tin and pat the mixture down to about ^{1}/$_2$inch/2.5cm thickness. Bake for about 20 minutes, and when cool cut into squares.

Cheese
See **Dairy products**.

Chocolate
See **Bedtime drinks** and **Sweets and chocolate**.

Coffee
See **Tea and coffee**.

Confectionery
See **Sweets and chocolate**.

Cream
See **Dairy products**.

Dairy products

Butter and butter substitutes

There's a problem with real dairy butter. It tastes great, it cooks well and it is unadulterated by the chemists' box of tricks, but it is nearly 65 per cent saturated fat. As with other 'naughty but nice' foods, use it sensibly. Buy a good-quality butter but don't eat too much.

The alternative for spreading is a good-quality margarine, high in polyunsaturates, low in saturates and cholesterol, with added vitamins. Don't spread it too thickly. For cooking, three fine oils – first-pressed olive, sunflower and sesame – are all available in organic form. Unfortunately they won't scramble eggs (so you had better have them only on your 'butter treat' days!).

In the world of butter substitutes, or yellow fats as they are known, new brand names and packages appear almost daily. Many of them rely on the traditional desirable image of butter to sell themselves, with pictures of cows gambolling in green meadows. And some of these products are, indeed, mostly vegetable fat but topped up with perhaps 15 per cent butter.

Butter's volume of market share has fallen by 10 per cent since the mid-1980s, while that of low-fat and dairy spreads has increased by 13 per cent. Among those who have remained faithful, tastes are moving towards continental-style pale butters with little or no salt, such as Normandy, Lurpak and Wheelbarrow. Manufacturers are increasingly using butter in processed foods, so if you want to be careful about your family's butter consumption read the labels carefully.

See also **Fats and oils**.

Cheese

The ancient art of cheesemaking disappears into the foggy mists of time. Men and women have created cheese from the milk of the camel, water buffalo, ass, mare, goat and ewe as well as our friend the cow. Today most European countries have their own special cheeses – France, for instance, has a staggering four hundred different varieties. The character, fragrance and texture of each have been perfected with patience, skill and imagination. The geology of the region, the air, soil, vegetation and rainfall, the time the cheese is allowed to mature and the utensils used all affect the uniqueness and flavour of natural cheese. And the best cheese is produced only at certain times of year.

Now cheese factories have to work all year round. They must continue to produce even when the cheese is not really worth making. Let's face it, some cheese is deadly dull – it cooks all right, but it has little flavour or texture to recommend it. High-yield dairy cows forced into an unnatural lifestyle don't necessarily produce best-quality milk: its keeping qualities and suitability for cheesemaking are considerably reduced.

Raw milk or pasteurized?

Connoisseurs believe that cheese is best made from raw milk – they find it superior in flavour and texture to the pasteurized product. In Britain, however, the concern about listeria (see Chapter 6) since 1989 has affected consumers' attitudes to soft and semi-hard raw cheeses. Parents for Safe Food suggest that for safety's sake you choose hard cheeses when eating out, especially for those people in the vulnerable health categories.

Soft cheeses

These cheeses are highly perishable and last no more than three or four days in the refrigerator. Cottage cheese is made from skimmed milk, with rennet added. (Rennet is an extract from the stomachs of suckling calves. If you find this objectionable, cheeses made with vegetarian rennet are sold in most health food shops.) The curds which result are cut and washed to produce that granular, creamy texture. A richer product is produced by adding cream. Cream cheese is made by adding a lactic 'starch' or rennet to cream. The resulting curds and whey are strained to make a product which is richer than cottage cheese. Curd cheese is made by allowing milk to 'turn' naturally. The resulting curds and whey are separated, and it is the curds that become curd cheese. Other typical soft cheeses include

Italian ricotta, Bel Paese and Mozzarella, Greek feta and French Brie and Camembert.

Semi-hard cheeses

This group of cheeses includes crumbly ones like Italy's Gorgonzola, Dutch Gouda and Edam, Britain's Stilton and France's wonderful Roquefort, made from ewe's milk. End a meal with any of these and fresh fruit, and you will turn it into a feast.

Hard cheeses

These cheeses, such as Italian Parmesan, are excellent for cooking. Grate them for use on vegetables, soup or egg dishes. Fresh Parmesan doesn't form nasty elastic threads as it melts, mixes wonderfully with pasta, rice, pulses and vegetables, and improves with age.

Nutritional aspects

Natural cheeses are a good substitute for meat as they contain protein and casein. Vitamins D and E, and the B vitamins, are also present (when cooking cheese always use low temperatures so as not to destroy these vitamins). But many cheeses are also high in fat, so take care. Cheese is a wonderful food, but like cream it must be treated with respect – don't eat large portions. A number of cheeses are available in both full-fat and low-fat versions, and skimmed milk cheeses are invaluable in slimming diets.

Nutritional content of cheese

	reduced fat cottage cheese	per 100g cheese plain fromage frais	English Cheddar
protein	13.3g	6.8g	25.5g
fat	1.4g	7.1g	34.4g
Kcal (energy)	78	113	412
water	80.2%	77.9%	36%
sugars	3.3g	5.7g	0.1g
sodium	380mg	31mg	670mg
potassium	89mg	110mg	79mg
calcium	73mg	89mg	740mg
magnesium	9mg	8mg	26mg
phosphorus	160mg	110mg	490mg
iron	0.1mg	0.1mg	0.2mg
copper	0.04mg	trace	trace
zinc	0.6mg	0.3mg	2.3mg

Cheese for children

For babies, you can do no better than buy cottage cheese in ready-packed cartons (not loose from the deli counter in supermarkets): it is a wonderful ready food. Young children also enjoy small amounts of hard cheese, but since these are often high in salt serve them with other foods which are salt-free. You can usually get unsalted Cheddar at health food stores.

Cheeses such as Cheshire may contain the colouring annatto, which can cause asthma and rashes and is poorly tested for safety. Choose the white rather than the yellow varieties for your children when you can.

Contrary to popular belief, cheese isn't hard to digest and it isn't constipating. Foods like cheese and hard-boiled eggs are held in the stomach until their proteins are digested to liquid.

Finally, if you are buying cheese for your children always go for 'real' cheese (see below), not the prettily packaged, bland, emulsified spreads which are designed to appeal to the young but aren't much good for them.

Go for real cheese

Natural cheeses are far superior to processed, which are pasteurized blends of cheese emulsifiers and quite a lot of water, made solid by hydrogenation of the butterfat. This type of cheese has good keeping qualities and will be safe in the fridge for an indefinite period, but you would be well advised to read the ingredients label – you may be paying a high price for a synthetic, poor-quality product. Cheese spread, for instance, could contain up to 60 per cent water, gums and gelatines. The distinguished American nutritionist Adelle Davis suggests that 'all processed cheeses should be strictly avoided', while her compatriot Clifton Fadiman says that 'processed cheese represents the triumph of technology over conscience'.

Imitation cheeses are products in which the butterfat content has been replaced by vegetable oil. This is combined with vegetable proteins (casein), stabilizers, emulsifiers, flavours and colours and sometimes extra water. These products are designed to replace or extend real cheese, and their use has spread with the popularity of pizzas because of their 'economic advantage' over real cheese.

Some ideas for cooking with cheese

Cheese popcorn

8oz/250g popcorn
3 tablespoons sunflower oil
Parmesan cheese, grated

Heat the oil in a large, heavy-bottomed pan. Add the popcorn, stir until each kernel is coated with oil and cover the pan. As soon as the corn starts to pop turn the heat down as low as possible. Don't shake the pan or lift the lid. When the popping has stopped sprinkle the corn generously with the grated Parmesan cheese.

Cream cheese and nut spread

8oz/250g low-fat cream cheese
4oz/125g finely ground nuts (cashews, pine nuts, walnuts or
    hazelnuts)
a little parsley, finely chopped

Beat all the ingredients together and refrigerate until needed. This spread is very good on hot toast, or in sandwiches for a child's packed lunch.

Cream

Cream is a treat, but we don't seem to regard it as such, and as a nation we are eating too much of it. Here is a bit of realism written in the magazine *Checkout* in July 1989 by the marketing director of Eden Vale. 'In the UK, cream is booming. There is a misconception that the consumer's preoccupation with healthy eating involves a reduction of things that are unhealthy. That is not the case. People see no contradiction whatsoever in consuming low-fat spreads, then having cream cakes to follow ....'

The Milk Marketing Board's promotional activity concentrates on both cream in cakes and fresh cream. The market for cream through retailers was worth £105 million in 1988, while expenditure on cream cakes stood at £66 million. Even 'healthy' eaters have been won over by these 'little luxuries' which are so accessibly priced. A producer drew attention to the irony in all this. 'During the mid-1980s there has been a strong growth in low-fat products. One of the results is that there was more fat around, which is basically free cream. The supply increased and the price came down.'

Here is a table of the fat content of various kinds of cream; compare them with whole full-fat milk.

Fat in cream

	percentage of fat
whole milk	3.9
half cream	13.3
soured cream	19.9
single cream	19.1
spray canned cream	32.0
whipping cream	39.3
double cream	48.0
clotted cream	63.5

Cream also contains water, casein, lactose and mineral salts. Pasteurized cream has undergone heat treatment, which destroys bacteria and prolongs its keeping quality, but reduces the nutritional value. Fresh dairy cream may be untreated; if so, use it quickly after purchase. Soured cream is cultured rather than sour.

Spot the difference

Good cream is easily digested by most people. It can be adulterated by adding potato flour and gelatine, but these give it a gluey, mealy texture and should be simple to detect.

The Milk Marketing Board is concerned about the similarities in packaging between dairy cream and non-dairy creamers, and would like the government to tighten up legislation to prevent imitation products being passed off as the real thing. Presumably they think you can't tell the difference.

Cream substitutes are based on vegetable oils and fats; modern technology has made them more like the real thing in appearance and taste. Clear labelling would help. When the words 'dairy cream' are omitted from a product you can assume that, whatever it may look like, it is not dairy cream.

Treat cream with respect

Parents for Safe Food think cream is a wonderful servant but a bad master, and children should not be encouraged to develop the habit. If you go away on holiday and have a Devonshire cream tea that's fine – but every day? You might as well main-line saturated fat straight into your veins and have done with it.

Eggs

It is, unfortunately, impossible to discuss eggs today without mentioning salmonella (see Chapters 2 and 6). Sad to say, this highly nutritious, useful item in our diet – nature's own convenience food – is now off limits for some. Professor Richard Lacey, Britain's leading microbiologist, says: 'The advice for the elderly, those over 65 years, people who are ill, pregnant women and babies under one year is that they should avoid eggs altogether, except in baking.'

When buying eggs always open the packet and check to see that they are clean and not cracked or damaged in any way. This doesn't guarantee safety, but it is a start. And don't think that the problem is just a home-grown one – imported eggs are no safer than eggs from the UK. Store them at room temperature and buy in small quantities, so that they can be eaten quickly. Don't use any eggs more than a week after their 'sell-by' date. If you want the nutritional value of eggs without the worry that you might be poisoning yourself or your children, use them only in baking or else hard-boil them for seven to eight minutes.

Nutritional qualities

The egg makes a useful contribution to our daily intake of vitamins A, B and D, iodine, iron and protein. The extent to which iron is absorbed is dependent on the other foods eaten at the same time; it has been shown, for example, that orange juice increases its absorption. However, because egg yolks contain very high levels of cholesterol and fat you are not recommended to eat more than three or four a week (including those concealed in bought and processed food).

What else is in an egg?

'The composition and flavour of an egg varies with the breed of the hen and its diet,' says *Larousse Gastronomique* of how it used to be. 'The best eggs come from poultry kept in the open and allowed to forage for worms and receiving the right balance of grains and greenery.'

But only a small proportion of our eggs are laid by such lucky birds. The rest are fed on processed feedstuffs which include our old enemy the additive. In December 1989 the *Grocer* ran an article which stated that: 'Between one and five colorants are mixed into the birds' feed to give a richer colouring to the egg yolks. One of these is Canthaxanthin (E161g) which MAFF banned from direct addition to foods for human consumption, though it is not opposing its continued use via feedstuffs.' As stated in Chapter 2, you should choose free-range eggs whenever possible, since the hens that lay them are less likely to have been given this kind of feedstuff.

Milk

In MAFF's 1989 *Manual of Nutrition*, cow's milk is described as 'the most complete of all foods, containing nearly all the constituents of nutritional importance to mankind; it is however comparatively deficient in iron and vitamins C and D'. We each consume half a pint of milk a day in Britain, with the skimmed and semi-skimmed varieties becoming increasingly popular. In the early 1980s, sales of low-fat forms were negligible; they now command more than 23 per cent of the market, a trend which continues to grow. And children still drink more milk than adults – despite the fact that since the early 1970s it has not been available to older primary schoolchildren. In 1986 children represented 12 per cent of the population and consumed 36 per cent of the milk – on its own, as a drink.

Nutritional value

All milk provides excellent nutritional value for money, and pasteurized milk (see p.155) can be included in the diet of anyone who has no ethical or medical reason for not doing so. It contains easily assimilated calcium and high-quality protein, and is a rich source of riboflavin. But whole or full-cream milk is very high in fat (nearly 23g in a pint, compared to nearly 10g in semi-skimmed and less than 1g in skimmed). Parents for Safe Food recommend changing to semi-skimmed or skimmed for your family, but not for babies below the age of two.

Calcium – essential for a healthy life

The calcium contained in dairy products is vital for all:

- growing children
- pregnant and breast feeding women
- menopausal and post-menopausal women.

Babies, in spite of their size, require more calcium than the average adult. It is easily absorbed by the intestine and the process is assisted by the lactose in milk. Calcium is, however, regularly lost in the urine and has to be made up from the diet to maintain healthy levels.

Too little calcium in the bodies of young children results in stunted growth and rickets (extreme bow-leggedness due to softening of the bones). In women who lose large quantities of calcium through repeated pregnancies and lactation, and in some old people, the deficiency may show as osteomalacia (decalcified bones). The primary problem in rickets and osteomalacia is lack of vitamin D, which results in too little calcium being absorbed.

After the age of 30 more calcium is lost than is retained. The female sex hormone oestrogen encourages the retention of calcium in the bones, so during and after the menopause, when the level of this hormone falls, women may become calcium-deficient. Osteoporosis, common in the Western world, causes the vertebrae to crumble and bones to fracture easily. Those who cut down on dairy products to reduce the risk of coronary heart disease and obesity may be substituting one danger for another.

Good bone building starts in childhood with a diet rich in calcium to protect your children's bones and teeth throughout their lives – which are now likely to be longer than those of their parents' generation. As Geoffrey Cannon says, 'It is not so much the years in your life as the life in your years.' To get the best of both worlds, eat more *low-fat* dairy products.

Most milk is pasteurized

Nearly all milk sold in Britain is pasteurized. Only 3 per cent of the total milk supply is untreated, and in Scotland untreated milk is banned altogether. The process involves heating the milk to 72°C (162°F) for about 15 seconds to kill any disease-causing bacteria. Some 10% of thiamin and vitamin B12 and 25% vitamin C are destroyed. In June 1989 the government announced that consumers should be allowed to decide for themselves whether or not to drink untreated (green-top) milk – but there would be new procedures and labelling requirements. The decision was a compromise response to the powerful opposition to a proposed ban as a result of the listeria outbreaks – a ban which had been supported by bodies concerned with public health.

In his capacity as organizer of the Association of Unpasteurized Milk Producers and Consumers, organic farmer Julian Rose, whose family have been producing this kind of milk successfully for more than 50 years, spearheaded the campaign to keep the right to sell it. In January 1990 he wrote to the Minister of Agriculture: 'We are most concerned with the proposal to put a health warning on bottles of unpasteurized milk as described in your statement to the Commons of 21 December 1989. This is clearly a discriminatory statement which could equally apply to many other foods currently carrying a considerably higher health risk.' He pointed out that unpasteurized milk had greater vitamin content, and that if a health warning were carried by such milk it would be the only food product ever to do so – putting it on a level with cigarettes, which killed thousands every year.

Despite the decision to leave the choice to the consumer, the controversy continues. There are still restrictions on the sale of such milk to shops and institutions. Government advice is that certain categories of people:

- the elderly
- pregnant women
- young children
- people diagnosed HIV-positive and AIDS victims

should avoid unpasteurized milk and milk products.

Different kinds of milk

This is what you get when buying the numerous different sorts of milk we see in the shops:

- skimmed milk has had almost all its fat removed. This leaves the protein and most of the minerals, including calcium – but the fat-soluble vitamins A and D are reduced (see **Vitamins and minerals**). Per 100g of milk, the total sugars are 5g and fat 0.1g
- dried skimmed milk may be fortified with vitamins A and D. Per 100g of milk, the total sugars are 52.9g and fat 0.6g; if it has added vegetable fat the total sugars are 42.6g and fat 25.9g
- semi-skimmed milk contains, per 100g, total sugars 5g and fat 1.6g
- pasteurized whole (full-cream) milk contains, per 100g, total sugars 4.8g and fat 3.9g
- Channel Islands milk (from Jersey and Guernsey breeds) contains, per 100g, total sugars 4.8g and fat 5.1g
- UHT (ultra-high temperature) milk is heated to approximately 130°C (266°F) for one or two seconds, then packed into special containers which protect it from light and oxygen. It has a shelf life of several months without refrigeration, but once opened it is as perishable as fresh milk. Vitamin C and folic acid losses may occur during prolonged storage. Sugars and fats are the same as in pasteurized whole milk
- homogenized milk has had the fat globules broken up mechanically and distributed throughout the milk so that they no longer rise to form a creamy layer on top of the milk. Nutritional value is similar to pasteurized milk.
- sterilized milk is prepared from homogenized milk, then heated to 120°C (248°F) for 20 to 60 minutes. Some 60% vitamin C and 20% thiamin are destroyed in the process to prolong shelf life.
- evaporated milk is prepared by the concentration of milk at low temperatures, when it is sterilized in cans at 115°C (239°F) for

15 minutes. Nutrient loss is similar to that in sterilized milk. Per 100g of milk, total sugars are 8.5g and fat 9.4g

- sweetened condensed milk is prepared similarly, but at lower temperatures since it contains added sucrose. Nutrient losses are similar to those that occur during pasteurization. Whole sweetened condensed milk contains, per 100g, total sugars 55.5g and fat 10.1g. Skimmed sweetened condensed milk contains, per 100g, total sugars 60g and fat 0.2g.

Pesticides in milk

MAFF has detected pesticide residues in milk. 'Generally low levels' of dieldrin, a substance now banned in the UK, were reported in the 1988 review of the working party on pesticide residues.

Storage – preserve those vitamins

All milk (except UHT and sterilized, which don't need it before opening) should be stored in a refrigerator. Don't buy more than you need at one go – it's better to buy fresh and more frequently. Riboflavin, essential for the utilization of energy from food, is destroyed by ultra-violet light, so don't leave your bottle of milk on the doorstep too long in the morning.

Home-made milk shake

See how your children enjoy this healthy and delicious alternative to a commercial milk shake:

> ½pint/10 fl.oz skimmed *or* semi-skimmed milk
> 3 tablespoons low-fat natural yoghurt
> a little runny honey (optional)
> fresh fruit.

Mix it all together in a blender.

Buttermilk

You may have seen buttermilk in the chiller cabinets of many supermarkets. It contains all the casein (which comprises 75 per cent of total milk protein) and mineral salts of regular milk.

As well as being a pleasant drink, it is useful for making soda bread and scones. Here is a recipe for an easily prepared, healthy pudding.

> ¾ pint/400ml buttermilk
> 8oz/250g wholemeal breadcrumbs
> grated rind of 1 lemon (organic and unwaxed)
> 2 tablespoons honey
> 2oz/60g raisins
> 1 teaspoon vanilla essence

Blend all the ingredients together, cover and chill in the fridge, where the mixture will thicken. Add more buttermilk if you prefer a thinner mixture.

Goat's milk and ewe's milk

'For centuries goats' milk was more used than cows' milk by the common people and a milking nannie was commonly taken on sailing ships,' wrote Dorothy Hartley in *Food in England*. She went on: 'Goats' milk was considered good for babies ... doctors knew that goats were usually very healthy and tubercular-free ....' Although TB has thankfully been dealt with, goat's milk and goat's milk products are now enjoying a revival of popularity – MAFF census statistics in June 1988 showed that there were then nearly 22,000 milking goats in England and Wales.

Ewe's milk is produced all over the British Isles. It is high in calcium and vitamins C and D, the fat is naturally homogenized and the milk is ideal for authentic live yoghurt and ice cream without additives. Unlike cow's milk, ewe's milk can be frozen with no apparent deterioration in nutritional content. Ewe breeders are becoming increasingly skilful at breeding and distribution and marketing, with domestic production of milk for Greek-style yoghurt parrying the imported kind.

British goat's milk products are winning prizes against foreign competition, and it is fervently to be wished that the goat-and-ewe sector does not become intensive as the market expands. Here is one area that can be protected from disaster instead of being rescued after a crisis.

Soya milk

Soya milk, and soya milk products produced from soya flour, are used by vegetarians and vegans as an alternative to dairy products. Anyone who wishes to convert to plant foods from dairy products should plan their diet very carefully, for plant foods are a poor source of such necessary vitamins as B12 and D, major minerals, calcium and essential amino acids, zinc and iodine (see **Vitamins and minerals**).

In *Let's Have Healthy Children*, Adelle Davis, America's queen of nutrition, advises caution over soya products:

> Since they contain no milk, sugar or lactose, they cannot support the growth of valuable intestinal bacteria which synthesize B vitamins, or form lactic acid, as essential to the absorption of calcium as is vitamin D.
> Soya milk is low in two essential amino acids, methionine and cystine, inadequate in calcium and deficient in iodine and vitamin B12.

If you are going for soya it is essential to buy fortified products and to see that your diet is properly adjusted to replace any deficiencies which may occur from the absence of animal and dairy products. But the story is not all gloom – soya milk does have some advantages. It is high in protein (used by the body for growth and repair) and lecithin (important to the body for fat transport), and contains about half the calories and half the fats of whole cow's milk.

Soya Health Foods manufacture around 150,000 litres of soya milk per month. Much of it is supplied to the major supermarket chains and health food wholesalers around the country. The popularity of their basic milk led them to add banana, chocolate and strawberry varieties to the range. Only natural flavourings and colourings are used, and apple juice is substituted for sugar. Ice Dream soya-based non-dairy frozen dessert is available in seven flavours.

Parents for Safe Food are sorry to end on a sour note, but in 1989 some doctors were concerned to discover that soya milk contained about 10 times as much aluminium as cow's milk. Soya milk is low in zinc, which normally competes with aluminium for absorption into the body – thus increasing the body's aluminium intake further. Health professionals believe it could have a toxic effect if it were to accumulate in the bones and brains of babies.

Yoghurt

A good source of protein and calcium, real yoghurt is a curdled milk product originating in the Balkans. There are two basic types – the live, healthy sort and the rest. The first kind is produced by combining two organisms, *Lactobacillus bulgaricus* and *Streptococcus thermophilus*, which cause fermentation of the lactic acid in the milk and give yoghurt its characteristic sharp flavour. This has a beneficial effect on the digestive process, assisted by the production of B vitamins within the body.

Bacteria are constantly at war in the intestinal tract – good germs versus bad ones. Some doctors advise their patients to eat live yoghurt to kill harmful germs. Seven natural antibiotics which occur in yoghurt have been isolated by scientists. But yoghurt whose cultures are killed by pasteurization loses its anti-bacterial power.

Nutritional content of yoghurt per 100g

	protein	calcium	cholesterol
whole milk yoghurt, organic	4.3g	140g	10
whole milk yoghurt, goat's	3.5g	120g	11
low-fat yoghurt, plain	5.1g	190g	4
Greek yoghurt, cow's	6.4g	150g	N
Greek yoghurt, ewe's	4.4g	150g	(14)
soya yoghurt	5.0g	N	0

	total fat	saturated	monounsaturated	polyunsaturated
whole milk yoghurt, organic	2.9g	1.7g	0.9g	0.2g
whole milk yoghurt, goat's	3.8g	2.5g	0.9g	0.1g
low-fat yoghurt, plain	0.8g	0.5g	0.2g	TR g
Greek yoghurt, cow's	9.1g	5.2g	2.7g	0.5g
Greek yoghurt, ewe's	7.5g	4.8g	1.9g	0.4g
soya yoghurt	4.2g	0.6g	0.9g	2.4g

N = present in significant quantities, but there is no reliable information on the exact amount
( ) = estimated value

Illusions of health

'Yoghurt has a halo of health,' said Nigel Hunter, marketing director of Eden Vale, in *Checkout* magazine in July 1989, 'and so consumers like to think they are being good when eating premium yoghurt.' He is quite right. What could present a healthier halo? The choice ranges over low-fat standard, very low-fat, children's, luxury, long life, Greek, mousse, yoghurt drink (fruited or plain) and natural yoghurt. Nowhere do you see the word 'live'. What you *will* see, if you read the labels, are:

- artificial sweetener
- natural flavourings
- sugars
- glucose syrup

- gelatine
- natural thickeners
- preservatives
- cream
- E additives.

The value-added market is growing rapidly and there is a keen contest for space in the chilled cabinet. Multipacks account for more than half of sales. Hunter says that 'the advantage of multipacks for the trade is that they tend to encourage greater consumption. Mothers will not refuse to give a child a yoghurt as a snack, because the alternative is likely to be much worse.'

Parents for Safe Food advise you to find a good natural farm yoghurt made from fresh separated low-fat milk (from cows, ewes or goats) and live yoghurt culture; eat it plain or add fresh or frozen fruit. Generally try to avoid too regular buying of the 'treat' varieties. A typical one picked at random says it has no artificial ingredients – good. But what it does contain is:

- cream
- sugar
- peach purée
- passion fruit purée
- glucose syrup
- gelatine
- natural flavouring
- natural thickeners guar gum, pectin, locust bean gum
- preservative E202 (potassium sorbate).

Should simple yoghurt be made so complicated? If you have a problem finding the Real Thing, Parents for Safe Food suggest that, since proper yoghurt is so easy to make at home, you look for a recipe and make your own. You won't regret it.

Yoghurt drinks

After a slow start, drinking yoghurt (13% sugar) has increased in popularity. A typical reduced calorie variety is sweetened by aspartame and preserved with potassium sorbate E 202. We think commercial yoghurt drinks are too processed so we suggest it would be nicer to make your own (see page 157).

Eggs
See **Dairy products**.

Fats and oils

British food contains far too much fat. There is no doubt or real debate about this fact. Eating too much fat throughout life is a major cause of a number of common killers: heart attacks, strokes, and other diseases of the circulation system, for example. In Britain now, around 250,000 people die every year from diseases of the circulation system. The number of people dying prematurely from heart attacks, under the age of 65, is higher in Britain than almost any other country in the world.

Much of the fat we consume is in 'hidden' forms – in processed foods such as sausages and pasties, cakes and puddings. A lot of it comes from milk and dairy foods like cheese, butter and the butter substitutes. And lastly some comes from frying fats – vegetable oils and lard – both used at home and in fast foods. The deep frying fats used for chips can vary:

- McDonald's and Burger King use beef fat blends (over 45 per cent saturated fat – see below)
- Kentucky goes for partially hydrogenated soya oil (around 20-25 per cent saturated)
- Wimpy use vegetable oil (around 15 per cent saturated).

Acid truths

There are several types of fat, or fatty acids, with different properties:

- saturated fatty acids (saturated fat). These cause raised blood cholesterol, which in turn increases the risk of heart attacks.
- unsaturated fatty acids (mono- and polyunsaturated fat). While all fat is heavy in calories and therefore liable to make you fat, both monounsaturated and polyunsaturated fats evidently have a good effect on blood fats.
- hydrogenation is an industrial process that converts unsaturated fat into saturated fats, a perverted kind of polyunsaturated fat called 'trans-saturates' or 'trans fatty acids'. The food industry likes it as it can create harder vegetable fats with a longer shelf life, but these trans-saturates are now a health hazard equivalent to naturally occurring saturated fats.

Good quality unsaturated oils are positively good for you. This is one important reason why fish is good for you. Whereas the fat in domesticated animals bred for meat is hard and unsaturated, the fat in fish, which are in effect wild creatures, is oily and saturated (see **Fish**). All whole cereals contain unsaturated oils, as do fresh vegetables, in varying quantity. Nuts and seeds are rich in unsaturated oils.

Vegetable facts?

Proud boasts on a packet that a product 'contains no animal fat' may be great for non-meat eaters, but they do not necessarily mean the fat is rich in polyunsaturates. ('Low in saturates' is the statement you should be looking for.) Some vegetable fats are high in saturated fat, especially the so-called tropical fats such as palm, palm kernel and coconut (see table below), which are probably just as bad for you, certainly in processed form, as saturated animal fats.

Fats and oils compared

	saturates	percentages of monounsaturates	polyunsaturates
beef dripping	45	50	5
butter	65	30	5
lard	40	50	10
coconut oil	95	5	0
corn oil	15	25	60
olive oil	15	75	10
palm kernel oil	85	15	0
palm oil	50	40	10
soya oil	15	30	55
sunflower oil	10	20	70

Spreading the fat facts

The butters and marges we spread on our bread and toast – yellow fats, to give them their trade name – supply nearly a quarter of the total fat in our diet. We buy some 2 billion packets and tubs of these spreads each year. Worth nearly £700 million, the yellow fats market is bitterly contested by the vegetable fat giants – led by Flora-makers Van den Berghs (owned by Unilever), Kraft and Dairy Crest – and the dairy fat producers promoted by the Butter Information Council.

The *Food Magazine* looked at over 40 butter substitutes and found none that had as much saturated fat as butter. But some reduced-fat spreads were little more than watered down butter, with the proportion of saturated fat just as high as in butter. Some dairy blend and low-fat spreads could be short on vitamins A and D, and there were hardly any non-butter spreads free of added colouring.

As much as 40 per cent of the fat in some margarines can be saturated. The best buy is polyunsaturated margarines, made largely from sunflower oils. Used sparingly, they can help cut back on saturated fat intake and total fat intake simultaneously.

Low-fat spreads are a blend of fat and water (more than half water), held together with emulsifying agents. They are aimed at people wanting to cut back on total fat. But don't be tempted to increase the amount you use, which defeats the whole purpose of the exercise. These spreads have about half the fat content of regular marge or butter, but it may be rich in saturates, so that a thin layer of sunflower margarine would give less saturated fat and possibly fewer calories than a thicker spreading of a so-called low-fat product. But if you like the taste of low-fat spreads take a look at some of the new extra low-fat products which, although expensive for a tub that is 60 per cent water, might offer the best way to achieve a low-calorie, low-saturate diet.

Definitions

- margarine must be at least 80 per cent fat, and at most 16 per cent water. The oils may be from fish and animal sources as well as vegetable, and will be refined, deodorized and bleached; they may also be hydrogenated. As with virtually all non-butter spreads, these products may be flavoured and coloured, and mixed with anti-oxidants and emulsifiers to produce a long-lasting, smooth blend
- half-fat butter has no legal definition, but is typically 40 per cent fat, 55 per cent water
- fat-reduced margarine has no legal definition, but is typically 70 per cent fat, 25 per cent water
- dairy spread has no legal definition, but is typically 70-80 per cent fat, 15-25 per cent water
- reduced-fat spread has no legal definition, but is typically 60 per cent fat, 35 per cent water
- low-fat spread has no legal definition, but is typically 40 per cent fat, 55 per cent water
- very low-fat spread has no legal definition, but is typically 25 per cent fat, 60 per cent water.

Fat content of butter, margarines and similar spreads

	percentage of fat by weight	saturated fat as percentage of total fat
butter	81–83	62–75
margarines		
Blue Band sunflower (c, h)	82	15

Co-op margarine (c)	81	–
Co-op silver (c)	81	–
Flora sunflower (c, h)	80	20
Good Life sunflower (c, h)	81	15
Granose vegetable (b, h)	82	–
Safeway vegetable (c, h)	83	–
Safeway soft (a, c)	81	30
Sainsbury's margarine (a, c)	80	35
Sainsbury's sunflower (c, h)	81	20
Stork (a, c)	80	40
Suma sunflower (b, h)	83	15
Tesco soya (c, h)	83	20
Tesco sunflower (c, h)	82	20
Tomar kosher (c, h)	–	–
Vitalite (c, h)	80	15

blends and low-fat spreads

Anchor half-fat (c, h, nv)	40	–
Clover (c, h, nv)	75	–
Clover light (c, h, nv)	40	–
Co-op Red Seal (c)	–	–
Delight (c, h)	40	30
Kerrygold light (c, nv)	39	–
Kraft Golden Churn (c, h)	75	20
Krona (a, c)	70	45
Outline very low (c, h)	28	20
Safeway low-fat (c, h)	–	–
Sainsbury's Devon spread (c, h, nv)	75	40
Sainsbury's golden (c, h)	39	25
Sainsbury's low-fat (c, h)	40	20
Sainsbury's sunflower spread (c, h)	39	20
St Ivel Gold (c, h)	39	25
St Ivel Gold Lowest (c, h)	25	25
St Ivel Shape (c, h)	39	25
Summer County (c)	72	35
Tesco half-fat creamery (c, nv)	40	65
Tesco sunflower spread (c, h)	40	20
Tesco soft spread (c)	72	30
Willow (c, h, nv)	78	–

Key:
a: includes animal or marine oil (excluding butterfat)
b: label says 'No colouring', but betacarotene added
c: added colouring
h: includes hydrogenated fat
nv: no vitamins added
-: no fat information on pack

Additives

Butter contains significant amounts of two fat-soluble vitamins, A and D. Food regulations have long required that margarine should also have these vitamins added during manufacture. But the regulations have never been extended to the recent generation of blended products and low-fat spreads, allowing manufacturers to cut costs by leaving out the vitamins. Several of these products do not mention any added vitamins (see table below).

Butter is permitted to contain certain colouring agents, but in Britain it rarely does so. Margarines and other spreads, however, nearly all have added colouring – usually betacarotene or annatto. Granose vegetable margarine declares on its label 'No colour or flavour added', but lists betacarotene in its ingredients and uses mono- and diglycerides and maltodextrin in the recipe – all of which are flavour-affecting agents. Similarly, Suma sunflower margarine declares no colouring or flavouring added, but the ingredients include betacarotene and mono- and diglycerides.

Pesticide residues in fat and oil

Some of the more persistent residues from pesticides find their way into the diet of animals and are stored in the fat in their bodies. So cutting back on animal fats has an extra advantage. In government tests residues were found in:

- nearly a third of sausages sampled
- nearly half of 150 burgers sampled
- nearly half of 177 cheese samples.

In a number of different surveys, well over half of all samples of milk, cream and butter revealed residues. Another government survey looked at 55 samples of eight types of vegetable oil. Refined oils showed no detectable residues, but some unrefined oils – all of them sesame seed – did.

Olive oil

Great faith is put in olive oil as a health food. The low levels of heart disease enjoyed by people living on 'Mediterranean' diets are given as evidence for the benefits of this traditional food. Other factors could be involved, too: more fish, fresh fruit and vegetables, fewer animal fats and hydrogenated oils. But as a replacement for fats such as butter, lard or hard margarine it can be recommended.

There is good evidence that olive oil, which is rich in monounsaturates, is as healthy as sunflower and other oils rich in polyunsaturates, and may actually offer some advantages. It appears to be able to reduce total blood cholesterol mainly by reducing one component

– the low-density lipoproteins – that at high levels evidently cause heart disease, while not reducing and possibly increasing a second component – the high-density lipoproteins – which protect us from arterial disease. Research on these factors is of great interest to countries such as Italy and Spain, which are anxious to promote olive oil exports.

Fat futures

At least nine companies are currently developing 'non-fat fats' to compete for the potentially huge profits to be made from guilt-free food. The leading contender, Olestra, expects to make over $1 billion a year in the USA alone. Big bucks for industry and the promise of small waists and long-lasting hearts for consumers – but can we really have our cream cake and eat it too?

Olestra is a type of sucrose polyester which our bodies, lacking the right digestive enzyme, cannot absorb. Its maker, US giant Procter and Gamble, is seeking US and UK approval to use it in 35 per cent of home cooking fats and 75 per cent of commercial frying fats. It could be widely used in everything from cakes to chip fat, and could contribute up to 5 per cent of a person's diet.

In 1987 it looked as if Olestra would get US approval on a wave of positive publicity. But the Washington-based Center for Science in the Public Interest criticized the company's safety tests because they used only one animal species instead of the normal two. There was also evidence that the absorption of fat-soluble vitamin A and vitamin E was impaired, and indications that the undigested material could interfere with intestinal functions.

In Britain, Olestra has been referred by MAFF to its Committee on Toxicity of Chemicals in Food and to the Novel Foods Panel of the Committee on Medical Aspects of Food Policy. But the approval process is shrouded in commercial confidentiality. Not only are British consumers kept in the dark but, unlike in the USA, this government does not require companies to submit all their data on a new product.

Another product close to arriving on the supermarket shelves, NutraSweet's Simplesse, has promoted its 'naturalness' because it is made from egg and milk proteins. Ray Dull from Experience Inc., who has studied fat substitutes, says that approval of Simplesse would be a test case for future foods: 'The ability of a company to take parts of a naturally occurring approved substance and change them for use in foods will be a regulatory issue.'

Add these fat substitutes to fluffy cellulose, a no-calorie flour substitute developed by the US Department of Agriculture and currently being marketed as Snowite Oat Fibre, mix in some artificial sweetener, sprinkle with traditional E numbers and you have a dish which is made entirely of cosmetic foods – one giant additive. And this is 'good' for us?

Fish

'We think of Britain as a meat-eating country,' writes Professor Michael Crawford in *The Driving Force*,

> yet history would seem to suggest otherwise. Sir Walter Raleigh persuaded Queen Elizabeth I to fight for Newfoundland for no other reason than the rich cod fisheries. One half of England's income was at that time dependent on fish. Mrs Beeton's cookery book, that great repository of traditional English recipes, also witnesses differently. Out of 340 recipes for main meals no less than 280 include fish or other products of fresh and salt water .... The traditional 'Cockney' food of Londoners was cockles, mussels, whelks, oysters, scallops, crabs – and a variety of fish from the Thames estuary.

But in Britain today average consumption of meat is over seven times that of fish: on average we eat a pathetic 5 ounces of fish a week, and that includes fish fingers, tinned fish, fish and chips, scampi – everything. Average consumption of fresh fish is just over one ounce a week.

Fish is a wonderful food

One of the great boosts you can give to your family's health is to switch two main meals a week from meat to fish. In any nutritionist's list of delicious and readily available superfoods that can form the basis of a good meal, fish is on or near the top. All fish are rich in vitamins and minerals – important when so much of our Western food is drained of nutrients during processing. Most are good sources of B vitamins, which nourish the nervous system. Many oily fish are rich in the fat-soluble vitamins A, D and E, which nourish the skin, bones and circulation system. Fish livers are concentrated sources of fat-soluble vitamins: many children, especially those who live in cities or don't eat much fresh food, will benefit from a daily spoonful of cod liver oil, sensibly recommended by the Ministry of Food 50 years ago.

Fish are also good or fair sources of many minerals, notably potassium, magnesium, zinc, iron and calcium. Potassium, magnesium and zinc nourish the digestive system, the heart and the metabolic system. The government's survey *The Diets of British Schoolchildren*, published in 1989, shows that most children are short of iron. There is now good evidence that iron not only nourishes the blood, but is also vital for proper mental functioning. Studies show that children who are short of iron do less well at school: they are tired, depressed, and can't concentrate. And around half of British children are short of calcium. The soft bones of small fish like sardines and pilchards are excellent sources.

Find a friendly fishmonger and ask for advice and information. There are fish for all pockets. The cheaper white, lean fish include the familiar cod, haddock, whiting and plaice. Halibut, turbot, sole, mullet, brill and monkfish are more expensive. Cheap oily fish include herring, mackerel, sprats and sardines. Farmed trout and salmon are quite cheap (but there are problems with this method of producing fish – see Chapter 2). Real wild trout and salmon are much more expensive, and are treats for a family feast.

Fish oil is healthy

The best news about oily fish is that their fat is positively beneficial to human health. Some fats are called 'essential' because, like vitamins and minerals, they are vital for health and life itself. All essential fats are polyunsaturated. And all oily fish are a rich source of essential fats. It stands to reason that the fat in a fish is soft and unsaturated: a herring or salmon would have a hard job flexing a body or flipping a tail full of lard.

Why are essential fats so valuable? As long ago as 1956 Dr Hugh Sinclair of Oxford University, now the most distinguished living British nutritionist, proposed that many common Western killer diseases, including heart attacks, are in part caused by a deficiency of essential fats in the Western diet. He and his followers have also proposed that a diet poor in essential fats is an important cause of degenerative diseases of the nervous system, including multiple sclerosis; and that a diet rich in fish nourishes the nervous system – including the brain. At the time he was ignored, but time and many scientific studies have proved him right – and his message is: eat more fish.

It is likely that we will keep our brains and nervous systems in better shape throughout life if we eat more fish than meat. And what we can do as a nation is to breed a new rising generation on lots of fish. This will require a new government pledged to clean up Britain's rivers and seas, and to fight in Europe for the rights of Britain's fishermen to increase their allotted catch of the staple sea fish the British have always enjoyed. As individuals, the time to switch to fish is when planning a family. The time when a baby is best nourished with the essential fats, vitamins and minerals from fish is when growing in the womb, and then early in life.

Nutritional content of fish

	calories per 100g	as percentage of calories		
		protein	fat	starch
white fish (cod, haddock, whiting, plaice, halibut, turbot, sole, mullet, brill, monkfish etc.)				
steamed, boiled,baked	100	85	15	-
fried	200	45	50	5
fingers, grilled	175	30	35	35
fingers, fried	250	20	55	25
oily fish (herring, mackerel, sprats, sardines, trout, salmon, tuna etc.)				
grilled, baked	200	45	55	-
small, fried	400	25	75	-
canned in oil	300	30	70	-
canned in tomato	150	60	35	5
seafood (lobster, prawns, shrimps, octopus, squid, whelks, cockles, mussels etc.)				
boiled	100	85	15	-
fried (say scampi)	300	15	50	35

These values are approximate and vary somewhat from fish to fish.

Tinned fish

If you can't find really fresh fish, or when you want to make a filling, nourishing, instant snack or meal, tinned salmon, tuna, pilchards and sardines are excellent family stand-bys. But never buy fish tinned in 'vegetable oil' or 'edible oil'. Brine (which you can drain off) or tomato are all right. The best choice is Mediterranean fish tinned in high-quality 'extra virgin' olive oil, worth every one of the few extra pence.

Pollution

It is a disgusting and disgraceful fact that some fish is now contaminated with industrial pollution, including heavy metals like mercury, lead and cadmium, especially around the Thames and Mersey estuaries; sewage; and radioactive effluent from Sellafield in the Irish Sea. How much does this matter, and what can you do about it?

It's probably best to avoid shellfish from British or any known contaminated waters. Generally, the level of contamination found in fish from the deep sea seems insignificant. One sign of a good fishmonger is that he knows where his fish comes from; if you prefer fish from the relatively unpolluted Arctic waters, or if you refuse to eat fish from the Irish Sea, say so, and see how knowledgeable he is.

Fish – the original fast food

What about fish and chips? Everything depends on the quality of the ingredients and the frying. A meal of fresh fish fillets in a batter made with eggs and milk, together with chipped unpeeled potatoes, fried in corn, sunflower or groundnut oil which is regularly replaced, accompanied by one or two big fat sweet gherkins, is delicious, filling and healthy. But if what's on offer is stale fish slapped into a vat of batter substitute and then fried in a sea of smouldering filthy fat of unknown origin, also used to fry chips made from reconstituted potatoes, don't buy. To be quite safe, if you like fish and chips, cook them at home.

What's in fish fingers?

Most fish eaten in Britain today is processed, and many children love fish fingers. For many years Trading Standards Officers have objected to the steady deterioration of the quality of the British fish finger. But the present government led by Mrs Thatcher believes in a free-for-all for food manufacturers and will not maintain compositional standards. In 1987 the Ministry of Agriculture promised legislation to ensure that fish products were labelled with minimum fish content. Two years later the *Food Magazine* reported that nothing had happened. On analysis, it turned out that the cost of the fish in selected fish fingers varied from £2.09 and £6.31 per pound, at a time when farmed salmon cost £4.25 a pound!

What is 'fish mince'?

And the story gets fishier. You might think that economy fish fingers are the best buy. Wrong. They contain 'fish mince' or 'frame mince' (also called in the trade 'engineered seafood'). Fish skeletons (or 'frames'), together with fish heads, guts and other waste, are squeezed between a moving rubber belt and the outside of a revolving perforated steel drum. The resulting paste is to fish what MRM is to meat, and what chipboard is to wood. By itself, fish mince is grey, gritty and can taste like cardboard, so it is perked up with:

- chemical sweeteners
- flavour enhancers
- colourings
- water soaked up with polyphosphates.

How can you spot fish mince? By the claims, descriptions and ingredients lists on fish products. The presence of flavour enhancers like monosodium glutamate is a give-away. Fish mince is in all sorts of fish products.

In 1987 the Ministry of Agriculture also promised that any fish product containing more than 10 per cent fish mince would soon by law have to declare this fact on the label. But by early 1990 nothing had happened: the interests of those manufacturers who are anxious to preserve the quality of their product, and of consumers, have once again been sacrificed to the dogma of deregulation.

Flour
See **Bread and flour**.

Fruit and vegetables

Fruit

The amount of fruit eaten by British children in 1989 had fallen by a third in four years, a report in *Today* newspaper revealed in August 1989, referring to a survey commissioned by the DHSS. The survey showed that parents were buying fifty per cent more fast foods such as baked beans, chocolate biscuits, packet desserts, frozen chips, and take-aways than homes without children. Children wield an important influence on what is consumed within the home, and Parents for Safe Food feel that adults need to persist in providing healthy, nutritious food. Start early, when your children are more biddable and not subject to peer group pressure from their junk-scoffing mates in the school playground.

Use fruit more often – it's one of the great convenience foods:

- eat fresh fruit when it's ripe and in its prime – if you buy seasonal produce it won't be expensive
- buy little and often so it doesn't become dry or mouldy, and therefore unappealing
- give your children fresh fruit as a between-meals snack
- serve it at the end of a meal instead of a sweet pudding.

Expenditure on exotics is rising

Although fruit and vegetable consumption has drastically diminished in some sections of the community, there has been an overall growth in spending on them. This is according to the January 1990 report of a survey conducted on behalf of Geest, the banana people, which showed that exotic fruits like mangoes, avocados and kiwi fruit were an area of real growth. Domestic expenditure on exotic fruits alone had quadrupled since 1978, to over £73 million.

Ron Parker, chairman of the Fresh Fruit and Vegetable Information Bureau, which worked in association with Geest on the report, said: 'The consumer research we carried out for the report shows that almost one in two housewives have tried kiwi fruit, and over 50 per cent have eaten fresh pineapple.' Consumption of melons, peaches and nectarines is expected to double in the next ten years as new varieties are developed and become more widely available. Mangoes, when ripe, are rich in carotene (1200mg per 100g), vitamin C (30mg) and potassium (190mg) – are predicted to be the new 'boom' fruit of the 1990s.

Old friends cold-shouldered

In the mid-eighties, thanks to insufficient advertising, our old friends – apples, pears, oranges and grapefruit – were suffering a long-term decline in popularity. (It's ironical to think that when Nell Gwynn was touting her wares three hundred years ago they, too, were considered exotic and desirable!) The total fruit market was worth £1 billion, and yet in the whole of 1985 little more than £1 million was spent on TV advertising of fruit. Just by way of comparison, during the same period almost £20 million was spent on promoting potato crisps and snacks, while £19 million went on biscuits and a massive £80 million-plus on chocolate (see **Sweets and chocolate**).

It was admitted that people in the fruit and vegetable industry had not treated their products as a food manufacturer would have done. The Apple and Pear Development Council believed that unless more advertising money was spent, fresh fruit would continue to lose ground to the producers of convenience and snack foods.

Why you should buy organic

Television, travel, immigration, job mobility and general affluence have brought about a great spurt of interest in exotic fruits, as we have seen. They are much cosseted on their way to market. Once they were varnished – coated in shellac – to preserve them for their journey from the Third World to the rich West. More recently fruit has been sealed in a combination of synthetic and natural waxes to inhibit premature ripening and decay. That is why Parents for Safe Food recommend that for fruits that are not peeled, or whose peel you use in cooking, you buy organic.

But of course washing and peeling only go skin deep, whereas some chemicals go rather further than that. Go to any fruit and vegetable market and you will see boldly stated on boxes of bananas 'Treated with thiabendazole' (a systemic fungicide – that is, one that creeps into the entire plant – also used in the treatment of potatoes). Peter Beaumont of the Pesticides Trust sees the way of the future as a steadily reducing dependency on the use of fungicides, by moving goods more quickly on a smaller scale, and storing them at lower temperatures with better ventilation. Treatments in storage, he said, presented special problems to monitoring groups: 'You can't see what's being done. Spraying in fields is more obvious!' For the present we have to live with pesticides and to press for determined reductions.

In 1984 Friends of the Earth launched their pesticide-free food campaign, on which the *Observer* ran an article. Things were bad. Thirteen out of 32 lettuces examined were found to be contaminated with chemicals including the persistent organochlorine pesticide lindane, which has been identified as a potential carcinogen and a substance that causes babies to be born deformed. (Remember that much-headlined 'barrel of death' washing around the English Channel and chased by the French Navy for weeks on end in 1988? That was lindane. It is banned in 15 countries.) DDT was also found on three samples of lettuce, although its use on this popular salad plant had been banned many years earlier.

One of the real nasties, aldrin, was found on tomatoes (though it had been banned for use on them) and on some other innocent-looking produce – spring onions, mushrooms and watercress. Aldrin, like lindane, is thought to cause birth defects and is a suspected carcinogen.

Some dreadful scare statistics arose from the 305 fruit and 178 vegetables tested:

- six different pesticides on tomatoes
- six on grapes and cherries
- eight on mushrooms
- overall nearly a third of mushrooms were found to have pesticide contamination
- important British fruits – apples, blackcurrants, cherries, gooseberries, peaches, pears, plums, raspberries and strawberries – showed 37 per cent with detectable residues
- major vegetables – beans, beetroot, broccoli, cabbage, carrots, cauliflowers, cucumbers, lettuce, mushrooms, onions, parsnips, peas, potatoes, tomatoes and turnips – showed 35.5 per cent with detectable residues.

One reason for all this is that consumers expect too much of food in terms of presentation, and not enough in terms of content. So true is this that James Erlichman opens Chapter 1 of *Gluttons for Punishment* with these words: '"My biggest problem is caterpillar shit," said Peter Atkins, a 40-year fruit and vegetable grower from North Kent. "It is green and slimy but it washes off easily enough and doesn't hurt anyone. But if Marks and Spencer finds any in my cauliflowers, they'll probably send back the whole consignment.'"

Nutritional value of fruit

It is from fruit that we obtain, in an easily assimilated form, essential minerals and vitamins, especially vitamin C. The amount varies greatly in different fruits. During cooking, some loss occurs. Guavas, blackcurrants, lemons, papaya, strawberries and oranges are among the richest in vitamin C. Apples, bananas, cherries, rhubarb, pears and peaches are examples of fruit which contain little vitamin C, but to compensate they have valuable amounts of other vitamins, minerals and fibre.

An apple a day

Pity the poor apple. The number of its varieties has shrunk from a one-time six thousand to the horrifyingly scant nine which now make up the bulk of British apple production. As true believers in wholefood and diversity, Parents for Safe Food share the concern of the organization Common Ground for the protection of old orchards, now in worrying decline. Neil Sinden of Common Ground explains: 'A modern commercial orchard will rarely contain more than two or three standard varieties of fruit, selected largely for their suitability for supermarket shelves.' In an old orchard, established to provide fruit for local needs, it is quite usual to find more than 20 varieties and a range of different fruits – plums, pears, apples, greengages – to provide a diversity of tastes and qualities to be enjoyed in their prime from August through to the following spring.

Now, quite apart from the pleasure of variety and choice, and the value of orchards to wildlife, for recreation and for their distinctive presence in the landscape, vigorous, widely spaced trees of different varieties are better able to cope with natural pests and diseases. Make the effort to seek out different apples, enjoy making fruit more fun, and help save our orchards.

Dried fruit

These are little packages of concentrated nourishment. They are high in fructose (so don't eat too many), and are very often much sweeter than in their fresh form. This is because they were left to ripen on the tree. They don't contain vitamin C, but are rich in potassium, iron and other minerals, and in vitamins A and B. Sun drying is the traditional method of drying fruit. Sulphur dioxide, heat drying and freeze drying are sometimes also used nowadays.

Tinned fruit

Fruit can be tinned in various forms:

- in natural fruit juice with no added sugar
- in sugar and water
- and in a sugar syrup.

It is a very useful addition to your store cupboard, but will inevitably have lost the water-soluble vitamins B and C. Be sure to choose the no added sugar variety.

Freezing fruit

If you are freezing at home, choose firm, sound, ripe fruit and take your instructions from a good freezer book. It isn't difficult, but it must be done properly. Many fruits need no sugar in open (flash) freezing (indeed it toughens some), while some hard, non-juicy fruits need to be packed in sugar syrup.

Vegetables

Like fruit, fresh veg are good for us. Although vegetables (including potatoes, which look so solid) contain between 78 and 95 per cent water, they still supply valuable quantities of essential nutrients: vitamins, proteins, fats, carbohydrates and mineral salts. And they are an important source of dietary fibre. All that for a relatively low price – certainly a low price compared to the 'added value' processed foods.

The nutrient content of vegetables is influenced by many factors during growth, harvesting and storage, transportation, selling and arriving in our kitchens. It will also vary according to their type, degree of maturity and amount of exposure to sunlight.

'Green vegetables are of nutritional importance because of the contribution to the daily intake of vitamin C, carotene (which, after absorption, is converted to vitamin A in the body), folic acid, iron, other minerals and dietary fibre.' So says MAFF's *Manual of Nutrition*. It goes on: 'They are especially valuable when eaten raw, as they will suffer no losses in cooking; there will be considerable losses of vitamin C from wilted vegetables.' On pulses it says: 'Peas and beans, fresh, frozen and dried, are richer in protein, B vitamins, dietary fibre and energy than green and root vegetables.' (See **Rice, other grains and pulses**.)

Pesticides and potatoes

In August 1989 James Erlichman told *Guardian* readers that to oblige the manufacturer, ICI, the government had relaxed new safety rules restricting the use of the controversial post-harvest potato 'protector' tecnazene. He said that ICI had been allowed to reduce the interval between applying the stuff and selling the potatoes from four months to six weeks. But, he added, the Ministry had been 'long aware that potato handlers grossly overuse the chemical during winter storage to prevent potatoes from sprouting and spoiling'. ICI have now been asked for a whole new range of studies to determine how toxic or carcinogenic the material might be; the report is expected by 1992. But Parents for Safe Food and Friends of the Earth have commissioned their own independent studies.

Andrew Lees of the latter organization said there was too much horse trading over tecnazene. 'It is evident that the government's own scientists remain concerned about the chemical breakdown products of tecnazene and what happens during cooking,' he said. There is also concern about the effects on fish, wildlife and drinking water when tecnazene is washed into rivers from potato processing plants. A pesticidal pestilence indeed.

Tecnazene apart, the potato is a wonderful vegetable that has sustained humankind through many troubled times. Its failure in Ireland in the mid-19th century killed 2 million people – a quarter of the population – and caused many more to emigrate. Academics today say that before the famine the Irish were very much healthier than after it, when those that survived had to alter their diets. Labourers who worked prodigiously hard had been putting away 10 to 12lb a day, said Dr Margaret Crawford and Professor Leslie Clarkson from Queens University, Belfast. In August 1987 the *Daily Telegraph* reported: 'The humble potato deserves a better place in the national diet, researchers in Ireland said ....' And they were quoted as saying: '"The incidence of diseases such as diarrhoea and dysentery increased in Ireland, contrary to the rest of the UK. Diets before the famine may have been monotonous but were rich in protein, carbohydrate, energy value, calcium and iron."'

Though much has changed in life – in protection against disease, and certainly in diet – since then, the nutritional properties of the potato remain the same. Brought to Europe from South America in the 1500s by the Spaniards (not Sir Walter Raleigh), the potato is a mighty force for good. And since it can be processed hundreds, maybe thousands, of different ways, it is far from absent in our diet. But in its whole form it is eaten far too little.

To quote MAFF again:

They [potatoes] provide the main source of vitamin C in many diets, even though their vitamin C content per unit weight is comparatively low. The amount is highest in new potatoes and falls gradually during post-harvest storage.

Instant potato powder flakes and granules are nutritionally equivalent alternatives to fresh potatoes only if the vitamin C and thiamin which are lost in processing are added back to the products.

Potatoes contribute more protein and iron than other vegetables to the average diet, because of the comparatively large amounts which are eaten. They are a useful source of thiamin, niacin and several other nutrients, including dietary fibre.

Long live the powerful potato, and may its tribes increase. It's encouraging to learn that Sainsbury's chain alone stocks 40 varieties. Now, if only they were organic ....

Home storage of vegetables

Young and seasonal vegetables will be naturally sweeter than older, stored produce. And fewer chemicals will have been used on them. As ever, buy organic when you can, and if you can grow your own, even better.

Put your leafy vegetables and salads, unwashed, in the crisper compartment in your fridge, in plastic bags. The moisture in the vegetables will keep them fresh for a time. With watercress, cut 1/2 inch off the stems and store it in the fridge in a covered dish containing about an inch of cold water.

Root vegetables should have their leaves removed before storing them in the fridge. And onions should never be stored with potatoes, because they make the poor spuds deteriorate rapidly. Store them away from each other in a cool, dark place (light makes potatoes go green, and in this state they are not safe to eat). Similarly, don't store apples near carrots – the ethylene gas given off by the apples will make the carrots taste bitter.

How to cook vegetables perfectly

Vegetables don't need complicated cooking. Lightly stir fry, steam or poach them in a small amount of boiling water, thus minimizing the loss of vitamin C, thiamin and other water-soluble nutrients. Never cook them longer than the point of 'just done'. Long cooking destroys texture, colour and flavour as well as nutrients.

Here is a meal to gladden the heart of every member of your family on a cold day.

Tranmere Scouse

This trans-Mersey recipe is a low-fat variation of the traditional Liverpool dish called Scouse.

2 tablespoons sunflower oil
1 1/2 lb/750g lamb fillet, sliced 1/4 inch/6mm thick
2 large onions, sliced

3 cloves garlic, crushed
2¹/₂pints/1.5 litres stock *or* water
4 medium carrots, roughly cut
2 small white turnips, sliced
2 large leeks, roughly cut
1¹/₂lb/750g new potatoes
3 sticks celery, chopped
fresh mint, parsley and rosemary (if available) *or* 2 tablespoons
    good dried mixed herbs
4oz/150g frozen peas
extra handful of chopped parsley, seasoning

Heat the oil in a large, heavy pan. Add the lamb fillet and seal it over a moderate to high heat, stirring all the time, for about 5 minutes. Then turn the heat down a little, add the onions and continue to fry until they are translucent. Add the garlic, pour the stock or water over the top and bring to the boil. Cover, and turn down to a simmer for 10 minutes.

Then skim off any fat and add the carrots, turnips, leeks, potatoes, celery and herbs, return to the boil, cover and allow to simmer for about 45 minutes, by which time the meat and vegetables should be tender. Add the peas, return to the boil and simmer again for 5 minutes. Turn off the heat, add the parsley and seasoning and allow to stand for 5 minutes before serving.

Raw food for health and flavour

But whenever possible eat your vegetables raw – sliced or diced carrots, courgettes, celeriac, fennel, cauliflower, mushrooms, peppers and many more are delicious. There's far more to salads than lettuce and tomatoes. For dressings, invest in some good flavour-some polyunsaturated oil and blend it with lemon and herbs; or mix yoghurt with lemon (grated peel and juice), herbs, finely chopped spring onions and a very little honey and seasoning to add flavour.

If your children are happy to eat raw fruit they will often eat raw vegetables as well. It is an excellent habit to encourage.

Frozen and canned vegetables

These do make very useful stand-bys – none more so than Italian tomatoes, as already recommended. Some veg are more processed than others. Here is the ingredients list for instant potato:

- potatoes (98 per cent)
- salt
- emulsifier E471
- tetrasodium pyrophosphate

- vitamin C
- preservative: E223
- anti-oxidant: E321.

And here is the list of contents of a can of 'mushy processed peas with no preservatives':

- processed peas
- water
- sugar
- salt
- colours E102, tartrazine, coal-tar dye E133 brilliant blue FCF.

A number of these additives will be found explained in all their glory in Chapter 4, but here's a reminder:

- E471 (monoglycerides of fatty acids) are possibly safe, but still controversial
- tetrasodium pyrophosphate (E450a) has a possible link to kidney damage in laboratory animals, and has a definite laxative effect.
- tartrazine and coal-tar dyes may cause asthma, rashes and hyperactivity, and have been linked to cancer in laboratory animals.

Do we need all these Es? Make sure you read the labels carefully before you buy.

Herbs, spices and aromatics

At last – something that is both cheap and good for us and for our children! Add herbs and spices to your cooking whenever possible, but use them sparingly so that they enhance rather than overpower the other ingredients. Those with delicate flavours should be put into soups and sauces towards the end of preparation and left long enough for the volatile oils to be released and absorbed. Aside from deriving pleasure from their aromas, by generous, sensitive use of spices and herbs we can draw from the food its intrinsic sodium and so reduce the need for added salt.

If you can get fresh herbs, so much the better (some supermarkets are now stocking them). If you can grow them yourself that is best of all, because you will know they are free of the entire range of pesty nasties, from aldicarb to zineb. You can grow your own oregano, marjoram, thyme, parsley, rosemary, sage and chives easily in the smallest patch outside, or in pots. (Watch out with mint – it's very invasive, so plant it in a pot rather than directly in the ground if you don't want it to spread triffid-like throughout your garden!)

If you can't either grow or obtain fresh herbs you can buy them dried, and on the whole they will still serve you well (though some, such as parsley, are not worth having unless they are fresh). Spices should always be bought whole rather than ground, as they keep better – use a pepper grinder or mortar and pestle to grind your own as and when you need them. Herbs are known, sometimes, to be irradiated against impurities, like animal droppings, picked up during the open-air drying process.

Homely flavourings

Mint has long been a part of our food – usually in its simplest British form as flavouring, courtesy of vinegar, sugar and water, for the Sunday joint of lamb. Likewise parsley with fish; thyme and parsley with poultry; sage (and onion) with pork, and mustard with beef. But although lots of herbs and spices were used in British cookery centuries ago (frequently to disguise tainted ingredients in the days before refrigeration and speedy distribution), their use gradually declined and our cooking became bland and uninteresting. It is only in the last 20 years or so, with the rapid increase in foreign travel and consumption of ethnic fast food at home, that we have found ourselves turned on once more to all sorts of different taste sensations.

Foreign exotica

Garlic, now commonplace, was hardly known to British housewives until the 1960s. It was 'something the French ate', and it was said you could smell them a mile off. Nowadays most of us eat garlic, which is very good for us. As for coriander, cumin and chilli, these are used in abundance – a real boon for making exciting what might otherwise be quite dull ingredients. Potatoes, says Indian cookery expert Madhur Jaffrey, taste one way when cooked with sesame seeds, another when stewed with soy sauce, and different again when fried with mustard and cumin seeds. And if you have ever wanted to make something special out of something mundane, put some bruised coriander seeds in olive oil and stir fry some spring cabbage very quickly – wonderful!

Many herbs have their own special associated foods, such as basil for tomatoes. Do pursue this lovely, distinctive, deep green, soft-leaved plant, originally from India but now more usually from the Mediterranean. It can also be grown in the sun, indoors or out, in Britain. Rosemary is classic with lamb, but also goes with soups, eggs and indeed fish. Likewise fennel blends with fish and just as comfortably with pork. Coriander goes with poultry (add lemon too) and with breads and in soups – but also, and more excitingly, where you would use English parsley. Tarragon fits with pretty well everything – but especially with chicken, where this tall, slim herb is most at home.

Make use of nature's gifts

We would be foolish indeed not to make as much use as we can of these gifts: herbs and spices and aromatics are three of the loveliest words in the culinary dictionary. With such a variety available now, we can do at home what until recently seemed possible only in restaurants. And since herbs and spices go a long way, they turn out to be among the cheaper occupants of our kitchen cupboards. What more could you want?

See also **Sauces, dressings and gravies.**

Honey

> 'If there's a buzzing noise somebody's making a buzzing noise and the only reason for making a buzzing noise that *I* know of is because you're a bee'. Then he thought another long time and said: 'And the only reason for being a bee that I know of is making honey.' And then he got up and said: 'And the only reason for making honey is so as I can eat it.' So he began to climb the tree.

Thus Winnie the Pooh. The very best health food shops have lovely displays of honey in jars and combs that would have delighted A.A. Milne's bear. Indeed, honey has an enviable image as a life-enhancer associated with that shining symbol of summer and warm early autumns, the bee.

Certainly honey does contain some good things: it is a delicately poised aggregate of carbohydrates in water with a little fat, some enzymes, protein, amino acids, vitamins and aromatic compounds. But never forget that honey is about 75 per cent sugar – and sugar, as this book has constantly emphasized, is something that we all need to cut down on.

Quality is important

Despite that, Parents for Safe Food are in favour of a little honey from time to time, because it is good for the quality of life. It is a natural product made by the good offices of the enzymes present in the bees' stomachs working on the nectar. The flavour will depend on what plants the bees have fed on, the climate where they are kept, and so on.

But do buy carefully. Nowadays there is a large market in 'produce of more than one country' honeys, which all end up in one jar; sometimes sugar is added to jack up the content. Try instead to obtain some that has been collected and packed locally. Wholefood companies sell some nice honeys collected from named flowers or perhaps from a selection of wild flowers.

Long live bees

Incidentally, Winnie the Pooh was wrong when he said there was only one reason for being a bee – to provide him with honey. He was, of course, a bear of very little brain. The bee's primary function is to sustain the state of nature as we have come to rely on it in all its glory, by helping to pollinate the flowers that make the world that much more wonderful and enduring.

Ice cream

Each of us sweet-toothed Britons is eating 4.5 kg (10lb) of ice cream *at home* every year. We eat 500 million of them out of doors or in cafés. We spend half a billion pounds on the stuff annually, and the manufacturers spend £5 million trying to get us to buy more. It is a huge part of the sugar addiction industry, and there are few things more pleasurable – even though much of it is junk. It is a lovable, huggable, smellable, unbeatable, all-year-round-but-especially-summer treatable indulgence – a seaside pleasure and a teatime treasure.

But what is it really?

Ice cream is mostly rich fat chemicalized, altered, whipped around, air-filled, softened, emulsified, stabilized, sugared, gummed, coloured and flavoured for the palate. There is a lot of second- and third-rate stuff around – some of what passes for ice cream in Britain won't pass in Europe or the USA. And when you eat it, ice cream is often a bit of a disappointment. Have you never experienced that slightly synthetic, that-wasn't-really-cream-was-it feeling, with a faint sugar burn in your throat – particularly after eating the soft stuff?

Soft ice cream, which accounts for one-sixth of street sales of iced confectionery, is made by reconstituting a commercial powder with water. Ice cream powder is made from concentrated skimmed milk to which fat, emulsifiers and stabilizers are added. The concentrate is then homogenized, pasteurized and spray dried before dry blending it with ground sugar. The resulting powder is about:

- 40 per cent sugar
- 30 per cent fat
- 25 per cent non-fat milk solids
- 2 per cent emulsifiers and stabilizers.

The powder is mixed with about two parts of water before going into the dispensing machine.

Good mouth feel

When it comes out it will have good 'mouth feel', as this appealing condition is known in the trade (without it, few processed foods would attract anyone at all), depending on the amount of air trapped in the frozen emulsion. Without any air, eating it would be like licking a hard 'ice cream' lolly – whereas too much air makes the ice cream collapse. (In her days as a food scientist for Joe Lyons, Margaret Thatcher once invented a new process for pumping more air into ice cream.)

The ice cream man cometh

Buying loose ice cream from mobile vans is convenient and fun. Less so are the bugs you may pick up as a result of poor hygiene. Modern state-of-the-art soft ice cream machines are self-pasteurizing and, according to Eric Brunner, who has researched them for the *Food Magazine*, the makers say that they do not have to be cleaned out for intervals as long as six weeks. Although the technique is recognized by the Public Health Laboratory Service, it depends (here we get technical) on heating the machine's interior to between 65.5 and 76°C for up to 35 minutes while the contents of the machine's reservoir are kept at 4°C. The pasteurizing temperatures are supposed to be monitored and recorded in a log book. There is a very high rate of food poisoning from soft ice cream – but few prosecutions.

Check for additives

If you buy your ice cream sealed from a supermarket it's probably safer, and the package will list what you are getting. The main nutritional difference between different types of ice cream is the use of additives (see Chapter 4 to remind yourself what those listed below are and do). Parents for Safe Food advise you to spend rather more than you want to on really good ice cream, having first checked the ingredients. Here is a very brief selection: the first two are upmarket, the last two are not.

Thayer's Real Dairy Ice Cream

- ingredients: milk, double cream, sugar, dextrose, butter, eggs (1.25 per cent minimum), emulsifier (E471), stabilizers (guar gum, xanthan gum, locust bean gum)

Myatt's Country Fresh Ices

- ingredients: whole fresh milk, double cream, sugar, natural flavour (vanilla), skimmed milk powder, dextrose, emulsifiers (monoglyceride), stabilizers (sodium alginate, guar gum)

Wall's Soft Scoop (box marked 'non-dairy fat, no artificial colouring')

- ingredients: skimmed milk, dextrose, vegetable fat, whey solids, glucose, syrup, emulsifier, stabilizers (sodium alginate E401, carob gum, guar gum), colourings (curcumin, annatto)

Co-op Ice Cream, vanilla flavour (box marked 'contains non-milk fat')

- ingredients: skimmed milk, sugar, vegetable fat, skimmed milk powder, dextrose, whey powder, emulsifier (glyceryl monostearate), stabilizers (guar gum, xanthan gum, carrageenan), flavouring, colouring (curcumin, annatto).

Now of course all four are fattening and sugary (the Co-op brand has three kinds of sugar), but the first (and more expensive) two are offering real double cream and many fewer additives. The non-milk fat in the Wall's and Co-op products is hardened (hydrogenated) and saturated – so that isn't much of a gain, is it?

In 1988, the London Food Commission carried out a major food survey and analysis of 11 ice creams, the results of which were published in the *News of the World* and are given in the following two tables.

How much air you get in ice cream

	average price	weight	cost per scoop	air
Bejam White Non-milk Fat	39p	476g	4p	***
Iceland with Non-milk Fat	42p	461g	4p	***
Lyons Non-milk Soft Scoop	61.5p	437g	6.25p	***

continued overleaf

How much air you get in ice cream *continued*

	average price	weight	cost per scoop	air
Tesco Non-milk Fat	49p	484g	5p	* * *
Treats Natural Non-milk	69p	493g	7p	* * *
Marks and Spencer Non-milk Soft Scoop	95p	506g	9.5p	* *
Sainsbury's Non-fat Brick	45p	552g	4.5g	* *
Wall's Blue Ribbon Non-fat	97p	511g	9.75p	* *
Tesco Real Dairy Ice Cream	139p	518g	14p	* *
Sainsbury's Natural Dairy	119p	572g	12p	* *
Loseley Old Fashioned Dairy	293p	721g	29p	*

All the ice creams were 1 litre packs, and the testers worked on the basis of 10 scoops to the litre. The more stars a brand gets, the more air it contains.

Value for money

	additives	double cream	egg	value for money
Sainsbury's	5	no	no	* * *
Loseley Dairy	2	21%	yes	* * *
Sainsbury's Dairy	4	no	yes	* *
Bejam	3	no	no	* *
Marks and Spencer	4	no	no	*
Tesco Dairy	5	1-2%	no	*
Wall's	6	no	no	*
Tesco	5	no	no	*
Iceland	5	no	no	*
Treats	6	no	no	*
Lyons Maid	5	no	no	*

Value for money is based on quality, and air and water content – three stars is tops.

Watch your intake

MAFF's *Manual of Nutrition* (revised edition, 1989) states: 'Ice cream can make a useful contribution to the daily intake of energy and calcium, particularly for people who have small appetites or who will not drink milk.' But eaten frequently between meals it falls into the same category as many other snack foods. Rich in fat and sugar, it reduces the appetite for foods such as vegetables, cereals and meat at the next main meal. It can also make you put on weight if you don't use up all the extra energy it provides. People confined to their homes, or who don't take regular exercise, should watch their intake.

Ice lollies

A word on ice lollies: they are mostly sugar and glucose in water, with a whole slew of additives to give different colours or flavours. If that's what you want for your children, well ... a lolly a week won't kill them. But you'd be much better freezing your own from fruit juice – you can buy sticks and moulds – or freezing peeled whole bananas.

See also **Dairy products**.

Jam
See **Spreads**.

Juices and soft drinks

The British have taken to fruit juices in a big way. In five years we have nearly doubled our juice drinking to an amazing £400 million worth. Orange juice is by far the most popular, although apple and various blended juices are also well liked. Supermarket own-label brands take most of the sales, with Del Monte, Just Juice, Delora and St Ivel Real following behind.

Doctors recommend us to eat lots of fruit and vegetables. Fruit juice seems an enjoyable way of eating fruit, but we do lose out on valuable vitamins (30-50 per cent of vitamin C) and dietary fibre (virtually 100 per cent). The fruit's natural sugar is no longer bound up inside the flesh, where it would take a long time to digest, but is all dissolved in the juice (see table below).

Don't be fooled – some warnings

You may decide you want a fruit juice, but watch out for the rip-offs! Packaged like a fruit juice, featuring fruit on the label and advertised on television for their fruitiness, cartons of fruit drink are easily picked off the supermarket shelves instead of real fruit juice.

What's the difference? The answer is a lot of added water – up to 95 per cent of the pack. And to make the product taste as sweet as juice they add sugar – up to the equivalent of 50 lumps in a 1 litre carton! Throw in some colouring agents, stabilizers and artificial sweeteners, and pack it in fruit juice-style cartons at fruit juice prices, and what do you have? A consumer con trick.

Read the labels. The big print on the front of the carton may say 'contains real juice' or 'a refreshing combination of six fruit juices', or 'made with concentrated fruit juice', but take a look at the small print on the back or the side of the pack. Real fruit juice should be just that – juice extracted from fruit and packed either fresh or reconstituted from concentrate. Some companies add a little vitamin C (to help prevent the colour from fading) and some add sugar (watch out for this if you're trying to cut down) to make a sweetened fruit juice.

The specific differences between drinks and juices, and between the many various forms of juice, are explained on p.79 in the section on labelling. In addition there are also:

- orange squash or orange crush: contains as little as 5 per cent real orange (juice)
- orangeade: may be less than 5 per cent real orange
- fruit nectars: contain between 25 and 50 per cent fruit juice and fruit pulp, depending on the kind of fruit.

Sugar in fruit juices and drinks

	equivalent of sugar lumps in a 250ml serving
juices	
orange juice	10
apple juice	11
grapefruit juice	9
grape juice	14
pineapple juice	11
juice drinks	
Five Alive fruit drinks	10-12
Del Monte Island Blend drink	10
Libby's Orange 'C' drink	9
still drinks	
Robinson's High Juice Crush	11
St Clements orange drink	11
Ribena blackcurrant drink	15

	equivalent of sugar lumps in a 330ml can

sparkling drinks

Coca-Cola	13
sparkling Ribena	16
Tizer	12
Lilt	15
Tango orange	13
7-up lemon and lime	12

In collaboration with the London Borough of Southwark, the *Food Magazine* also checked juices and drinks for their fruit content. This is what they found:

Fruit and colouring in fruit drinks

	estimated percentage of fruit	price per litre ready to drink	added colour
Britvic 55	55	£1.08	no
Capri-sun (various)	10	86p	no
Co-op Sun-up Tropical	under 45	76p	no
Del Monte Island Blend	under 55	53p	yes
Del Monte Orange Burst	under 45	53p	no
Five Alive Mixed Citrus	under 55	59p	no
Five Alive Tropical	under 55	59p	no
Libby's Orange 'C'	15	45p	yes
Libby's Blackcurrant 'C'	5	47p	yes
Libby's Hi-Juice Um Bongo	25	£1.00	no
Libby's Moon Shine	under 45	£1.00	yes
Presto Apple with Vitamin C	10	36p	no
Ribena Blackcurrant	5	59p	yes
Ribena Orange and Apricot	under 10	£1.00	no
Safeway Orange 'C'	under 45	47p	yes
Sainsbury's Hi-Juice Orange	15	80p	no
Sainsbury's Fruit Cocktail	under 45	79p	yes
Sainsbury's Tropical Fruit	under 45	55p	no
St Clements Original Orange	10	57p	no
St Clements Tropical Fruit	10	57p	no
St Michael Sunfruit	under 45	85p	yes
Sungold Mango Nectar	50	85p	no
Supreme Hi-Juice Orange	20	47p	no
Supreme Apple Drink	under 8	41p	no
Supreme Grapefruit Drink	under 45	41p	yes
Supreme Tropical Cocktail	under 45	52p	yes
Thomas Hi-Juice Orange	under 16	96p	no

Although freshly squeezed juice sounds a lot better than pasteurized or UHT juice, the difference is not that great (though the price often is). The vitamin C content of the treated juices is still nearly 75 per cent that of the fresh product:

Vitamin C in orange juice

	vitamin C per 100g
freshly squeezed	47mg
frozen reconstituted	38mg
UHT/pasteurized carton	34mg
canned, unsweetened	35mg

Pesticide residues in juices

A concern highlighted by the use of pesticides like Alar in apples is the possibility that some agrochemical residues may get concentrated when fruit is juiced. Alar becomes a potent cancer-causing chemical known as UDMH when apples are processed into juice. Several samples of apple juice tested by Parents for Safe Food in 1989 were found to contain significant traces of Alar, and it is possible that other pesticide residues might also be present in such products.

Ministry of Agriculture reports of pesticide tests in fresh fruit do not identify the sprays and residues found, but do show that post-harvest chemicals used during fruit storage can be detected – 37 out of 46 samples of UK apples showed residues. MAFF surveys of juices have not been published in detail. One study of 48 samples of citrus juice drinks found 34 with either one or both of two post-harvest treatment chemicals.

Soft options

When it comes to soft drinks no one expects much fruit – but nor might they expect the wide range of additives. Additives are dealt with in detail on p.55, but here is a quick checklist of those which people who drink a lot of soft drinks should watch out for. (If this list worries you – and it probably should – there's a recipe for orange barley water on p.205.)

- sugar (see table on pp.81–2). Sugar levels may not be higher than those in fruit juice, but that just shows how surprisingly sweet fruit juice is! A typical can of cola contains the equivalent of a dozen lumps of sugar, and other drinks may be sweeter still
- artificial sweeteners: may be saccharine, which has to carry a health warning in the USA, or aspartame (Nutrasweet), which is a hazard for people suffering from phenylketonuria

- caffeine: a standard can of drink like Coke, Pepsi or Dr Pepper contains about as much caffeine as a cup of instant coffee
- phosphoric acid: phosphorus competes with calcium, so excess phosphorus in the diet may adversely affect your calcium levels
- benzoates: commonly used preservatives, which in some people can provoke asthma and skin rashes
- colourings: many of these are associated with adverse effects in some sensitive people. The brown 'caramel' used in cola drinks is a complicated chemical treatment of sugar, and is under suspicion for causing possible health problems.

Fizzy, fruit-flavoured drinks have very little nutritional value, offering virtually empty (sugary) calories and water. Here are some comparisons.

Nutritional values of coffee, fizzy drinks and juice

	instant coffee (one cup, black)	Coca-Cola (one regular can)	fizzy lemonade (one regular can)	pure orange juice (250ml carton)
energy (calories)	3	130	70	80
sugar	0.2g	35g	18g	20g
protein	0.4g	—	—	1g
fat	—	—	—	—
useful minerals				
calcium	4mg	13mg	16mg	21mg
iron	0.1mg	—	—	11mg
zinc	—	—	?	0.7mg
copper	—	0.1mg	—	0.1mg
magnesium	10mg	3mg	—	21mg
vitamins				
A	—	—	—	20mcg
B1	—	—	—	0.2mg
B2	—	—	—	0.1mg
niacin	0.6mg	—	—	0.7mg
B6	—	—	—	0.1mg
B12	—	—	—	—
folates	—	—	—	16mcg
C	—	—	—	80mg
D	—	—	—	—
E	?	—	—	—
caffeine	50mg	45mg	—	—

– = none   ? = not quantified

Meat

We are brought up to believe in the pomp and pageantry associated with the Roast Beef of Old England, and find it hard to believe that there's anything fundamentally wrong with meat. But while it is not a purpose of this book to stop you eating meat, the fact is (as shown in Chapter 2) that much meat, poultry and meat products are unhealthy and unsafe, and if you do eat meat, you must buy, cook and eat it carefully.

Truths and fallacies

Some commonly held notions about meat – for and against – need examination, too. Much of what is said about meat is exaggerated, misleading, or just plain wrong.

'We need meat for health and strength.' Misleading. Meat is a good source of a number of essential nutrients; that is true. Red meat is rich in B vitamins and is a good source of minerals, including iron and zinc. But so are other foods. Oily fish, for example, are rich in these and also other essential nutrients. So are whole grains, and nuts. We need the nutrients in meat, but we do not need meat, because these nutrients are readily available in other foods.

'We need the protein in meat for growth and performance.' Again, misleading. Meat is indeed a rich source of protein. Earlier this century scientists believed that animal protein was superior to vegetable protein, and this belief lingers on. This is why mothers are encouraged to feed their children with lots of cow's milk and dairy products, and why athletes still sometimes train on steaks. The truth is, though, that the protein from a balance of grains and pulses is just as good as that from meat.

'The British have always been a meat-eating nation.' Exaggerated. Animals have been domesticated and hunted for meat since before the Romans came to Britain, certainly. But few people, not even the rich, ate meat every day until very recently, and the common people ate meat only on high days and holidays. The image of the Roast Beef of Old England is an image of feasting; meat-eaters in Britain today often eat feast food every day.

'Meat causes heart disease and cancer.' Exaggerated. Some of the propaganda against meat is also off the mark. It has been proved beyond reasonable doubt that, eaten in the quantity now typical in Britain and other Western countries , saturated, hard fat is a major cause of heart disease and some common cancers. A quarter of the saturated fat in the British food supply comes from meat. But over half comes from milk and cheese, butter, margarine and other fats. Meat is not the main problem.

'Everybody would be better off as a vegetarian.' Ethically, this may be so: the factory farming of animals is an outrage that most meat-eaters ignore. But nutritionally this is untrue. The best-quality meat is an excellent food, and cheap cuts should be a source of savour and goodness in pies, casseroles, stews and soups. But almost all meat and poultry now on sale is low quality, and much is very fatty, adulterated and contaminated. The problem for the meat-eater is to find good meat.

Best buys

So whether or not you eat meat is a matter of choice. You and your family will not be stronger or healthier because of eating meat rather than another good source of protein. On the other hand, if you enjoy high quality meat as part of a diet rich in whole, fresh food, you will eat very well.

What kind of meat is best to eat? If you eat the carcass meat on sale in butchers' shops and supermarkets:

- go for lean meat
- cut the fat off
- don't add fat or oil in the cooking.

Apart from that, whether you eat beef, lamb or pork is almost entirely a matter of taste.

For poultry the answer is similar. We are encouraged to believe that chicken and other poultry is lean – and so it was, once upon a time. But now most of the calories supplied by intensively reared birds come from fat. So, as with meat, the healthy choice is:

- cut away the fat and the skin
- don't add fat when cooking
- drain away the fat produced by grilling or roasting.

In other respects there's not much to choose between chicken and turkey – but duck and goose are much fattier (see below).

Freedom means leanness

The freer an animal, the better the quality of its flesh. Lamb is therefore a marginally better choice than beef or pork; better still is mutton from older sheep, but that's difficult to find nowadays. The best choice is game meat: expensive venison, or cheap rabbit.

Half or more of the calories supplied by red meat come from fat – highly saturated fat, too. By contrast, fewer than a quarter of the calories in game meat are from fat, and simply because the animals range free and eat a natural variety of foods, this fat is a lot less saturated. In days gone by, poor people who lived in the country poached deer, rabbit and hare; and only a few generations ago the working classes ate rabbit as a savoury addition to stews, almost as a staple food. These were good eating habits.

Likewise with birds. Although duck and geese are very fatty, their fat is better quality, because these birds resist the imprisonment that battery chickens endure. When you cook goose or duck, take care to drain all the fat off the bird.

The best choice, though, is wildfowl: birds that fly and eat what they want. The flesh of wild duck and goose is quite different from that of the domesticated variety: darker, tastier and more nourishing. How much fat there is on the bird depends on the season. Pigeon, quail, partridge, grouse and other gamebirds are sometimes available in big supermarkets with fresh meat and poultry counters, and in butchers and even fishmongers. Try them.

Meat: nutritional values and drawbacks

	calories in 100g	as percentage of calories			good news	warnings
		protein	fat	starch		
carcass meat (beef, lamb, pork)						
joint	300	25	75	—		contaminants; fatty
organic joint	300	25	75	—	free of contaminants	fatty
lean meat	200	50	50	—		still fatty
meat products (sausages, burgers, pies etc.)						
burgers	300	33	55	12		fatty
sausages	350	10	78	12		additives; fatty
pies	400	10	70	20		avoid!
poultry (chicken, turkey)						
whole bird	250	35	65	—		
lean meat	175	65	35	—	leaner than carcass meat	
game (deer, rabbit, wildfowl)						
animal	150	75	25	—	essential fats	
bird	200	60	40	—	essential fats	

NB This is a rough guide only: all values are off the bone, and vary considerably from joint to joint and animal to animal.

Safety in organic husbandry

The really healthy, safe choice is meat from organically reared animals. Such animals are free-ranging; no type of factory farming is allowed. Their feedstuffs are themselves organically grown; additives and contaminants in feed are banned, and no healthy animal is allowed to be drugged. And when you buy organically reared meat, you are supporting green agriculture, good for your health and that of your family, good for the countryside, good for the environment, and good for the planet.

The trouble is, though, that organically reared meat is often hard to find, unless you live near a mixed farm displaying the Soil Association symbol, or in or near London and a few other big cities which have organic butchers.

Quality, not quantity

The essential message about meat is: less quantity, more quality. There's no need to make meat or poultry the centrepiece of main meals. Try using it southern European fashion, in small quantities to flavour stews and soups. Consider non-meat pizza and pasta. Serve a smaller, better-quality Sunday roast with three or four veg that are family favourites, and plenty of them. Better still, eat meat just once or twice a week, as most people still did until the late 19th century, when the mechanization of slaughterhouses was perfected and meat could be mass-produced cheaply. And finally, eat more fish, which is so good for you (see **Fish**).

Meat is feast food. Enjoy high quality meat when you have something to celebrate. Use cheap cuts for flavour in cooking. And as a citizen, support every organization opposed to chemicalized factory farming, and all other forms of mass manufacture of animals for meat.

Milk
See **Dairy products**.

Miso
See **Tofu and miso**.

Nuts and seeds

Nuts
Nuts should be prized more highly – they are so much more than Christmas fare to be left to sour in their shells on the sideboard while the New Year bills come in. They are excellent sources of protein

(over 15 per cent) and carbohydrate (the same percentage), which makes them ideal for vegetarians.

They are also high in fat (45-60 per cent). Many of course are grown for their fat – the tropical oils, coconut and palm, in particular – and when hydrogenated (hardened) this fat becomes extremely saturated. It is used in margarine (see *Butter and butter substitutes* under **Dairy products**).

When mixed with dried fruits nuts make a very nutritious food source. But there can be problems: some dried fruit is preserved in paraffin (see **Fruit and vegetables**). Nuts are a good source of the B vitamins but contain no vitamin A or C. Dried fruit has no vitamin C either. When they are central to a diet, therefore, nuts must be supplemented by fresh fruit and vegetables.

No nuts for the under-fives

Dietician Isobel Cole-Hamilton says: 'Children under five should not be given whole nuts or even splintered nuts to eat, as it is possible for them to inhale the small parts which can become lodged in the lung and cause choking. Smooth nut butters and nut milk are, however, useful foods for young children.' (See **Spreads**.)

Care with peanuts

As a snack (see **Bag snacks**) peanuts have a massive following, but there have been scares in connection with aflotoxin, a potent carcinogen produced by mould growth often found in crops exposed to damp. Careful screening and sorting can virtually eliminate aflotoxin from nuts. Though there were problems with certain peanut butters a few years ago, there is no known current problem of any size.

Unusual newcomers

Apart from peanuts, familiar nuts for ready eating include brazils, cashews and almonds. There are also some divine lesser-known nuts moving into wider distribution in Britain. Two of these, pistachios and pine nuts, are highly recommended: both are expensive, but used sparingly and imaginatively they can enhance many meals.

In her book *Mediterranean Cookery*, Claudia Roden writes of the importance of pine nuts in the cuisine of these countries, suggesting that 'their unique flavour is brought out if they are very lightly roasted under the grill or gently fried in a dry frying pan. They are often used in both savoury and sweet dishes, are often partnered with fried onions, and go into meat fillings.' Combine them with basil and olive oil to create pesto, a fabulous classic pasta sauce that will turn a packet of wholemeal spaghetti into a feast fit for the gods!

Seeds

Also excellent for nutrition, seeds abound in good health food shops. For the under-fives, the same safety rule applies. Though smaller than nuts, seeds are still easy to choke on.

Sunflower seeds are rich in the B vitamins and provide a good source of protein and minerals. They produce a highly prized and reasonably priced unsaturated oil with which you should cook, and which can be turned into a very healthy butter-substitute spread (see **Fats and oils**, and *Butter and butter substitutes* under **Dairy products**). Sesame seeds, high in protein, are another joy, calorie-packed and producing a 50 per cent unsaturated oil which is becoming increasingly popular in good home cooking. Alfalfa seeds are a good source of vitamins B12 and K – watch them sprout, and eat them as soon as they do. This is just a small sample selection and there are many, many more – try out a number of them and see which your family likes best.

Oils
See **Fats and oils**.

Pasta

The story goes that macaroni was invented in Naples in the 13th century by an impoverished man who had a desire to provide a tasty, economical food for everyone. Sadly for him, his recipe was stolen by a shrewd neighbour who grew famous for her 'angels' food' – when the King of Naples sampled her macaroni he declared it to be 'divine'. Who would quarrel with him?

This food was invented for people with limited choice – those who are on a low income, who have kids to feed, or bad feet, or a poor bus service. A 500g (1lb) packet of dried pasta made from durum wheat compares favourably in price with anything you could buy in tins, boxed, or from the freezer cabinets. It keeps well in a dry store cupboard, and it really is fast food. Pasta doubles its bulk when cooked, so one 500g packet will feed a family of six. When they see how much the grown-ups are enjoying it, your children won't refuse it. And because it's high in carbohydrates it's a great energy provider – it's only fattening if you use the richer (and admittedly delicious) of the thousands of possible sauces.

Nutrients in pasta

	per 100g	
	white spaghetti, boiled	wholemeal spaghetti, boiled
protein	3.6g	4.7g
fat	0.7g	0.9g
Kcal (energy)	104	113
sugars	0.5g	1.3g
fibre	1.8g	4g
sodium	trace	45g
potassium	24mg	140mg
calcium	7mg	11mg
magnesium	15mg	42mg
phosphorus	44mg	110mg
iron	0.5mg	1.4mg
copper	0.1mg	0.18mg
zinc	0.5mg	1.1mg
sulphur	46mg	67mg
thiamin	0.01mg	0.21mg
riboflavin	0.01mg	0.02mg
vitamin B6	0.02mg	0.08mg
folates	4mcg	7mcg

Fresh pasta

Some supermarkets and delicatessens now sell fresh pasta; the 'envelope' kind is ready filled with cheese, spinach, meat and so on. Don't be taken in too readily by these apparent delights – they do vary immensely in quality, and they are much more expensive than the dried version which requires just a little effort from you to prepare the accompanying sauce. If you do buy pasta in this form, remember that it only has a very short life – eat it soon after purchase, and only buy from shops that have a good turnover.

Tinned pasta

There are, of course, tins of pasta for your store cupboard if you really only have time to open a can. A tin would probably serve two small eaters or one person with an appetite. Here are three typical cans picked from a supermarket shelf:

Crosse and Blackwell Family Spaghetti in a rich tomato sauce, free from added preservatives, colour and flavouring, made from 'the finest durum wheat', covered with 'lashings of our rich tasty sauce, which contains all the goodness of 7oz of tomatoes':

- tomatoes
- cut spaghetti
- water
- sugar
- salt
- modified starch
- onion
- hydrogenated vegetable oil
- garlic
- herbs and spices.

Buitoni Ravioli with Tomato and Meat Sauce, 'made to an Italian recipe':

- water
- tomato purée
- durum semolina
- meat
- rusk
- onions
- sugar
- textured soya protein
- carrots
- salt
- modified starch
- beef fat
- hydrolysed plant protein
- spices
- citric acid.

Heinz Macaroni Cheese, 'free from artificial colour and preservative'; the label adds that 'reflecting today's consumer tastes, the levels of added salt and sugar in our recipe are kept at the minimum possible without impairing your enjoyment of the traditional Heinz flavour':

- water
- cut macaroni
- cheese
- vegetable oil
- dried skimmed milk
- salt
- modified cornflour
- cornflour
- mustard
- emulsifiers

- sodium polyphosphates
- natural flavouring
- flavouring enhancer monosodium glutamate
- colour betacarotene.

You can open a tin and eat the contents five minutes later, or wait another 10 for a plateful of freshly boiled spaghetti and a simple but delicious sauce made from fresh ingredients. The former would cost between £1 and £2 to feed a family of four. The latter, made from a packet of wholemeal organic spaghetti costing roughly 75p, and with a sauce like the one costed out below, would be about the same but provide second helpings:

- in 2 tablespoons sunflower oil (10p) fry 2 chopped rashers of bacon (30p) with a chopped onion (10p)
- add 4oz/125g sliced mushrooms (30p) with a large sliced leek (25p)
- at the end of cooking, add a handful of frozen peas (10p)
- and some chopped parsley (10p) and seasoning.

The choice is yours!

Pizza

Pizzas are now to be found everywhere in Britain, brought here by the Italian chefs of the 1950s. Complete restaurant chains are devoted to the pizza, and for home consumption they are now available frozen and chilled in every supermarket. They are particularly popular with children and are beginning to rate amongst other favourites such as burgers and fish fingers, both in school meals and at home.

Basically a pizza is made from a bread dough base with any sort of topping which you wish to put on it. Mostly, however, they have a topping based on melted cheese. The two main types of pizza are deep pan and the ordinary thin kind. The principal difference is that the deep pan pizzas contain more raising agent and have a lighter texture; they do not necessarily contain more bread dough.

Nutritional value

The nutritional quality of a pizza depends on whether the base is made from wholemeal or white flour, on the relative proportion of base to topping, and on the ingredients used in the topping. A pizza can be a complete meal if it has a thick base with some vegetables in the topping as well as a small amount of meat, fish, eggs or cheese.

Many pizzas, however, contain large amounts of cheese and fatty meats in their topping and are therefore very high in fat.

All bought pizzas and pizza bases contain some sort of preservative, flavourings and/or colourings. If you make them at home you don't need to use these additives. Here are the ingredients of a typical bought British pizza, neither better nor worse than any other in its place in the scheme of frozen processed foods:

- wheatflour
- tomato
- Mozzarella cheese
- water
- onions
- yeast
- animal and vegetable fat
- salt
- modified starch
- soya flour
- natural flavourings
- sugar
- herbs and spices
- flour improvers E300, 920, 924, 927
- preservative E302
- thickener E415
- emulsifiers E471 and 472.

Pizza like mamma made

In terms of value for money, pizzas are one of the foods which are considerably cheaper to make yourself than to buy. This includes in particular French bread pizzas, which are very popular with children because they can make them themselves — cut a French stick down the middle, place your cheese topping on the cut side and then put it under the grill. Choose good cheese such as Bel Paese or Parmesan, and other healthy toppings — fish, good meat, olives, crushed garlic, canned or fresh tomatoes, onions and herbs. Have enormous fun with pizzas, but don't eat too many of them, even the home-made kind.

Puddings

Many people eat light desserts and jelly if they are trying to lose weight, thinking that jelly is nothing but water. Wrong! Jelly cubes are made with sugar. (They also contain gelatine – vegetarians should be aware of this, as gelatine is animal-based.) A 600ml (1 pint) packet of jelly can contain up to 75g (3oz) of sugar — nearly

100 ml (20 teaspoons). If canned fruit is added to the jelly, the sugar content is increased even more.

And those 'light' jellies and desserts are always flavoured with chemical additives and colouring. A full ingredients list from a typical packet strawberry jelly is instructive:

- sugar
- invert sugar syrup
- glucose syrup
- water
- gelatine
- natural colours (beetroot extract, annatto)
- citric acid
- acidity regulator (sodium citrate)
- acetic acid
- strawberry juice
- flavouring
- lemon juice
- artificial sweetener (sodium saccharine).

Jelly is, incidentally, extremely easy to make at home. If your children like it, find a recipe and feel confident that they are eating something containing minimum sugar and relatively safe fresh fruit juice.

And if you're into whips, here's a chemistry set to engage the brain. The ingredients list from a packet that trails the legend 'No artificial colours and preservatives' goes like this:

- sugar
- modified starch
- vegetable oil (hydrogenated)
- dried skimmed milk
- gelling agents (disodium monophosphate, sodium pyrophosphate)
- whey powder
- caseinate
- flavourings
- thickener (xanthan gum)
- vitamins (vitamins C, A and D)
- iron
- colours (betanin and annatto).

Is this a pudding? Do you want your kids to eat such things? It is worth a little extra time in the kitchen. Encourage your children to regard puddings as a treat for weekends and holidays, when you can try some of the recipes given elsewhere in this book.

The best pudding of all

If you really can't spare the time to make puddings – and even if you can – why not go for the healthiest alternative of all: beautiful live yoghurt and/or fresh fruit?

Rice, other grains and pulses

Like pasta, grains and pulses are cheap, nutritious and can form the basis for a huge range of dishes, both savoury and sweet. They don't need refrigeration, and a little goes a long way. With a little planning, pulses and grains will provide a proper balance of nutrients and fibre, so use them often. Parents for Safe Food suggest that with such a good variety of basic foodstuffs to choose from, healthy food need never be boring. The Indian diet of dal, rice, bread and yoghurt can make a wonderful contribution to a healthy diet for children and adults. Only the unimaginative could say that such food is boring.

Rice

> What is the matter with Mary Jane
> She's perfectly well and she hasn't a pain
> And it's lovely rice pudding for dinner again
> What is the matter with Mary Jane?

So wrote A.A. Milne. Poor Mary Jane was bored — she needed her dinner made with more imagination. Food was very bland in the 1920s, especially in the nursery. But today there is certainly no need to be bored with rice, which is a wonderfully amenable food and combines exceptionally well with a whole variety of pulses, wheats, vegetables and dairy products, fruit and nuts, fish and meats.

Rice is a grain, very low in fat and rich in gluten (the protein complex in wheat and rye). It originated in India and China, and gradually spread through the Middle East to Europe.

Types of rice

There is a wide variety of rice from which to choose. In general choose short-grain for puddings, because it will absorb liquids; and long-grain for savoury dishes (except risotto) where you want the grains to remain separate. Italian arborio makes perfect risotto; Japanese and glutinous rice are short-grained, plump and sticky, good to eat with soup. Wholegrain brown rice has a delicious, nutty flavour.

Nutritional value of rice

	brown rice	per 100g white rice, easy cook	rice pudding, canned
protein	6.7g	7.3g	3.4g
fat	2.8g	3.6g	2.5g
Kcal (energy)	357	383	89
carbohydrate	81.3g	85.8g	14g
sugar	1.3g	trace	8.2g
fibre	3.8g	2.7g	N
iron	1.4mg	0.5mg	0.2mg
potassium	250mg	150mg	140mg
calcium	10mg	51mg	93mg
magnesium	110mg	32mg	11mg
phosphorus	310mg	150mg	80mg
folates	49mcg	20mcg	N

N = nutrient is present in significant amounts, but there is no reliable information as to the exact amount.

Other grains

Here is a list of other grains apart from rice. They are cheap to buy, fun to cook and nutritious to eat. Give them a try.

- barley flakes: these make a nutritious soothing orange and barley drink (see recipe below), good for when children are ill or at any time instead of sugar- and additive-packed soft drinks
- bulgar or cracked wheat: has a nutty taste, with a firmer texture than rice, and can be bought in different-size grains. The finer grains, which don't need to be cooked, are good for salads, while the medium or coarse grains are used for pilau dishes. Bulgar is a good source of phosphorus
- couscous: meaning 'crushed small', this is the national dish of Morocco, Algeria and Tunisia. Steam it and serve it as a separate dish with stew or broth
- millet flakes: cook with nuts to make good, crunchy biscuits
- semolina: resembling very fine-grained bulgar wheat, it makes excellent pilaus and puddings, and goes well in soups. Buy it in small quantities and use it quickly, since it goes lumpy when stale

- whole hulled millet: toast in a dry, heavy-bottomed pan until the seeds are light brown to bring out the nutty flavour before cooking. Millet has a firm, grainy, slightly fluffy texture when cooked
- wholewheat berries: these make a wonderful addition to home-made bread. For breakfast, pick them over, wash and drain, pass them through a coffee grinder and mix with an equal amount of finely chopped nuts. Then add honey and milk to taste.

Orange barley water

- 2oz/60g barley flakes
- 1 tablespoon raw brown sugar or honey
- 1 orange or lemon (preferably organic)
- ½ pint/300ml boiling water

Put the barley flakes in a jug. Add the sugar or honey. Squeeze the orange or lemon and add both the juice and the squeezed skins. Pour the boiling water on top, cover, and leave to cool. Strain before serving. If the mixture is too thick, add more water.

Pulses

Pulses — peas and beans — have a very long history and have even been discovered by archaeologists among Stone Age relics in caves. However it is only quite recently that the rich Western world, worried about world population and food shortages, has paid much attention to the nutritional value of the centuries-old traditional peasant diet based on pulses, grains, vegetables and dairy products.

There is now an ever-increasing variety of pulses appearing in health and wholefood stores; and do use your local Greek, Italian, Indian or Chinese food markets if you are lucky enough to have them nearby. It is best to find a shop with a quick turnover, for its stock will be fresher. Pulses do not perish easily, but long storage can make them very hard. Buy small quantities and store them in containers with close-fitting lids.

Nutritional value

Although beans are not a complete food, their protein is not second-class (and they are certainly a very cheap source of protein). There are different types of protein which complement each other, and when put together in a meal they will provide you with all the required nutrients. Apart from protein, beans are a good source of vitamin B6 (approximate average 0.4mg per 100g), potassium (1.16g), iron (6.7mg) and fibre (25g).

Nutritional content of pulses

	mung beans	per 100g soya beans	masur dal (red split lentils)	chick peas
protein	22g	34.1g	23.8g	20.2g
fat	1g	17.7g	1g	5.7g
Kcal (energy)	231	403	304	320
carbohydrate	35.6g	28.6g	53.2g	approx 50g
fibre	approx 22g	N	approx 11.7g	approx 15g
iron	8mg	8.4mg	7.6mg	6.4mg
magnesium	170mg	265mg	77mg	160mg
calcium	100mg	226mg	39mg	140mg
potassium	850mg	1.68g	670mg	800mg
folic acid	140mcg	100mcg	35mcg	180mcg
vitamin B1	0.45mg	1.1mg	0.5mg	0.5mg
vitamin B2	0.2mg	0.31mg	0.2mg	0.15mg
carotene	24mcg	24mcg	60mcg	190mcg

N = nutrient is present in significant amounts but there is no reliable information as to the exact amount.

Cooking with pulses

Always wash pulses well and pick them over to remove any small stones or husks. Lentils don't need soaking, but you should soak the thicker-skinned varieties of beans (like soya) overnight in twice their volume of water. Rinse the pulses again and put them in unsalted cold water to cook (never add salt to pulses while they are cooking because it toughens their skins). Likewise don't add bicarbonate of soda, which will destroy some of the vitamins and minerals. Red beans contain a toxic substance but this is destroyed by boiling the beans for ten minutes before simmering until tender.

If you want to make beans more digestible, parboil them and rinse them again before final cooking. Another trick if you find them hard to digest is to add small quantities of asafoetida (a resin and digestive) or fresh coriander (a digestive) and ginger.

If the beans are fresh, after soaking bring them to the boil and let them simmer for about an hour. Older beans will take much longer to cook. But be careful not to over-cook, which spoils their texture. Lentils will only take about 25-35 minutes to become tender.

Any liquid left after cooking can be saved for soup. Cooked pulses will keep in the fridge for several days, and you can freeze them. Serve with rice and yoghurt, and some stir-fried vegetables and/or meat, to make a highly nutritious, value-for-money meal for all the family.

Nothing much wrong with baked beans

Should you want to keep it really simple, Whole Earth do a tin of organically grown baked beans. Ingredients:

- organic haricot beans
- apple juice
- organic tomato purée
- sea salt
- apple cider vinegar
- guar gum
- onion powder
- spices
- tamari soy sauce
- kelp
- herbs.

Heinz produce a tin of no added sugar baked beans. Ingredients:

- beans
- water
- tomatoes
- modified cornflour
- salt
- spirit vinegar
- hydrolysed vegetable protein
- artificial sweetener – saccharine
- spices.

Home-baked beans

Alternatively you could buy haricot beans and cook your own. This recipe makes a tasty, substantial meal for a hungry family. The quantities given for the sauce are not exact – make it according to your family's tastes.

1 lb/500g haricot beans (organic if possible)
herbs (a bouquet garni in muslin is best, because it is easy to
     remove later)
1 bay leaf
1 clove garlic, crushed
1 onion, stuck with cloves

And for the sauce:

chopped onions
olive oil
1 large tin tomatoes
tomato purée
lemon juice
a little raw sugar or honey
salt and black pepper
herbs

Rinse the beans well and let them soak overnight in water to twice the depth of the beans. Drain, and put them in a heavy-bottomed pan. Cover with plenty of water and add the herbs, bay leaf, garlic and onion. Bring to the boil and simmer until tender — about 1½-2 hours. Drain, and remove the onion, herbs and bay leaf. Pre-heat the oven to 170°C (325°F/gas mark 3).

Make the sauce by first frying the onions in the oil until translucent. Then add the other ingredients, tasting as you go, and let them cook together, stirring, for about 10–15 minutes. When the sauce is ready, stir the haricot beans in. Rub a heavy pot with a little olive oil and spoon in the beans and tomato sauce. Cover the pot with a tight-fitting lid and bake for 1-1½ hours.

Sprinkle with chopped grilled bacon (unless you're vegetarian) and parsley, and serve with good wholemeal bread.

Salt

Salt is mixed into every kind of food. Salt and pepper are the two condiments on the tables of the nation. The word 'salt' has a sense of prized value: the expression 'worth his salt' refers to Roman days when soldiers were part paid in salt. 'Below the salt' refers to medieval days, when inferior guests at a feast were seated below a point midway down the table, marked by the pot of salt. Salt is embedded in our language and our culture. So how can it be bad for our health?

We have a special taste for salt. The tongue has sensors to detect salty (and also sweet) foods, and savour them; and also bitter and sour foods, and spit them out. This natural, built-in attraction to salt is the vital clue to its dangers, when consumed excessively.

The chemical name for salt is sodium chloride. Sodium is a mineral which, just like vitamins, is a vital nutrient: without salt we die. The body uses sodium together with potassium, another vital mineral, to maintain its balance of water. The body is designed to consume more potassium than sodium. In nature all raw, whole foods are good sources of potassium and – apart from meat – very low in sodium. This is why humans, and animals, have evolved a natural taste for salt, as a signal to seek it out.

No chance of deficiency

Scientists who have studied gatherer-hunter peoples still living in remote areas of the world have shown that humans can get by perfectly well on a gram of salt a day. If you ate nothing but whole, unsalted cereals and raw vegetables and fruit, you would get enough sodium just by eating bread made as it normally is, with salt as part of the recipe. The only healthy people in Britain who could possibly suffer salt deficiency are very heavy manual workers or road runners on a hot summer day. Until such time as you are called upon to shovel coal in a steel mill, or to build a bridge over the River Kwai, forget any stories you may have heard about the dangers of salt depletion.

Processed food creates metabolic imbalance

Our problem in Britain, in common with other Western countries, is that manufacturers understandably exploit the natural taste for salt and add it to every kind of processed food. And at the same time potassium is lost in the manufacture and cooking of food. In general, British food is marginal to low in potassium, and high to vastly too high in sodium. Average consumption of salt in Britain is around 10-12g a day, whereas the World Health Organization's recommended daily intake is 5g. So the natural balance between potassium and sodium in the body is thrown out.

Pork contains over four times as much potassium as sodium; in contrast, bacon contains four times as much sodium as potassium. There is a hundred times as much sodium in canned vegetables and soups as in fresh vegetables. A single helping of a number of popular ready-to-eat breakfast cereals can contain more than a gram of salt. The amount of salt in peanuts is peanuts; but there is half a gram of salt in a 50g packet of salted peanuts. Four-fifths of all salt in British food is added during manufacture; only one-fifth is added at table.

Vested interests

Scientists in America are sure that salt consumption is a big public health problem, and an important cause of the epidemics of high blood pressure and strokes suffered in Western countries. Some years ago the Consumer Frauds division of the Attorney General's department in New York stopped Campbell's claiming that their canned soups were healthy, because of their high salt content. (Campbell's soups are no more salty than other canned soups).

In Britain the Salt Data Centre, funded by the British salt manufacturers, says salt is fine. If you see a newspaper headline saying in effect: 'Salt OK, says top doc', as likely as not the report will be of an occasion organized by the Salt Data Centre. Take such claims with a pinch of salt (as long as you then chuck it over your shoulder).

Low-salt diets

A low-salt diet cannot do you and your family harm, and will certainly be healthy. Throw away your salt cellar, stop adding salt when you cook, and use herbs instead (see **Herbs, spices and aromatics**). Unsalted food – vegetables especially – tastes strange at first. But in time you will prefer food tasting of itself rather than of saline solution. Be patient. After a few weeks your taste buds will be retuned, and salted foods will taste awful!

The more potassium and the less sodium you eat, the better. All whole foods are high in potassium, low in sodium. Most processed foods are high in sodium, and are often low in potassium, therefore eat heaps of vegetables and fruit. Vitamins and minerals and fibre come with the potassium, so a low-salt diet is altogether a healthy diet. And here's a bonus for slimmers: some people become rather swollen with extra water on a typical high-fat diet. Once you kick the salt habit, you may lose a few pounds and inches.

Salt in food

	parts per thousand	
	potassium	sodium
butter (salted)	0.1	8.7
cornflakes	1	12
Danish blue cheese	1	14
kidneys (grilled)	3.4	2.7
milk	1.5	0.5
muesli	6	1.8
salmon (poached)	3.3	1
salmon (smoked)	3	19
sausages (grilled)	2	10
tomatoes	3	trace
tomato soup	1.8	4.6
yoghurt (natural)	2.5	0.7

Sauces, dressings and pickles

These items form only a tiny part of most people's diet, and are therefore nutritionally not important. However it is important to remember that, if you are one of those who likes to tip the sauce bottle over practically everything they eat, you are consuming considerable amounts of fat and sugar.

Ketchup-type sauces

Most savoury sauces and pickles contain relatively large amounts of sugar. Tomato ketchup, for instance, is approximately a quarter sugar. And in sweet pickles there is more sugar than any other single type of vegetable. The reason sugar in used in these products is to give them the right sort of thick consistency. Not many people realize they are putting sugar on their chips – but they are.

Salad dressings

These are almost always high in fat. Mayonnaise has considerably more fat than salad cream, as do French dressings. The nutritional importance of French dressing depends almost entirely on the type of oil used. If you use olive oil or any of the polyunsaturated oils the dressing will be better for you than one made with saturated oil (see **Fats and oils**). On the other hand, whatever type of oil is used the calorie count remains the same.

Yoghurt-based salad dressings can be delicious. Remember, however, that if you are using Greek yoghurt the fat content is relatively high (approximately half the fat of single cream).

White sauces

You can either make these yourself or buy packet mixes. As ever, the packet mixes contain large numbers of additives, whereas home-made sauces do not. It is a good idea to use semi-skimmed rather than full-cream milk, to cut down the amount of fat used. Also a small amount of a strong-tasting cheese will give as good a flavour as a mild-tasting one, but with the benefit of a lower-fat sauce.

Check the contents

Sauces are now available in cans and cartons, and these have fewer additives than the packet mixes. Always check the ingredients list to be sure of what you are actually buying. Here's an example (gravy granules – just add boiling water, says the package):

- starch
- hydrogenated vegetable fat
- salt

- wheatflour
- beef fat
- colour (caramel)
- beef stock
- hydrolysed vegetable protein
- hydrolysed beef protein
- beef extract
- yeast extract
- emulsifier (435)
- spices.

And what's with these hydrolysed proteins (we've met their equivalent in fats many times already)? Geoffrey Cannon says: 'Hydrolysed protein analyses out chemically just like the real thing (protein as in beans, wheat, or meat). Hydrolysis enables manufacturers to use anything suitable on the market to make a base, a slurry, an instrument on which the technicians can play tunes with chemical additives. Real food cannot be played with in this way.' In essence, hydrolysed protein is a flavour enhancer which has been chemically downgraded.

Stock cubes

Those poor old battery layers go to make chicken stock when they've had it in the reproduction business. Here they are in interesting company:

- hydrolysed protein
- salt
- chicken meat
- wheatflour
- bone stock
- yeast extract
- flavour enhancer (621, 635)
- colour (caramel)
- sugar
- chicken fat
- flavouring
- parsley
- onion
- turmeric
- pepper.

Now those flavour enhancers are monosodium glutamate (MSG) and sodium ribonucleotide, which were dealt with in Chapter 4. But just to refresh your memory ... the first is described in Additives: Your Complete Survival Guide as 'toxic to sensitised people, causing flushing, headache and chest pain' (Chinese Restaurant Syndrome). In Britain it is banned from baby food – as is the second of this unholy pair, with which it is frequently combined in processing. These two additives deserve each other, but do we deserve them?

Much the same goes into beef stock cubes, except that the beef bits come rather lower down the ingredients list. So can Parents for Safe Food recommend nothing in this line without these sour expressions of disapproval? Yes indeed!

Vecon, from Modern Health Products, contains no artificial colours, flavours or preservatives, and is approved by the Vegetarian Society. Its ingredients are:

- hydrolysed vegetable (soya and maize) protein
- water
- dehydrated vegetable powder (onion, celery, tomato, carrot, parsley, garlic, paprika, spinach, beetroot, celery seed, horseradish)
- yeast extract
- yeast powder
- glycerine of vegetable origin
- seaweed powder (containing natural iodine)
- ferrous sulphate
- vitamin C
- niacin
- betacarotene
- thiamin (B1)
- riboflavin (B2)
- vitamin B12.

The good guys in bottled sauces

Ever ready to accommodate traditionalists where possible, Parents for Safe Food speak up for people who enjoy the Original and Genuine Lea and Perrins Worcestershire Sauce. It contains:

- malt vinegar
- spirit vinegar
- molasses
- sugar
- salt
- anchovies
- tamarinds
- shallots
- garlic
- spices
- flavouring.

No colours or preservatives. OK, there are two sugars – but you don't put much L and P on food, so enjoy it when you want a bit of a buzz.

And a good soy sauce is also recommended, but again don't drench things in it. The contents of a good one are just soya beans and water (though you'll often find salt).

Shakes

Once a nutritious blend of fresh fruit and milk, the modern fast food shake contains for the milk part:

- skimmed milk
- sugar
- vegetable fat
- glucose syrup
- whey powder
- carrageenan
- carob gum
- guar gum
- sodium carboxymethyl cellulose
- flavouring
- mono- and diglycerides of fatty acids
- sodium citrate.

And for the strawberry part:

- sugar
- water
- flavouring
- citric acid
- preservative: sodium benzoate
- colours: sunset yellow and carmoisine.

That list came from Wimpy, but it is typical of many fast food outlets. It contains thickeners derived from seaweed and cotton, along with colours and preservatives known to provoke reactions in sensitive people. Carrageenan (the seaweed-derived thickener) is reported to increase the risk of stomach ulcers and is a possible risk of cancer in the gut, at least in laboratory animals. Sodium benzoate and the colouring agents, both of them coal-tar dyes, are associated with hyperactivity, asthma and skin rashes in sensitive people, especially children.

The other main ingredient which can be considered a health hazard is, of course, sugar. Milk is naturally sweet, but many milk shake recipes use a lot of added sugar, bringing the total up to surprisingly high levels.

Added sugar in milk shakes

	total sugars as sugar lumps
Wimpy shake (standard 400ml)	17
McDonald's strawberry shake (regular 285ml)	13
average of 21 take-aways (300ml)	15
home-made from milk shake powder (300ml)	13

The powder sold to make your own shakes at home is 98 per cent sugar. Here's a quick, delicious, healthy summer version that your children will love (and there's another shake recipe on p.157).

Quick strawberry shake with real strawberries
- 10 ripe strawberries
- ½ pint/300ml semi-skimmed milk

Whizz it all up in the blender to create a lovely smooth shake with the sugar equivalent of only about eight lumps. You can use frozen fruit as an alternative.

Soup

Soup is a warming, comforting, nutritious bowlful that mothers everywhere have always made. Or so it should be – and the ads for the bought product foster that image. Unfortunately the reality is not always like that. Let's take three spring vegetable soups, one from a packet, one from a tin, and one made from fresh ingredients, and compare them.

First the packet
The ingredients of the packet, when reconstituted, are:

- vegetables (red peppers, carrot, onion, swede, leek, celery, peas)
- salt
- starch
- hydrolysed vegetable protein
- hydrogenated vegetable oil
- flavour enhancer (monosodium glutamate)
- sugar
- yeast extract
- hydrolysed beef protein
- malt extract

- citric acid
- flavourings
- spices
- bay.

It doesn't contain any added artificial colourings or preservatives (it says so on the package). But it does contain certain other less than welcome ingredients, like saturated fat, sugar and bumped up flavourings. To be fair, it would make quite a nice, warming meal with good 'mouth feel' if you served it with some decent wholemeal bread.

Next the tin

Here are the contents of a decent can of spring vegetable soup:

- water
- potatoes
- carrots
- peas
- cornflour
- swedes
- rice
- salt
- flour
- cabbage
- hydrolysed protein
- modified cornflour
- chives
- herbs
- spices
- natural flavourings
- colour betacarotene.

There are three lots of flour in that list, and like all canned food this soup has had to be processed at very high temperatures, reducing the nutritional value.

Either of these two bought soups will provide sustenance, but they are not suitable for long-term daily nutritional needs. Here, on the other hand, is a home-made soup which does fulfil that requirement provided you can spare 40 minutes to make it.

And now the Real McCoy – Suffolk spring vegetable soup

These quantities will serve eight – for a smaller number reduce the ingredients accordingly, or else use the preparation time really effectively by making the larger quantity and freezing some for another day.

- 2 tablespoons sunflower oil
- 1 tablespoon olive oil
- 2 medium onions, roughly chopped
- 2 cloves garlic, crushed
- 3 medium carrots, sliced
- 2 small turnips, sliced
- 1 small parsnip, sliced
- 3 medium leeks, sliced
- 3 sticks celery, roughly chopped
- 1 dessertspoon good mixed dried herbs or chopped fresh herbs
- 2³/₄ pints/1.6 litres boiling water
- 1 dessertspoon Vecon vegetable stock extract
- 8oz/250g small new potatoes
- 4oz/125g spring cabbage or sprouting broccoli, finely sliced
- 4oz/125g frozen peas
- 3 spring onions, chopped small
- 1 small bunch parsley, chopped
- sea salt
- freshly ground black pepper

In a good-sized, heavy-bottomed pan heat the oils. Add the onions and garlic and stir until translucent. Don't let them brown. Add the carrots, turnips and parsnip and stir for 2-3 minutes, then add the leeks and celery. Stir for another 2 minutes. Sprinkle in the herbs, and stir again. Cover with the boiling water and Vecon stock. Add the potatoes, bring to the boil and simmer for 20 minutes.

Then add the cabbage or broccoli. Bring back to the boil for 5 minutes and add the peas. Cook for a further 5 minutes, then switch off the heat and allow the soup to stand for 5 minutes. During this period add the spring onions and parsley. Season to taste with salt and pepper, and serve piping hot with good fresh wholemeal bread.

Nearly as good as home-made

A recent development in the world of soup is the 'fresh' products that some supermarkets and small grocers are now stocking. They contain good wholesome ingredients, and it's such a relief to read the instruction 'Eat within one day of purchase' – clearly there aren't any preservatives to make it last longer. Here is the contents list of a watercress soup:

- chicken stock (water, chicken, onion, salt, pepper)
- watercress
- double cream
- wheatflour
- onion

- butter
- salt
- pepper.

Delicious! With butter and double cream it wouldn't, however, be wise to buy these soups every day – which brings us to their one drawback: they're expensive. But then you pays your money and you takes your choice ....

Instant nothing

We end with a small warning. In every supermarket you will find packets declaring themselves to be 'instant'. If you should be tempted to buy them for 'convenience', remember that apart from a few calories they contain no nutritional value whatsoever. Here is a typical list of ingredients:

- modified starch
- salt
- dried glucose syrup
- flavour enhancer (monosodium glutamate)
- hydrolysed vegetable protein
- dehydrated chicken
- beef fat (with E320)
- natural lemon flavouring
- onion powder
- dehydrated tomato
- spices
- herbs.

This is part of what Dr Tim Lang, formerly of the London Food Commission and now of Parents for Safe Food, calls the movement towards non-food food, which Parents for Safe Food are committed to putting in reverse.

Spices
See **Herbs, spices and aromatics.**

Spreads

When many people of a certain age were growing up, jam was *the* steady treat – jam sandwiches, jam tarts, jam rolls, jam with cheese, jam sponges – and you wouldn't think twice about the sugars or the nutritional value. It was just good to have it.

Today, jam is just one of a vast number of spreads. While nonetheless popular, it has to take its place in a wide range of other things you put on other things to make a snack: lemon curd, honey,

marmalade, Marmite, Bovril, meat and fish pastes, patés, cheese
spreads, nut butter, vegetarian patés and spreads, and sandwich
spread.

Vecon makes a nice vegetarian spread, and if you like a bit of mild
traditional processing on your bread there is Heinz sandwich spread,
which contains no artificial colouring and preservative and should be
refrigerated after opening. Its ingredients are:

- chopped vegetables (white cabbage, gherkins, carrots, onions, pimentos)
- spirit vinegar
- sugar
- vegetable oil
- eggs
- modified cornflour
- salt
- spices
- dried skimmed milk
- acetic acid
- stabilizer xanthan gum
- natural flavouring.

There are many worse foods than this.

Marmite and Bovril are very high in salt – too high for young
children – but low in fat. All the other savoury spreads are relatively
high in fat and, according to dietician Isobel Cole-Hamilton, they
tend to be made from left-over bits of meat, fish or cheese which have
been mixed up with other types of fat, additives, spices and
flavourings. Vegetarian patés and spreads, she says, are generally
made from vegetable fats and hydrolysed protein.

For sandwiches it is better to use real meat or fish rather than
spreads and pastes. But for occasional snacks, and to encourage
children to eat more bread, a thin layer of one of these products is no
problem.

Likewise sweet spreads are not a cause for concern unless someone
gets a 'jam habit'. Many shop jams – even the better ones – are
crammed with sugar. Here are the ingredients of a reputable brand of
blackcurrant jam stating 'pure fruit with no artificial preservatives or
colours':

- glucose syrup
- blackcurrants
- sugar
- gelling agent
- pectin

- citric acid
- acidity regulator: sodium citrate.

Sugar content is 66 per cent, fruit content 25 per cent. Always read labels carefully, and go for a high fruit content and reduced sugar – these jams are now widely available even in run-of-the-mill supermarkets.

But things can be even better than that. Some shops stock the Whole Earth range – fine jams with no sugar added at all (fruit contains plenty of fructose of its own – so why add sucrose?). The ingredients of its cherry jam are:

- apple juice
- cherries
- gelling agent: lime pectin.

The highly recommended Whole Earth range also encompasses apricot, blackcurrant, blueberry, hedgerow fruits, mixed berry, raspberry, Seville orange and strawberry.

For fabulous organic peanut butter, trust the Whole Earth people again. They add no sugar and take great care to inspect their peanuts for any sign of aflotoxin (see **Nuts and seeds**). The ingredients are:

- roasted organically grown peanuts
- unhydrogenated vegetable oil
- sea salt.

Note that the fat is not hardened and thus remains unsaturated.

Sugar

The less sugar you eat, the better: that's the simple message. Like hard, saturated fats, and like alcohol, sugar is bad news. For, as the Health Education Authority says in its booklet *Guide to Healthy Eating*: 'Sugar gives you "empty calories" – that is, calories with no other nutrients: no vitamins, no minerals, no fibre, no protein.'

'Eat less sugar' – official

In December 1989 the Department of Health published the latest official word on sugar, a report of its expert Committee on Medical Aspects of Food Policy called *Dietary Sugars and Human Health*. As summarized in a government press release, the report recommends: 'Everyone should limit sugar consumption for the good of their health.' Other conclusions of interest to parents include: 'Those at greatest risk are children, adolescents, and the elderly .... Sugars should not be added to bottle feeds for babies and young children and they should not be given sugared drinks .... Those providing food for families and communities should reduce the frequency with which sugary snacks are consumed.'

The craving comes early

What's the matter with sugar? This is what the Department of Health said over ten years ago in its booklet *Eating for Health*: 'This food has the disadvantage that it is so pleasant to taste that people usually develop a craving for it. Sugar is not very filling and it is therefore one of the easiest foods to eat in excess of energy requirements, and the excess is stored as fat. The consumption of sugar in this country is one of the largest in the world.' These words are still true.

A house divided

How much less sugar should you eat, for the sake of your health? The Department of Health hates setting targets, in case anybody takes them seriously and actually does eat less sugar. This would upset the Ministry of Agriculture, Fisheries and Food, the official sponsors of the giant food manufacturers, who depend on cheap fats and sugars to make money. So for clear guidance you have to go to reports published by independent medical bodies.

The British Medical Association recommends that everybody will do well to cut sugar consumption in half. So does the Royal College of Physicians. So does the World Health Organization in its global report on prevention of diseases by means of good food, published in 1990. But when the government-funded Health Education Authority published the advice 'aim to cut down the amount of sugar you eat by a half', this clear recommendation was censored by the government. A leaked letter from a Whitehall civil servant explained, saying, 'A less definite form of words, e.g. "Watch your sugar intake", would be preferable for us.'

Some myths exploded

Many common ideas about sugar, some perpetrated by industry, are misleading or wrong. For example: 'Sugar in processed food and sugar in fruit is the same thing.' Misleading, and essentially wrong. It is perfectly true that commercial, 'refined' sugars, and naturally occurring sugars in fruit and vegetables, are identical when analysed chemically. The most common commercial sugar, sucrose, is concentrated out of sugar cane or sugar beet. The sugar industry is very keen to suggest that anybody who wants to avoid commercial sugars should stop eating fruit, too. But there are a couple of fundamental differences between the two.

First, sugars in fruit come as part of a nourishing package. You can't eat fruit without eating vitamins, minerals and fibre as well: and the water in fruit makes it bulky and satisfying (see **Fruit and vegetables**). By contrast, the package of which commercial sugars are part, has little or no nourishment (as in soft drinks and sweets), or is often combined with hard fats (as in cakes, biscuits and chocolate). Second, what happens to any food in our bodies is biochemical, not chemical, and in concentrated form sugar has bad effects. This is how the Scottish Health Education Group puts it: 'Eating refined sugar causes a rapid rise in blood sugar levels and puts a strain on the body's control mechanism. Following this a rapid fall in blood sugar level may occur, resulting in light-headedness and a feeling of hunger. Diabetes is the extreme example of this.'

'Sugar gives you energy' is another common but misleading idea. The reason why commercial sugars are often called 'empty calories' is that calories is all they contain. The industry spends tens of millions of pounds a year putting it about that sugar gives you energy (calories); that energy is a form of nourishment; and that therefore sugary foods are nourishing.But the very last food that a basically sedentary population needs is food with calories but without nourishment. A wholemeal sandwich, or a baked potato, or a plate of pasta, or a banana, help you work, rest and play, because these good foods not only supply energy (calories) but also protein, fibre, essential fats, vitamins and minerals.

A hundred pounds of sugar a year – each

'Sugar comes only in packets.' Wrong. Packet sugar is made of only one type of sugar: sucrose. Over the years sales of packet sugar have dropped rapidly. At the same time, average consumption of sugar (or, more correctly, sugars) is still around 100lb a year on average for every man, woman and child in Britain. This is equivalent to just under a kilo packet of sugar every week. The reason is that, as fast as sales of packet sugar drop, the manufacturers stuff sugars of all varieties back into processed foods.

In 1990, of the 100lb of sugar everybody eats on average, around 70lb is hidden in processed foods. The industry dislikes the term 'hidden sugars', just as it dislikes 'empty calories'. Sugars are hidden, because manufacturers are not obliged by law to state the total quantity of sugar in their products. And they are also allowed to use a multitude of names on labels for different types of sugar, thus confusing the consumer.

'Sugar and sucrose are the same thing.' This is wrong. Look at the ingredients lists on food labels and you will find a number of items ending in '-ose': these include sucrose, glucose, fructose, maltose and lactose. These are all sugars. You may also find the word 'sugar' surrounded by other words, as in 'soft brown sugar', 'raw cane sugar' or 'pure unrefined sugar', all designed to make you think you will do yourself good by eating the product. These too are all sugars, as are the customized items with names such as barbados or demerara or muscovado. It is true that some brown aromatic sugars have some nourishment in them, as do honey and molasses. But all commercial sugars:

- rot your teeth
- make you fat

and, especially when combined with hard fats, increase your risk of:

- heart attacks
- diabetes
- gallstones
- kidney stones.

Concentrated commercial sugars, as in soft drinks and confectionery:

- cause blood sugar swings and therefore mood swings.

Too much sugar all round

'Sugars are only found in sweet foods.' Wrong. Sugars are a dream ingredient for food technologists: they are also preservatives and bulking aids, as well as cheap sweeteners, and they give what the trade calls 'mouth-feel'. Watch out for sugars in baby foods, breakfast cereals, canned soups, vegetables and fruit, and even in meat products.

A hundred years ago the sugar trade, then concentrated in the West Indies, first started dumping sugar on Britain in the form of cheap jams, biscuits and confectionery for the working classes; and the national palate has remained degraded and corrupted ever since. The products represented by the trade association, the Biscuit, Cake, Chocolate and Confectionery Alliance (known to wags as the Sweet Fat Alliance or Sweet FA for short) employ 100,000 people, and turn over almost £5 billion a year. BCCCA spokesman John Hardy has said: 'The name of the game is influencing the government. Once they realize our industries account for 12.5 per cent of all consumer spending, they'll start listening.'

The cover-up

Government as well as industry is evidently keen to conceal just how sugary British food is. In 1986 an official report, *The Diets of British Schoolchildren*, was leaked and made the subject of a Granada TV programme. Armed with statistics from the report, nutritionist Caroline Walker put together a typical British teenager's food for a month: mounds of sugary, fatty food were revealed on screen. She said:

> Children now eat more cakes and biscuits than fruit or vegetables (excluding potatoes) ... more sweets than wholemeal and brown bread. Taking into account all the sugar in soft drinks, cakes and biscuits, confectionery, ice cream, flavoured yoghurts, and all the other processed foods children eat, their total consumption of sugars must come to at least one-fifth of their total energy (calorie) intake. This is a nutritional disaster.

The report, finally published in 1989, was then brushed aside by Education Minister John Butcher as out of date – which indeed it is, in a way. The signs are that the food supplied to children, especially by fast food joints in the street and by privatized caterers in schools, is getting fattier and more sugary year by year.

The remedy

What can you do? As a consumer, if you take sugar in tea or coffee, the best advice is to go cold turkey, brace yourself for a month of craving, and look forward to the day when your taste buds are once again in good shape and you can enjoy the natural sweetness in food. Don't fall back on chemical sweeteners, widely believed to be toxicologically dodgy, which keep you on the sweetness hook.

Eat as much fruit as you like. After a while you will notice that many vegetables too are sweet: carrots, for example, and even onions. Cut out sweet snacks and eat fruit instead, or a sandwich if you are hungry. Supermarkets now stock plenty of sugar-free processed foods: breakfast cereals, for example. Stop buying soft drinks and colas; drink fruit juice instead, if you can afford it, and water if you can't. Support those supermarkets whose own-label brands own up to the percentage of added sugars. Write to your MP, saying that manufacturers should by law be obliged to state how much sugar is contained in their products. People from industry say we want sugar added to our food. Prove them wrong.

See also **Honey**.

Sweets and chocolate

What can parents for Safe Food tell you that you don't already know about candies, sweets and chocolate bars? You know they have lots of sugar in them. You also know that they are terribly attractive to most children, and that much of the industry's advertising is aimed directly at them. And if you've read the section on **Fruit and vegetables** you'll recall that in the mid-1980s something in the order of a staggering £80 million was laid out on advertising by the chocolate producers, to remind everyone of how much more pleasant life could be if they eat these very 'more-ish' treats. (The problem of sugar addiction, and its attendant physical and psychological symptoms, is dealt with under **Sugar**.)

Sweet sponsorship

Under a sponsorship agreement, Mars bars and M & M's chocolates are the official snack foods of the 1990 Soccer World Cup in Italy, with rights to pitch-side advertising at the 12 stadia where the 52 matches will be played. The TV audience is likely to be around 26 billion: all potential sugar addicts. This will give the brands more worldwide exposure than ever before – more than they could have dreamed of 30 years ago. The companies will be expecting quite some return on their investment with that kind of exposure. Are we right or are we right?

Obviously manufacturers are in business to sell their wares. All quite legitimate. What their friendly, highly coloured packaged products may do to the body is not their primary concern. But it is ours, as Parents for Safe Food.

The battle over our children's teeth

Recently, Cadbury Schweppes have been battling for the milk chocolate buttons and white chocolate market with Nestlé, who took over Rowntree's and make Milky Bar. Total sales of milk chocolate buttons are worth around £25 million a year, with Cadbury having 80 per cent of the market, Nestlé 15 per cent and own-label the remaining 5 per cent. Milk chocolate buttons mainly sell to children between the ages of one and four, and in the *Grocer* of 16 December 1989 were described as 'chocolate for beginners'.

By the time children reach fifteen, more than 90 per cent of them have tooth decay. By the age of five, more than half of small children have decay, even in their first set of teeth. The sweet habit or addiction is usually acquired very early in life. Dentistry costs Britain a billion pounds a year – a lot of money and a lot of pain. The Swiss have come up with a fine scheme: a logo of a smiling molar surmounted by an umbrella on packets of confectionery indicates a tooth-friendly product. Could it happen here? We think so.

Fat and sugar content of sweets and chocolate

	percentage per 100g	
	sugars	fat
boiled sweets	86.9	—
fruit gums	42.6	—
liquorice allsorts	67.2	2.2
toffees, mixed	70.1	17.2
chocolate, milk	56.5	30.3
chocolate, plain	59.5	29.2
chocolate, fancy filled	65.8	18.8
Bounty bar	53.7	26.1
Mars bar	65.8	18.9
Milky bar buttons	59.0	32.0

What can parents do?

Parents for Safe Food advise anyone who is raising children not to give them things with added sugar when they are babies. When they are toddlers, and if they have got interested in confectionery, one square of chocolate or a single sweet after a meal will be least harmful to their teeth. It will also prevent the psychological problems associated either with being deprived of something that their little friends may have, or the emotional association that sweets can have with treats. Try to channel this emotional association into a more positive direction – instead of a sweet as a treat, why not give a non-edible prize like a book or a little toy?

All this and additives too

Let's look at some of the things these little children will soon enough be buying themselves with their pocket money if we don't catch them young and train their innocent palates. Here is a popular packet of 'sherbet-style' boiled sweets, nearly 96 per cent of which is sugar. They do contain small amounts of minerals, but have no fibre and a huge calorie content. All this plus colouring additives E100, E141, E120 and E160b – old enemies encountered elsewhere in this book, but just to recap:

- E100 curcumin or turmeric (an Indian herb): some evidence of thyroid damage in test animals
- E141 chlorophyllins: presumed safe
- E120 cochineal (an insect extract): suspected of causing food intolerance
- E160b annatto (a tree-seed extract): may cause asthma and rashes; poorly tested for safety.

Sherbet indeed! And these sweets work out at more per pound than most fruit, even in winter.

Now here for the toddler is a bag of dolly mixtures containing:

- sugar
- glucose syrup
- gelatine
- hydrogenated vegetable oils
- modified starch
- fat-reduced cocoa powder
- citric acid
- flavourings
- colourings E100, E104, E110, E124, E127, E131, E132, E150, E153.

Let's take a closer look at those colours:

- E100 was in sherbet (see above)
- E104 quinoline yellow, E110 sunset yellow FCF, E124 ponceau R, E127 erythrosine BS, E131 patent blue V and E132 indigo carmine are all coal-tar dyes
- E150 are caramels
- E153 is carbon black.

All these present us with the same disturbing story as before: they may provoke food intolerance, skin rashes, hyperactivity, asthma, allergic reaction and cancer.

Are we down-hearted? No!

Should sweeties designed for small children with immature immune systems contain such potentially dangerous ingredients, however small the amounts may be? Parents for Safe Food think not. But don't be down-hearted. Get angry. Write to the manufacturers and demand better ingredients.

And here are two really nice, quick recipes that you (or, indeed, your children, since there's no dangerous boiling sugar involved) can make at home. Certainly there is sugar in them — but you can't make sweets without *some* sugar. Regard them as a special treat and feel happy that you are controlling the amount of sugar in your children's diet — somewhat!

Nut Creams

3oz/90g low-fat cream cheese
2oz/60g clear honey
4oz/125g desiccated coconut
2oz/60g mixed nuts, finely ground

Work all the ingredients together in a bowl until evenly mixed. Shape into a bar. Chill in the fridge until required, them cut into bite-sized pieces.

Sesame and carob fudge

1oz/30g sesame seeds
2oz/60g polyunsaturated margarine
1oz/30g carob powder
2oz/60g clear honey
1oz/30g soya flour
3oz/90g ground almonds
1 teaspoon vanilla essence

Toast the sesame seeds in a dry frying pan until browned. Cream the fat and carob powder until well mixed. Add the honey, flour, almonds and vanilla and mix thoroughly. Sprinkle the sesame seeds on a clean, dry working surface. shape the 'fudge' into a roll, coating it with the toasted sesame seeds. Chill in the fridge until required, then cut into pieces.

See also **Bedtime drinks**.

Tea and coffee

Tea and coffee are powerful drugs: legal, of course, available in every supermarket and corner shop, enjoyed in almost all households – but drugs nonetheless. If you disagree, try a little experiment. Go without any tea and coffee for a week, and see what happens. If all you miss is a sense of agreeable and sociable refreshment, then it's unlikely that your usual tea or coffee drinking habit is doing you any harm. And, as likely as not, you usually drink no more than four or so cups a day, or else prefer a weak brew. But your week of abstinence may give you a sharp shock.

A shock to the system

Some time ago, hospital doctors were worried about the evident ill-effects of general anaesthesia on many surgical patients who, for several days after their operations, suffered appalling headaches and nausea, similar to a severe alcoholic hangover. Eventually a smart medical detective solved the mystery. He looked into the significance of the fact that, around the time of a major operation, patients are not allowed to eat or drink anything for some days – they are 'nil by mouth'. The sick headaches had nothing to do with anaesthesia, but were the pains of withdrawal from heavy cuppa habits. The patients who suffered most were those who drank 10 or more cups of coffee a day. Tea also caused withdrawal symptoms. Chemically, both coffee and tea are very complex; but the chemical with the poisonous effect is probably caffeine.

Take care with caffeine

In heavy doses caffeine is addictive, certainly unhealthy and probably dangerous. Too much chemical stimulation of the body causes jitters, bad temper, poor sleep and eventual exhaustion. Specific ill-effects of a high caffeine intake include palpitations (pounding and sometimes irregular heartbeat) and dangerously raised blood cholesterol levels. Some studies also suggest that caffeine can cause raised blood pressure and also cancers.

Cup for cup, coffee is more potent than tea. A breakfast cup of freshly brewed coffee contains about 80mg of caffeine; instant coffee, about 60mg; tea, about 40mg. A sensible maximum daily caffeine dose is now reckoned to be about 250mg – three or four cups of average strength coffee, or six cups of tea. (Cola drinks also contain caffeine: see **Juices and soft drinks**.)

Dealing with the problem

Does this mean that the only really healthy choice is to cut out tea and coffee altogether? No. For a start, you can switch to decaffeinated varieties. (They won't, of course, give you the jolt of the standard stuff.)

Secondly, the Chinese and Arabs who first identified the medicinal value of tea and coffee were right. Tea contains tannins, catechins and fluoride, that protect against infections and tooth decay. They, or other elements in tea, may also counteract the harmful effects of caffeine on the heart. And caffeine is indeed a pick-me-up: one cup of coffee in the morning boosts energy and concentration for up to six hours.

The danger is the addictive quality of caffeine. If you crave it in the afternoon and evening, you are in the danger zone. A useful tip is to drink it only in the morning. Weak tea is the better drink after midday.

Avoid coffee in pregnancy

But pregnant women should avoid caffeine in any form – in cola drinks and chocolate, as well as in tea and coffee. Caffeine crosses through the placenta into the baby growing in the womb. There is some evidence that in heavy doses it increases the risk of birth defects. In any case, it's sensible to obey the instinct that babies should not be born with caffeine in their bloodstream. You can judge the possible addictive effect on your body. A tiny baby cannot.

For the same reason, it is best not to give pre-school children coffee. If they like tea, then two or three cups daily won't hurt. But fruit juices are better; and pure water is fine. (see **Water**).

Herb teas

As well as conventional tea, every well-stocked kitchen will include a range of herbal teas, which contain no caffeine, are delicious and refreshing, and have medicinal qualities. Many herbs commonly grown in Britain are healthful:

- rosemary is good for colds and other infections
- peppermint helps digestion
- dandelion stimulates the liver and kidneys
- camomile is soothing and relaxing.

And mixtures of fruit and flowers are nourishing and pleasant in the morning.

It has been suggested that herbal teas can be poisonous. This is as silly as saying that medicines are poisonous. Of course it is true that some herbs are potent and can have ill-effects; but you won't find these on sale in the shops.

In France, Germany and Italy, people drink herb teas in the afternoon socially, much as we British drink Indian tea at teatime. Many British supermarkets and most health and wholefood shops stock a range of safe, mild herb teas.

Tofu and miso

Japanese cookery is based upon three soya products:

- tofu, a custard-like cake made from soya milk in a process similar to cheesemaking
- miso, a paste made from fermented soya bean, wheat or rice and salt
- soy sauce, which is used to enhance the flavour as foods are cooked, and to mix into dips.

These products are available in specialist oriental grocers, in your local health food shops and in some supermarkets. Read the labels. Soy sauce doesn't need added salt.

Tofu is never boring

There are restaurants in Japan that serve a six- or seven-course meal in which the chief ingredient is always tofu, without its ever becoming boring! Although it does not have much flavour of its own it absorbs other flavours easily, so it is used in numerous dishes. It can be sautéed, boiled, steamed, grilled, used to garnish soups, rolled in cornflour and deep fried, scrambled with eggs, and mixed with sesame seeds to make a dressing for other raw or cooked foods. Though low-caloried, it has a high nutritional value (approximately 8 per cent protein, 4 per cent fat, 4 per cent carbohydrate and up to 90 per cent water) and a comforting texture.

Fresh tofu will spoil after three or four days in the refrigerator, but the Japanese have invented an instant powdered product which can be stored almost indefinitely. When reconstructed it will keep in the fridge for up to 10 days.

Miso – *no two are alike*

Miso is used to flavour soups and stews, as an ingredient in marinades for vegetables and fish, and as the basis for the preparation of grilled foods. Aka miso is a reddish colour, while shiro miso is white. It varies in taste, and no two are exactly alike, because in Japan the miso maker varies his ingredients to his own taste.

This is a product that improves with age. In Japan it is kept in wooden vats for up to 10 years without spoiling. At home, even when opened, it will keep for as long as a year at room temperature.

Here is a traditional recipe for a rich, nutritious soup which is made in Japanese country households. It is eaten at breakfast and right through the day: a huge pot will be cooked in the morning and then be reheated, getting more tasty as the day goes by.

Misoshiru

2½pints/1.5 litres vegetable stock
4oz/125g miso paste
1 small carrot and white turnip, very finely sliced
6oz/175g tofu
sea salt to taste
1 spring onion (including the green part), finely sliced

Put the stock in a heavy-bottomed pan and set a sieve over the pan. Rub the miso through the sieve. Mix it well into the stock and bring to the boil. Add the turnip or carrot, if you are using them. Cut the tofu into approximately ½ inch/1.5cm dice and drop them into the pan. Simmer for a minute or two and add a pinch of sea salt. Pour into bowls and serve, garnished with the spring onions and Japanese rice.

Vegetables
See **Fruit and vegetables**.

Vinegar

A wonderful adjunct to many meals, vinegar has a long history that goes back to Old Testament times. It is a fermented product that can be made from malt, wine, cider and many other sources. Vinegar is an excellent substance, but it tends to acquire the reputation of whatever it is used in, or with. In good cooking it is a joy. But as a pour-on reviver of not very nice food, when everything seems to be soaked in it, it isn't up to much at all. And vinegar forms part of all manner of bottled sauces, from the better brand leaders to some real rubbish.

And there's worse. In *The Food Scandal* Caroline Walker and Geoffrey Cannon warn: 'You might be interested to know that a curious development took place in the flavouring industry many years ago. For brown vinegar has often been replaced by a by-product of the petroleum industry. The brown stuff that is sprinkled on your bag of chips may not be what you had bargained for.' Check when you are eating fish and chips out – one euphemistic term for the brown stuff is 'non-brewed condiment'.

The good things about vinegar

Let's turn quickly to the real stuff. Good cider vinegar is full of mineral salts, potassium in particular, and it can have a very beneficial effect on the body's metabolism, increasing the alkaline activity and thus providing a balance to the acid in the system.

Chemistry apart, a good vinaigrette, home-made in a trice, is a delightful addition to a salad. But please don't make it with malt vinegar – that's strictly for chips, chutneys and pickles. Proper vinaigrette requires wine or cider vinegar – and unsaturated oil if you value your family's health.

Quick and easy fresh herb vinegar

It's easy to blend your own herb vinegars:

> just wash and dry any fresh herbs (tarragon, easily grown in a plant pot in the summer, is a classic example), slip the leaves down the neck of a bottle of wine vinegar or cider vinegar, then let it stand for a few weeks and then use it (there's no need to strain it).

Vitamins and minerals

Two of the great untruths of our time are 'There's no such thing as good or bad food, there are only good or bad diets', and 'You get all the vitamins and minerals you need in a normal, balanced, varied diet.' These claims are propaganda devised by government and industry, designed to give you, the consumer, a warm, comfortable feeling. If you care about food you will have heard or read 'experts' reassuring you with phrases like these, repeated so often in the 1980s that they have become chants of complacency.

Of course there is bad food. The shops are stuffed with bad food. Hundreds of millions of pounds are spent every year in Britain advertising bad food. The giant food manufacturers who make processed products out of cheap fats and sugars, tarted up with chemicals so that they look, smell, taste and feel wholesome, which if we eat them are eventually likely to silt up our arteries and guts and make us diseased, are saturating the market with bad food.

And what does a 'normal, balanced, varied diet' mean? Well, it means what the Department of Health and the Ministry of Agriculture, Fisheries and Food say it means, which is a diet supplying the official recommended daily amounts of energy and protein, plus a number of vitamins and minerals officially recognized half a century ago as important for human health: vitamins A, B1, B2, B3, C, D, calcium and iron. For over 50 years manufacturers have been encouraged to 'fortify' or 'enrich' processed foods with these 'scheduled' nutrients, and to boast about any of their products that happen to be rich sources of one nutrient or another.

You could readily make a 'balanced' meal – breakfast, say – from ready-to-eat breakfast cereal (vitamins B1, B2, B3, iron) sprinkled with sugar (energy) and covered in plenty of full-fat milk (energy, protein and calcium), plus a glass of 'health' fruit drink (vitamin C) and a white bread and margarine sandwich (vitamins A, B1, B3 and D, calcium and iron). In the official 'balanced' diet there is no need for any vegetables or fruit, nor indeed for any fresh food at all, apart from cow's milk.

Short on standards

You may find this hard to believe, but in Britain there are no officially recognized standards for fibre; nor for essential fats; nor for more than a dozen vitamins and minerals now known to be just as important to health and life itself as the handful of 'scheduled' nutrients.

And judged by official standards, the government survey 'The Diets of British Schoolchildren', published in 1989, shows that around a quarter of all 14-year-old British boys are short of vitamins B1 and B2. Most 14-year-old girls are short of vitamin B2. Scientists in America and Britain have identified a 'junk food disease' among children, caused by lack of B vitamins, which nourish the nervous system. The symptoms include nightmares, sleeplessness, lethargy and mood swings: in tests, these always improved with vitamin B1 supplements. British scientists concluded that 'the withdrawal of thiamin [B1] fortification of processed cereals would have serious implications for public health'.

Calcium is needed to build bones. A third of all 11-year-old boys, and a quarter of all 11-year-old girls, are short of calcium. The figures for 14-year-olds are even worse: just over half of all boys and girls are short of calcium. Lack of calcium and exercise weakens bones in adult life. Half of all British women over the age of 70 suffer bones so weak and brittle that a fall causes broken legs or hips.

The figures for iron are worse still. Most boys and girls are short of iron. The survey shows that only one in 20 girls aged 11 and only one in eight 14-year-old girls are above the official standards for iron intake. One in three British girls are far short of the standard, below two-thirds of the recommended daily amount. Careful studies of children at school show that pupils who are short of iron are nervous and fearful and lose the ability to learn. Is your child short of iron? The answer is probably yes.

Yet the official line is that the 'normal, balanced, varied' British diet is sufficient. Manufacturers can muck food about and manipulate it as much as they like, stuff it with processed fats and sugars, turn it into a chemical cornucopia, hydrogenate it, hydrolyse it, extrude it, bombard it with gamma rays; and yet, at the end of the production line, and after a month or a year on the shelf, more than enough vitamins and minerals remain.

True? No. And judged by international standards, most adults and children in Britain are short of other vitamins, for example B6, folic acid (another B vitamin) and vitamin E. Of these:

- vitamin B6 may protect against menstrual disorders
- folic acid almost certainly protects against birth defects like spina bifida
- vitamin E probably protects against cancers.

These conditions are common in Britain.

By the same standards, most British people are short of the minerals and trace elements potassium, magnesium, zinc, copper, selenium and chromium. Of these:

- potassium protects against high blood pressure
- magnesium against heart disease
- zinc against anorexia
- selenium probably against cancers
- chromium possibly against diabetes.

These conditions are also common in Britain.

Take folic acid. This vitamin is found in many fresh foods, especially leafy vegetables. During the 1980s British scientists have proved beyond reasonable doubt that birth defects, notably spina bifida, are caused by gross deficiency in folic acid, together with associated nutrients. British women are usually grossly deficient in folic acid: young women on average consume between one-sixth and one-quarter of the amount recommended in America for pregnant women. The rates of spina bifida in Britain are among the highest in the world.

Officially, the scientific case is regarded as unproved. A big experiment has been mounted: women who have already had a spina bifida baby are divided into two groups, some of whom are given folic acid pills, while the others receive a dummy pill. The doctors are waiting to see what happens. Behind the scenes, while the Department of Health has not 'scheduled' folic acid, officials at the Ministry of Food have quietly encouraged manufacturers to add it to processed foods. Hence the appearance of folic acid in the ingredients lists on ready-to-eat breakfast cereal packets.

Advice for parents and others

So what are you to do about vitamins and minerals? The good news is that if you and your family eat plenty of whole, fresh food, you will consume plenty of vitamins and minerals. If you are healthy, lead an active life and eat lots of wholegrain cereal, fresh vegetables, salads and fruit, your consumption of all kinds of nutrients will be up to the standards set in America, Russia, and other countries whose governments care about the quality of food their citizens eat. You and your family will probably have no need of supplements if, in addition to eating whole, fresh food, you are healthy and live far away from pollution.

But what should you do if your children eat sweet, fatty junk food outside the home? And what's the best advice for young children, adolescents, pregnant women, the elderly, and people faced with lousy food in schools, canteens and hospitals? Or for people who eat only small amounts of food – slimmers, for example? And what can you do about the fact that pollution (including car fumes and cigarette smoke) and drugs (including the contraceptive pill) rob the body of nutrients?

Health insurance

There is no substitute for whole, fresh food. That said, it is sensible and prudent to take well-balanced multi-vitamin and multi-mineral pills every day. Most pills on the market are not much good because they only supply vitamins and minerals scheduled in Britain, or else because they are unbalanced in other ways. Well-balanced pills supply all the vitamins and minerals scheduled in America up to the US Recommended Daily Amounts (US RDAs). These are the supplements to look for. Find a good chemist who understands what you mean when you ask for supplements supplying US RDAs and who knows the right amount to give children.

Pregnant women are likely to be offered vitamin or mineral supplements for themselves and, later, for their babies. These are better than nothing: accept them. But the really vital time to take supplements is before conception. A woman of child-bearing age who is taking recommended supplements, originally devised for pregnancy, is ensuring her health and that of her baby. And a well-nourished mother is less likely to suffer illness and depression after birth.

The supplements offered to mothers and babies on the National Health Service only supply nutrients recognized and 'scheduled' by the Department of Health and are therefore incomplete protection. A much better choice again is supplements including vitamins and minerals recognized in America, scaled up for pregnant women, down for babies and young children.

Useful warnings

Here are some warnings, though:

- pregnant women are often given too strong doses of iron supplements. Don't accept iron pills in doses of more than 30mg a day
- it's never a good idea to take individual vitamins and minerals, because they all work in combination. Too much iron throws out its natural balance with zinc, for example. Everybody should stick to multi-vitamin and multi-mineral pills
- don't take 'megadoses': pills supplying amounts of vitamins or minerals way above the Recommended Daily Amounts. The percentages of the RDA should always be listed on the label.

An exception to these warnings is vitamin C, which many reputable people swear by – in doses up to a gram a day – as protection against colds. And you may disregard these warnings if you have a prescription for vitamins and minerals, designed for your individual needs, devised by a doctor or qualified therapist whom you trust.

Does all this mean that typical British food is now so bad that you will do well to protect yourself and your family against its ill-effects with vitamin and mineral supplements? Yes.

Water

'British water is safe, which is more than you can say for a lot of countries.' That's an official statement, from a government minister. And that's what we have been brought up to believe. Until recently we have taken the safety of our water supply for granted, and have enjoyed little anti-foreigner jokes about Montezuma's Revenge and Gippy Tummy. But now foreigners are making little jokes about Maggie Belly, and we British are complaining that our water looks, smells and tastes bad.

Danger! Dirty water

The stories of water in the late 1980s were stories of privatization and of contamination. In 1988 thousands of people in Cornwall became ill with nausea, stomach ache, diarrhoea and ulcers, as a result of their water supply being contaminated with aluminium. In 1989 toxic bugs seethed in the drinking water around Swindon, and worms crawled out of the taps in London suburban homes. Typical of hundreds of national newspaper stories was a *Daily Mirror* front page lead in September: 'Danger: your dirty water'. The European Commission had announced its decision to sue Britain because in various parts of the country our water is contaminated with lead, which causes brain damage, nitrates, which may cause cancer, and aluminium.

An antiquated system

Our Victorian sewage system, reservoirs and treatment plants guaranteed Britain clean and wholesome water in their day, and were the pride and envy of the world. But our water system has been allowed to deteriorate, and in many overloaded areas is now literally past breaking point. Together with our elected representatives in Parliament, we have forgotten that water, like other utilities, needs continual investment. As with food, if we want clean, healthy tap water we will have to pay for it.

Do-it-yourself pollution

British water has become an alphabet soup of pollution, some of which comes from chemicals added deliberately. A total of 100,000 tonnes of aluminium sulphate (alum) is added to water supplied from upland reservoirs, to eliminate any peaty colour and to make it sparkle. In soluble form like alum, aluminium destroys brain function, and is widely believed to be a key cause of premature senile

dementia or Alzheimer's disease, which now afflicts over half a
million people in Britain.

Fluoride, a poisonous waste product of the iron, steel and
aluminium industries, is now designated as good for public health
and added to many British water supplies because it protects against
tooth decay. So the metal and sugar industries are pleased. It also
causes mottled teeth, which can be put right by capping. So the
dental profession is pleased, too. Evidence that fluoride causes
cancer is hotly debated. Anti-fluoridation campaigners object to the
mass medication of their drinking water.

Chlorine is added to disinfect water contaminated with sewage
and other poisons, especially in urban areas. A number of American
studies show that people who drink chlorinated water are more
likely to suffer cancer of the bladder and colon. There is new
evidence that chlorinated water is a cause of leukaemia in children.
The industry says that chlorine is 'absolutely no health hazard
whatsoever', while admitting that it makes water smell and taste
foul.

Every day tons of drugs are flushed into the sewage system, either
thrown away or excreted. Fears that traces of hormones in tap water
from remains of the contraceptive pill might cause trouble, especially
for small children, surface from time to time. Perhaps more worrying
are traces in tap water of the intensely poisonous drugs used to treat
cancer patients. Scientists say that so far any such traces are
undetectable and probably not a problem.

Hazards from farming

Biocides, the collective name for pesticides, insecticides, herbicides
and other toxic agrichemicals, pollute the water supply where land is
intensively farmed. Government has tried to cover up the hazard
caused by lethal pesticides such as aldrin, dieldrin, endrin and
lindane, already present in water in some areas at levels above agreed
safety levels. Independent scientists fear a 'toxic time bomb' as
poisons such as these continue to soak into ground water.

Factory farming causes other forms of contamination, too. In
Britain in 1988 four thousand cases of agricultural pollution of rivers
were reported – three times the number 10 years previously. The
urine and excrement of animals crowded indoors is concentrated
into a slurry which is up to a hundred times more toxic than raw
sewage. This muck is then run off into rivers, accidentally, or on
purpose by farmers who shrug off the small fines imposed if they are
caught. Speaking at the trade fair Muck '89, junior Agriculture
Minister Richard Ryder said: 'Every farmer must do his bit.'

In the last 50 years the amount of chemical fertilizer put on the land has increased from 60,000 to $1^1/2$ million tonnes a year, at a current annual cost to farmers of around £250 million. Anything from a tenth to a half soaks through the land into underground sources of drinking water, or else runs off into rivers in the form of nitrates. A million British people, especially in intensively farmed East Anglia, drink water containing over the European limit for nitrates which, some scientists say, cause cancers. The official line is that there is no problem.

Industrial wastes

Countless toxic chemicals used by industry drain into watercourses and then into the water supply. Just one example: the wood preservative tributyltin oxide (TBTO), which makes dog whelks grow extra sexual organs, caused a scare in 1989 when 150 gallons, together with lindane, leaked into the River Wey in Surrey. A company spokesman said: 'We know the stuff is very nasty and we are very sorry.' The effect on husbands and wives in the stockbroker belt has not been reported.

Phosphates from detergents and industry, and other chemicals, form a soup in reservoirs which breeds algae: microscopic plants that shimmer blue-green and kill off other life. In 1989 dogs and sheep died after drinking from Rutland Water. 'While no conclusive link has yet been established between the algae and the deaths of the dogs and sheep, tests have shown poisonous algae in the water and we have decided on precautionary measures,' said a spokesman for Anglian Water, adding that the tap water of the 700,000 people served from the reservoir was 'absolutely safe'.

The heavy metal lead destroys intelligence. 'It is the government's policy to ensure that exposure to lead is reduced wherever practicable,' read an official statement in December 1989. Some scientists believe that the fall of the Roman Empire was caused by lead from water pipes and other sources. Around two million British people drink water with lead concentrations above maximum levels permitted in Europe.

Trouble at waterworks

Called in to investigate 'worms' crawling out of taps in London in the summer of 1989, Dr Peter Barnard of the Natural History Museum said: 'These larvae grow into a non-biting breed of midge. They are green and translucent and my wife thinks they look horrible but they really don't do any harm at all.' The authorities told fussy drinkers to strain their drinking water through muslin, and then boil it. The problem was caused by bugs breeding in filter beds.

Some 125,000 miles of water mains in England and Wales are lined with bitumen and other types of coal tar pitch which, when tested on animals, cause skin, throat and gut cancers. A Thames Water Authority survey reported in 1988 showed that one in a hundred samples of water was four times over the European maximum limit, but also said it would cost £1 billion to reline the tarred mains. Chemicals formed from tar and pitch are much the same as those produced by cigarette smoke.

Thousands of miles of British sewers are collapsing, and one in five sewage works discharges human excrement into rivers. In West Yorkshire the turds in Bradford Beck are known to the locals as 'Barnsley Trout'. In the run-up to privatization, the 10 English water authorities declared profits amounting to over £1 billion. Professor Ron Packham, chief scientist at the government- and industry-funded Water Research Centre, has said of privatization: 'There will be a conflict between the interests of the shareholders and the interests of improved water. You can save money by letting the water quality deteriorate. There is clear evidence that this is going on now.'

And worse is to come

Is the contamination of British drinking water a menace to our health? As with food health and safety issues, it's possible to come to different conclusions from the same evidence. Government and industry representatives say that our water is safe; but then they would, wouldn't they? Environmental and consumer groups say that our water is unsafe; but they can be, and often are, accused of scaremongering. It's fair to say that whatever toxic load there is in drinking water will become heavier as a result of privatization.

Ideally we will all do well to follow the example of the Queen and the Prime Minister, who know what is going on and who both drink spring water. But the Queen and the Prime Minister both have plenty of money, and don't have to lug gallons of bottled water home from the shops. However, there comes a time in the life of everybody in Britain who cares about health - a time to consider avoiding tap water. What are the alternatives?

The bottled water industry

If you can't afford anything else, think of Britain as a Third World country and boil water before drinking it. This will kill bugs but will not, of course, affect inorganic contamination – chemicals, metals and so forth. If you have the money, you can go further and not only drink mineral water, like the Europeans, but also cook in spring water.

Sales of bottled water in Britain rocketed in the late 1980s, and the market is now worth over £200 million a year. There are two types:

- mineral water, which may be still or carbonated, and which makes health claims for its content of minerals
- spring water, which makes health claims only for its purity.

The French and Germans, who drink 50 times as much bottled water as the British (11 gallons a head a year, compared with under two pints), are water connoisseurs. Some leading brands do have therapeutic qualities: Vichy, for example, which is salty, is drunk as an aid to digestion. If you want really pure water, avoid those in plastic bottles. Otherwise it's mostly a matter of taste and price. Perrier, the market leader, is very fizzy. Evian is cheaper but uninteresting. The bubbles in Badoit are less aggressive than those in Perrier. The Italian San Pellegrino has a fresh, salty taste. Patriots can choose between Highland Spring, Malvern, Buxton Spring, Brecon and other native spring waters.

Early in 1990 traces of an intensely toxic chemical were found in Perrier water, and the company prudently decided to withdraw all tainted water from the world market. The sad fact is that few wells and springs anywhere in the world can now be guaranteed to be absolutely pure. Bottled water remains purer than tap water, though.

Jug filters

These jug filters use replaceable activated carbon and gravity to reduce the toxicity of water, but you get what you pay for. Jugs, of which Brita is the best known, do not claim to remove fluoride or nitrates, for example, and do not eliminate biocides or metals. The current best buy, as recommended by *Which?* magazine, is the Waymaster Crystal.

Technology under the sink

If you are prepared to spend as much on a water filtration system as on a good hi-fi system to get rid of all the nasties in your water, you have two choices:

- reverse osmosis
- distillation.

Of these the better choice is reverse osmosis, as used by patients on home kidney dialysis, who must have pure water. The bigger (and more expensive) versions supply three to five gallons a day, but do not turn your kitchen into a laboratory; they tuck under the sink, supplying water through a special tap, and make a conversation piece for friends and neighbours looking for a J-cloth or a plunger.

A warning, though. Install a home water filter only if you are prepared to maintain it according to the manufacturer's instructions. Scare stories about bacteria building up behind filters and then breaking through, have some basis: there are cowboys in the filter business, and even a good system needs careful attention.

Mid-price filters costing between £50 and £150 are now on the market. They use activated carbon impregnated with silver, and technology originated designed for spacemen. These are the option for people who want to eliminate more contamination than jugs can cope with, but who can't afford reverse osmosis machines, which sell at around £500.

If you want high-quality water you will have to pay for it. Small children are most at risk from contaminated water, and a home filter system, or at least a good jug, is a choice to consider along with Wendy houses and teddy bears.

9 A Message of Hope for the Future

A challenge both to the consumer and to the manufacturers: let's have real food

The nature, substance and quality demanded

Many people first get interested in food because they are worried – worried about additives, about BSE, about pesticides, about what is done to food before it gets into the shops. Some pundits from the food industry or the government dismiss these worries as the neuroses of over-anxious parents out of their depth, hyped up by the media. But besides being absurd and sometimes patronizing about genuine concerns, this argument is wrong in a legal sense.

British consumer law states that food shall be 'of the nature, substance and quality demanded'. It's that word 'demanded' which is important. The food trades are legally bound to deliver what the consumer wants. The Food Safety Act 1990 has, thank goodness, retained that key phrase.

The problems which have emerged in the 1980s and which this book describes would never have existed if the food trades had taken those words seriously. Whoever goes shopping for the salmonella that is found in most frozen chicken? What parent would consciously take risks with BSE in meat or with additives in processed foods?

Flouting the spirit of the law

One simple conclusion to be drawn from the events of the 1980s is that the spirit of the food law was being routinely flouted – and the public was eating the results. Not surprisingly, once the public started to pick up the rumours and press reports, confidence was lost.

A lot of this book has been about what's gone wrong. But the reason why Parents for Safe Food came into existence is that its members are optimists. If the people who control food production have made stupid decisions in the past, then surely they can be encouraged to see sense and produce better food in the future.

Time for change: consumers first

Daily, unconsulted, we have all been eating and drinking a cocktail of pesticide and fertilizer residues, additives and the results of irrelevant new technologies that often result only in further over-production. Humans have been unwitting guinea pigs. And it has clearly got to stop. Or at the very least the public must be given a choice: we must know what we are getting, why it is there and who says it is all right.

This book has argued that there is no need for the food industry to make money this way. From the mid-19th century to the early 20th, after extensive campaigning, tough anti-adulteration laws were passed in Britain and many other countries. Let's face it – food adulteration is nothing new.

Take two basic foods, bread and tea. In the 18th century white bread was regarded as more sophisticated and therefore more desirable (we are still fighting the legacy of this attitude today). Unscrupulous bakers produced the desired whiteness by adding all sorts of foreign substances to their flour: alum, chalk, lime, white lead and ground-up human bones from the charnel-houses. (We should, perhaps, be thankful that whatever else today's food manufacturers have imposed on us, it isn't cannibalism!) Tea was very expensive right up to the end of the 19th century, and therefore vulnerable to exploitation – counterfeiters sold the dried leaves of trees, coloured with verdigris or other poisonous substances.

So our food has always been mucked about with. We can either throw up our hands in despair, or we can look on the positive side. The legislation enacted in the past to outlaw these practices didn't cause the food industry to collapse.

What price harmony?

It is possible that European 'harmonization' in the 1990s could lead to food and dietary standards dropping to the lowest common denominator. The Single European Act says in principle that the highest standards of health, and of environmental and consumer protection, should apply to food. But will they in practice? Food irradiation has already been used to conceal too high bacterial counts in food, and EC pressure is forcing unwilling member countries to legalize this practice.

But what an opportunity harmonization presents if it is tackled in the right way – if all countries of the EC could be harmonized *upwards* to the level of the best that's available. Why shouldn't we British, for instance, share the top-quality fruit and vegetables that our neighbours in France insist on?

A shopping list – six steps to Heaven

So what do we all want from our food? What goals should we set for the 21st century? Here's a shopping list. Add to it. Discuss it with your family and friends. Talk to your Members of the British and European Parliaments. Make your voice heard. It's your food and your health.

1. Real food

Everybody has the right to good, honest, unadulterated food. One vision for the next century is the hi-tech route: better drugs, better 'natural' additives, better plant strains and foods via biotechnology. The hi-tech enthusiasts say there is no alternative, and that their critics want to turn the clock back to the bad old days of muck-and-magic farming and lousy food with a short shelf life.

The other vision, and the one endorsed whole-heartedly by this book, says the answer is not more hi-tech solutions and over-processed 'non-food food' (as the industry itself calls it). We don't want to eat stuff so depleted of nutrients that they have to be added back in by the manufacturers (who trumpet the fact on the packaging as if they were doing us a favour); and we want additives to be severely restricted.

2. Sustainable farming

Farming needs to move to more organic production and integrated pest management. Farmers who have become agrochemical junkies should be helped to kick the habit. Welfare of land and livestock should be a priority.

3. Tough production standards

From farm to factory to shop and kitchen, it is time for better training and hygiene. Good manufacturing practice should be encouraged by appointing more law enforcement officers to help prevent problems. Packaging should be more environment-friendly, steering a line between good hygiene and the avoidance of waste and pollution. Temperature controls need to be improved all down the food chain. All new fridges and freezers should be manufactured with built-in thermometers and warning monitors – and without ozone layer-damaging CFCs.

4. More education and information

The balance of information has gone too far in favour of the food industry. In 1988 it spent £570 million on advertising in the United Kingdom alone – about the same amount as is spent by the National

Health Service on treating heart disease. But advertisements and marketing don't constitute proper, impartial food education.

The subject of food education is not included in the new school core curriculum. What a mistake! Every child needs to be taught how to handle, serve and respect food. And any new educational drive should be directed to all areas of the community, not just to schools. If the government could manage to give good practical advice when hard-pressed in wartime, why not now?

5.   Consumer consultation

During the post-war intensive farming boom consumers have felt squeezed out by the bureaucrats. Even as late as 1988, at a time of growing consumer awareness and activity, the National Farmers' Union met the Minister of Agriculture, Fisheries and Food 38 times, and the government-funded National Consumer Council just twice. The Minister will not say how many times he had meetings with agrochemical or food manufacturers. This imbalance of access must change. We should press for a separate Ministry of Food.

6.   Pleasure

Food can easily be a drag. Don't let it be. Love it. Enjoy it. Keep it safe. In so doing, you'll be safeguarding your own and your family's and friends' health, and you'll be getting more out of life.

Bibliography

The following titles have been used in the preparation of this book.

ANDROUET, Guide to Fromage, Aidan Ellis.

BENDER, Arnold E., Directory of Nutrition and Food Technology, Butterworth.

BIRCHER, Ruth, Eating Your Way to Health, Faber.

BODY, Sir Richard, Agriculture: The Triumph and the Shame, Temple Smith.

BODY, Sir Richard, Red and Green for Farmers, Broad Leys.

BOYD ORR, Lord, Food, Health and Income, Macmillan.

BRAUDEL, Fernand, Structures of Everyday Life, Collins.

BURNETT, John, Plenty and Want: A Social History of Diet, Nelson.

BUTTON, John, Green Pages Directory, Optima.

BUTTON, John, How to Be Green, Optima.

CANNON, Geoffrey, Fat to Fit, Pan.

CANNON, Geoffrey, The Politics of Food, Century.

CANTER, David, Cranks Recipe Book, J.M. Dent.

CARSON, Rachel, Silent Spring, Penguin.

CLAYTON, Bernard, New Complete Book of Breads, Simon and Schuster.

CLEAVE, T.L., The Saccharine Disease, John Wright.

CONWAY, Jean (ed.), Prescription for Poor Health, LFC/Maternity Alliance/SHAC/Shelter.

CRAIG, Francis and Phil, Britain's Poisoned Water, Penguin.

DAVID, Elizabeth, Italian Food, Penguin.

DAVIS, Adelle, Let's Cook It Right, Unwin.

DAVIS, Adelle, Let's Get Well, Unwin.

DAVIS, Adelle, Let's Have Healthy Children, Unwin.

DRUMMOND, J.C., and A. Wilbraham, The Englishman's Food, Jonathan Cape.

DUDLEY, Nigel, This Poisoned Earth, Piatkus.

EDWARDS, David, and Peter Bazalgette, BBC Food Check, BBC Publications.

ELKINGTON, John, and Julia Hailes, The Green Consumer Guide, Gollancz.

Food Magazine, LFC.

ERLICHMAN, James, Gluttons for Punishment, Penguin.

GIEDION, Siegfried, Mechanisation Takes Command, OUP (New York).

HARTLEY, Dorothy, Food in England, Macdonald.

HENRY DOUBLEDAY RESEARCH ASSOCIATION, More Muck and Magic, National Centre for Organic Gardening.

HOBHOUSE, Henry, Seeds of Change, Sidgwick and Jackson.

HOWARD, Sir Albert, Farming and Gardening for Health or Disease, Faber.

IRVINE, Sandy, and Alex Ponton, Green Manifesto, Optima.

JACOBSON, Michael F., Complete Eaters' Digest, Doubleday.

JAFFREY, Madhur, Eastern Vegetarian Cooking, Jonathan Cape.

LACEY, Richard, Safe Shopping, Safe Cooking, Safe Eating, Penguin.

LASHFORD, Stephanie, The Residue Report, Thorsons.

LAWRENCE, Felicity, Additives: Your Complete Survival Guide, Century.

LOBSTEIN, Tim, Children's Food, Unwin.

LOBSTEIN, Tim, Fast Food Facts, Unwin.

LONDON FOOD COMMISSION, Food Adulteration and How to Beat It, Unwin.

McCARRISON, Sir Robert, Nutrition and Health, Faber.

MAFF, List of Approved Products for Farmers and Growers, HMSO.

MAFF, Manual of Nutrition, HMSO.

MAFF, Report of Working Party on Pesticide Residues, HMSO.

MILLSTONE, Erik, and John Abraham, Additives: A Guide for Everyone, Penguin.

MINCHIN, Maureen, Breast Feeding Matters, Alma/Allen and Unwin.

MINTZ, Sidney, Sweetness and Power, Viking.

MONTAGNE, Prosper, Larousse Gastronomique, Hamlyn.

NATIONAL ACADEMY OF SCIENCES (USA), Diet, Nutrition and Cancer, Washington National Academy Press.

NATIONAL ACADEMY OF SCIENCES (USA), Recommended Dietary Allowances, Washington National Academy Press.

OPEN UNIVERSITY, Healthy Eating, Rambletree/Pelham.

PASSMORE, Reg, and Martin Eastwood (eds), Human Nutrition and Dietetics, 8th edn, Churchill Livingstone.

PAUL, A.A., and D.A.T. Southgate, McCance and Widdowson's 'The Composition of Food' and 2nd/3rd/4th supplements, HMSO.

PORRITT, Jonathon (ed.), Friends of the Earth Handbook, Macdonald.

PRICE, Weston, Nutrition and Physical Degeneration, Price-Pottinger Foundation, California.

RANKEN, M.D. (ed.), The Food Industry's Manual, 21st edn, Leonard Hill.

ROMBAUER, Irma, and Marion Rombauer Becker, Joy of Cooking, Bobbs Merrill.

ROYAL COLLEGE OF PHYSICIANS, Medical Aspects of Dietary Fibre, Pitman Medical.

SELECT COMMITTEE ON NUTRITION AND HUMAN NEEDS (US), Dietary Goals for the US, US Government's Printing Office, Washington.

SHOARD, Marion, The Theft of the Countryside, Temple Smith.

STEINBERG, Rafael, The Cooking of Japan, Time-Life.

STOPPARD, Miriam, Feeding Your Family, Penguin.

STUART, Malcolm (ed.), The Encyclopaedia of Herbs and Herbalism, Orbis.

TROWELL, Hugh, and Denis Burkitt, Western Diseases, Edward Arnold.

TUDGE, Colin, Future Cook, Mitchell Beazley.

WALFORD, Roy, Maximum Life Span, Norton.

WALKER, Caroline, and Geoffrey Cannon, The Food Scandal, Century.

WALSH, Jan, The Meat Machine, Columbus.

WATTERSON, Andrew, Pesticides: A User's Handbook, Gower.

WEBB, Tony, and Tim Lang, Food Irradiation: Myth and Reality, Thorsons.

Which magazine, Consumers' Association.

WINNER, J.P. and David, The Coming of the Greens, Fontana.

WOKES, Frank, Food: The Deciding Factor, Penguin.

WYNN, Margaret and Arthur, Prevention of Handicap and the Health of Women, Routledge and Kegan Paul.

YUDKIN, John, Pure White and Deadly, Penguin.

SOURCES

McCance & Widdowson's The Composition of Foods (Fourth Revised Edition) *Nutritional content of pulses, sweets, chocolate.*

Cereal and Cereal Products; The Third Supplement to McCance & Widdowson's The Composition of Foods (Fourth Edition) *Nutritional content of biscuits, bread and flour, cakes, pasta, rice, baby food, breakfast cereals.*

Milk Products and Eggs; The Fourth Supplement to McCance & Widdowson's The Composition of Foods (Fourth Edition) *Nutritional content of dairy products, cheese, cream, yoghurt.*

Useful Addresses

The following organizations are associated with the movement for better food, a better environment and better standards all round.

Association for the
Protection of Rural
Scotland
14a Napier Road
Edinburgh

British Trust for
Conservation
Volunteers
36 St Mary's Street
Wallingford
Oxfordshire

Chickens' Lib
PO Box 2
Holmfirth
Huddersfield
West Yorkshire

Common Ground
45 Shelton Street
London WC2H 9HJ

Compassion in World
Farming
20 Lavant Street
Petersfield
Hampshire

Consumers' Association
2 Marylebone Road
London NW1

Council for the
Protection of Rural
England
4 Hobart Place
London SW1

Council for the
Protection of Rural
Wales
Ty Gwyn
Welshpool
Powys

Earth Resources
Research
258 Pentonville Road
London N1 9JY

Food Magazine
88 Old Street
London EC1

Friends of the Earth
26 Underwood Street
London N1

Greenpeace
30 Islington Green
London N1

Green Party
10 Station Parade
Balham High Road
London SW12

London Food
Commission
88 Old Street
London EC1

Marine Conservation
Society
9 Gloucester Road
Ross-on-Wye
Hereford and Worcester

National Association for
Clean Air
136 North Street
Brighton
East Sussex

National Centre for
Organic Gardening
Ryton on Dunsmore
Coventry
Warwickshire

National Trust for
Scotland
5 Charlotte Square
Edinburgh EH2 4DJ

Parents for Safe Food
Britannia House
1/11 Glenthorne Road
London W6

Pesticides Trust
20 Compton Terrace
London N1

Royal Society for the
Prevention of Cruelty
to Animals
Causeway
Horsham
West Sussex

Soil Association
86/88 Colston Street
Bristol

Transport 2000
Walkden House
10 Melton Street
London NW1

Women's Environmental
Network
287 City Road
London EC1

Woodland Trust
Autumn Park
Dysart Road
Grantham
Lincolnshire

World Wide Fund for
Nature
Panda House
Godalming
Surrey

Index

Acknowledgements

The following individuals and organizations gave their assistance, advice, inspiration, information or time during the preparation of this book: Jonathan Aitken MP, Phillida and Simon Albury, Sir Francis Avery Jones, Baby Milk Action Coalition, Tina Bailey, Peter Beaumont and the Pesticides Trust, Sir Richard Body MP, Dr Denis Burkitt FRS, Liz Castledine, Dr M.E.W. Chambers, Dr Charlie Clutterbuck, Derek Cooper and the Guild of Food Writers, Sue Cousins, Professor Michael Crawford, Reg Davis-Poynter, Keith Dickenson, Eve and James Doughty, Nigel Dudley, James Erlichman, Professor John Garrow, Alan and Jackie Gear and the Henry Doubleday Research Association, Geri Gibbons, Dr Alistair Hay, Dr Kenneth Heaton, Dr Michael Jacobson, Al Meyerhoff of the National Resources Defence Council, Professor Philip James, Gabrielle Jones, Professor Richard Lacey, Andrew Lees and all at Friends of the Earth, the staff, associates and council of the London Food Commission, Dr Alan Long, Anne Mauldon, Dr Peter Mansfield, Dr Melanie Miller, Dr Erik Millstone, Professor Jerry Morris, Ralph M. Nader, Jim Sugarman and Associates, Debo Norman, Paul and Sue Norman, Alison Osborn, Dr T.R. Penistan, Jonathon Porritt, John Reid Enterprises, David Rose, Professor Geoffrey Rose, Sir Julian Rose Bt, Margaret Sanderson, Professor Aubrey Sheiham, Dr Hugh Sinclair, Dr Hugh Trowell, Caroline Walker, Dr Andy Watterson, Lawrence Woodward, Arthur and Margaret Wynn, Dr Walter Yellowlees, and the Children.

As editors we have been uncommonly fortunate in our mentors and fellow contributors: Geoffrey Cannon, Isobel Cole-Hamilton, Sue Dibb, Tim Lang, Tim Lobstein and Tony Webb.

We have had fine support from Steve Brown, Gae Exton, Esther Jagger, Fiona MacIntyre, Simon Prytherch, Gail Rebuck and Pamela Stephenson. A special thank you is due to Olivia Harrison for inviting us on the adventure in the first place.

Joan and Derek Taylor
Spring 1990

Contributing Authors

Geoffrey Cannon: Ch. 4 Additives (excluding table); Ch. 8 Alcohol, fish, meat, salt, sugar, tea & coffee, vitamins & minerals, waters.

Isobel Cole-Hamilton: Ch. 8 Ice Cream, nuts & seeds, pizza, puddings, sauces &c, soup, spreads.

Sue Dibb: Ch. 5 Advertising, packaging; Ch. 6 Storing, cooking, convenience foods, food poisoning, eating out; Ch. 7 Lifting the veil on secrecy, vested interests.

Tim Lang: Ch 9.

Tim Lobstein: Ch. 5 Labelling; Ch. 7 Who to complain to &c; Ch. 8 Baby food, breakfast cereals, fats & oils, juices & soft drinks, shakes.

Joan Taylor: Ch. 5 Retailing; Ch. 8 Biscuits, bread & flour, cakes, cereal bars, dairy products, fruit & vegetables, pasta; rice, grains & pulses, soup, sweets and chocolate, tofu and miso.

Derek Taylor: Ch. 1, 2 & 3; Ch. 4 Food processing; Ch. 8 Bag snacks, bedtime drinks, herbs &c, honey, ice cream, nuts & seeds, sauces, soup, spreads, vinegar.

Tony Webb: Ch.4 Irradiation.